Advance Praise for Vera Jo Bustos'

A MINDFUL JOURNEY

"*A Mindful Journey* is an inspirational story that provides relevant life lessons and applicable perspectives to give readers a much needed mental edge."

—**Alan Stein Jr.**, author of *Raise Your Game: High Performance Secrets from the Best of the Best*

"*A Mindful Journey* is a definitive 'chase your dreams' book that keeps you captivated from tip-off to the final buzzer."

—**Jim Afremow, Ph.D.**, bestselling author of *The Champion's Mind*

"Vera Jo shares a riveting tale that transcends basketball; a story of not only what it takes to realize your dreams, to become a professional athlete but also of what it takes to realize self-transformation and leave a legacy of kindness, compassion, and gratitude."

—**Michelle Kirk, Ph.D.**, Performance Psychology Consultant

"*A Mindful Journey* is truly a journey that elicits every thought and emotion from the reader; it's relatable, heart-wrenching, surprising, funny, challenging, and encouraging. Vera Jo opens up her world to us in a vulnerable yet captivating way that makes it hard to put this book down!"

—**Ronald Nored**, Charlotte Hornets Assistant Coach, NBA

"Going through *A Mindful Journey* with Vera Jo is truly inspirational. She tells us and shows us that with a dream, hard work and faith anything can be accomplished. Vera made me feel like I was on this journey with her. It is a true celebration of human potential, personal excellence and what it takes to overcome self-doubt and adversity."

—**Alaura Sharp**, Division I Women's Basketball Head Coach

"Bustos is genuine and vulnerable as she takes you on a journey through Greece as well as to the inner parts of her mind. I had a hard time putting the book down as I felt pulled into her story as though I were there. She craftly weaves in many underlining lessons that we all could learn from as she shares her journey. Her experiences come to life in a way that challenges the reader to grow their mindset."

—**Tami Matheny**, Mental Game Coach and author of
The Confident Athlete

"A confirmation of the power of grit, persistence, and chasing—and reaching—one's dream. The reader is taken along a joyful journey through the eyes of the author."

—**Larry Mortensen**, former Coach and Athletic Director
at Adams State University

"*A Mindful Journey* takes us on a fascinating trip about an aspiring professional basketball player chasing her dreams. Not only do we get to see a behind-the-scenes look at traveling abroad and pursuing a professional basketball career, but Vera Jo invites us to come inside her mind. The book is written in an easy-to-read manner and is an honest, transparent, and entertaining look at her journey of self-discovery. This is a must-read for all young adults as they pursue their dreams and try to become the best version of themselves."

—**Jamy Bechler**, host of *Success is a Choice* podcast
and author of *The Bus Trip*

"*A Mindful Journey* teaches us through Vera's experience how to build mental toughness, how to stay in the moment and focused, and shows us the beauty of how a life lived in the present can open you up to amazing learning and growth opportunities. If you are a young athlete who wants to understand the work (physical and mental) that it takes to excel at your sport or in life read this book, but be warned you may come away with a sudden urge to eat ice-cream."

—**Valerie Alston**, MA, CMPC,
Master Resilience Trainer- Performance Expert
with Army Resilience Directorate and Owner of *Valston Coaching*

A MINDFUL JOURNEY

ABOUT THE AUTHOR

Vera Jo Bustos is an engaging communicator and a leading expert in challenging aspiring minds to reach their peak performance level, fight complacency, and chase excellence.

She has an extensive background and experience in building team dynamics, creating a high performance culture, training and building strong and emerging leaders, and teaching what it takes to build resilience and mental toughness.

Today, she travels the country speaking and teaching hundreds of students, athletes, and business professionals at conferences, conventions, workshops, school assemblies, and one-on-one trainings.

To inquire about a possible appearance or training — please visit Mentality Solutions at www.mentalitysolutions.com.

Connect with Vera Jo
Facebook: @VeraJoBustos
Instagram: @MentalitySolutions
Twitter: @VeraJoBustos
www.mentalitysolutions.com
www.vjselite.com

A MINDFUL JOURNEY

An Adventure of Discovery and Transformation

VERA JO BUSTOS

DESERT RIDGE PRESS
New Mexico

DESERT RIDGE PRESS

Copyright © 2020 by Vera Jo Bustos

Visit the author at www.mentalitysolutions.com

Desert Ridge Press, LLC., New Mexico.

Book Design by Shelli Clemenceau

ISBN: 978-0-578-66191-9

Library of Congress Control Number: 2020907215

Printed in the United States of America

———◉———

For my family.

*And for those who are
courageous enough to pursue their dream.*

———◉———

AUTHOR'S NOTE

To write this book, I relied on my personal blog and journal kept during my time in Greece, consulted with several people who appear in the book, and reflected on my own memories. Due to the language barrier, I documented some conversations and translated to the best of my ability—based on inflection, body language, gestures, and the small understanding I have of the language. The story you are about to read is the adventure I experienced through my eyes, thoughts, and emotions.

PROLOGUE

Now what?

I am a basketball player without a uniform, a 3-point specialist without a target. It's July of 2011. Three months ago, I exhausted my eligibility at Adams State University. I have a sports psychology degree in hand, but not a NCAA Division I pedigree professional teams desire.

My dream is to play overseas. Guards my size, 5-foot-8, can be found everywhere, especially in Europe. LinkedIn is not the option. Agents wait-list me, if they even list me at all. I might be invisible, but I won't be ignored. And I have internet.

I searched for coaches and agents on the Euro-basket website. I sent friend requests and messages on Facebook. I set my basketball status to available. More than one hundred wanted no part of me. One finally did. His name is Thomas.

I had my doubts. Thomas never did. It took a month, but Thomas found a team, the well-known club of Aris, in Thessaloniki, Greece. A week before my departure the deal fell through. Aris couldn't come up with the money to pay my contract.

Getting knocked down is part of life. Getting back up is living. I do what I've always done since I was a little girl. I worked, I prayed. My competitive nature sprouted like an uncontrollable weed since I was in elementary school, playing against boys, expecting to be the best.

I carried that relentless pursuit through high school where I was named athlete of the year for the state of New Mexico on three separate occasions. I packed it and took it to Adams State University in Alamosa, Colorado, where I earned All-American honors, set school records and helped lead my team to two postseason playoff appearances, including a Sweet-Sixteen berth. In 2019, the school inducted me into the Hall of Fame.

My pursuit was currently with me, in Denver, where I had set up my training base. It was a Tuesday in late August. I checked my email first thing that morning. I saw one from Thomas. He found another team in Thessaloniki ready to sign me. If I accepted the terms, I would be on a plane in three days.

I drove from Denver to my hometown of Las Vegas, New Mexico. I'm sure I exceeded the speed limit. I autographed the contract. I packed. I said my goodbyes. I left Albuquerque on a Friday. I boarded the plane, the one taking me to my dream. I buckled my seatbelt.

Now what?

Arrival – Day 1

It's happening. I'm about to live my dream.

At least, that's what I was telling myself as I settled into seat 38-K for the initial sixteen hours of a trip that would take me from New Mexico to Greece.

Life always had a way of working out for me. Well, it did in the past. Not that goals came easily. I worked—tirelessly—for my accomplishments. But in hindsight, everything turned out better than I imagined. Signing a contract to play professional basketball in the top division in Greece was a continuation to the amazing blessings God afforded me.

Yet, there I was, lost in this new world that was being thrown at me at warp speed, not knowing where to turn or what to do. Everyone around me was speaking at the speed of sound in languages I couldn't decipher. There was discomfort percolating deep inside me, boiling into the uncertainty of where I was heading and into the fear of the unknown.

It took all of one heartbeat to sense the transition of a new culture and life as the plane soared farther from home and closer to Thessaloniki, Greece—my new home for the next eight months, a journey of 6,223 miles. Thanks, Google!

I spoke to a few strangers after arriving at the Frankfurt airport. They replied with blank stares. I was the alien. It's their country, not mine. Best to keep my mouth shut and simply blend.

My olive skin helped. In my mind, I was a European traveling with ease throughout the continent. It lasted until I opened my mouth or failed to understand the particular foreign language that was spoken to me. After people realized I was American, I couldn't decipher whether they were surprised, repelled, or intrigued. My first impression of the Frankfurt airport and being in a foreign country was not pleasant.

After walking off the plane into a tunnel that funneled everyone into the main airport, I made a wrong turn into a dead end. By the time I made my way back to where we had all disembarked, the crowd was gone. I stood alone in the dimly lit lobby. The feeling was terrifying. I didn't stay stationary. I quickened my pace. I continued to walk down the hallway, hoping to see a sign, or a person I could ask for directions. Pictures of landscapes hung along the walls provided color to the otherwise bland hallway that seemed to go on forever.

Finally, I came across an employee standing on an electric scooter. As I approached him, I'm sure he saw the terror in my face. He slowed as he anticipated I wanted to ask him a question.

"Excuse me, sir, could you tell me how to get to the B gates?"

A face without expression quickly turned to agitation. His brow furrowed. His mouth tightened. I wasn't sure if it was because I was asking for directions or because I asked for directions in English. He muttered something so fast I couldn't determine whether it was English or German.

"I'm sorry, I didn't understand what you said. Which way do I need to go?"

"Arghhhh." His response was a scowl. "Go that way!" He pointed over his shoulder, his thick German accent echoing off the walls. Before the silence returned he sped off.

"Well, that was helpful."

My breath muffled my words and my feelings.

After finding my way to the B gates, I finally found an information board that clarified which gate I needed to get to. I also found a clock with the local time and realized I had less than forty-five minutes before my flight departed to Thessaloniki. Now, I was in panic mode.

Anyone who saw me walking through that airport would have thought I was training for the speed-walking marathon in the Olympics. I'm sure I was a comical sight to the people-watchers at the airport. I zoomed by a café where a man was sitting with his legs crossed, drinking a coffee as he read a book. He wore a funny looking hat that reminded me of one worn by a character from an old 1950s film. I flew past a Duty-Free shop where tourists were buying last-minute goodies and souvenirs. I didn't even peruse the fancy sunglass and watch stores I passed along the way, only noticing they were empty (with good reason, being so overpriced).

I reached my gate with a few minutes to spare before boarding. Not exactly the same feeling as hitting a last-second, game-winning shot, but I'll take it. When my breath joined me, I found a seat in the crowded waiting area to compose myself. Between my speed walk and the adrenaline flowing through my system because of the fear of missing my flight and being stranded in that unpleasant airport for the night, my heart was racing and my sweat was soaking. In the few minutes before boarding, I pulled my phone out from my backpack and opened my text messages.

Mom:

Made it to my gate safe, but not so sound (I'll tell you later). About to board my final flight to Thessaloniki. Text when I get there. Love you.

Send.

#

My nose was glued to the window for the entirety of the flight and my final Greek destination. I was amazed by the different shades of blue off the Greek coastline of the iconic Aegean Sea. From a bird's-eye view, Greece looked incredible. As we landed in Thessaloniki, the entire plane erupted with applause. Not sure what that was all about, but I clapped, too. I impatiently waited for the passengers in front of me to deplane. The excitement and exhilaration of finally stepping foot in Greece was overwhelming. I walked down the stairs that had been pushed up against the plane and made my way onto a bus that carried us to the terminal.

I found baggage claim then waited for more than twenty minutes with no sign of my luggage. A female employee came up to me and said something in a language I concluded was Greek. After looking at her with a blank stare, I think she realized I didn't speak Greek.

"Do you have your ticket?" she asked in English.

I dug through my pockets and handed her my ticket stub.

"Ah yes, your luggage has been lost."

She instructed me to make my way to the management desk to fill out paperwork to have my luggage delivered to me once it was found.

"Great."

I took that thought and headed toward what looked like the exit.

"What now?"

Looking around, I wondered where I'd find the one person I would recognize since I couldn't leave this place on my own.

I walked out of the airport and was relieved to see my coach. Immediately, he greeted me with open arms. After the long trip and multiple flights, I needed a friendly face and a warm hug. I had spoken with Coach Andreas a few times over Skype and Facebook messenger prior to my arrival. So I knew what he looked like, to an extent. But meeting someone in person for the first time is always different versus any kind of cyber communication.

More genuine, and real, of course.

Coach Andreas was a very handsome man who looked to be in his late thirties or early forties. His hair was black with a hint of gray at his roots. His eyes were gentle and his smile was luminous. I got a good vibe from him when we had communicated previously over the computer, but once I met him in person, I knew right away I was going to like him.

The overwhelming feeling of being out of my element and comfort zone dissolved as quickly as cotton candy in a puddle. I was thankful for the warmness and welcome I received. Now I understand how one gesture, one kind word, one act of kindness can make all the difference in the world. My excitement and sense of adventure returned.

The drive to the Apollon Kalamarias facilities, my new club, was enticing, and once more my nose was glued to the window. I found it hard to pay attention to my coach, who was talking to me about the team and the upcoming few days. I was simply soaking in the scenery. His accent made it even harder to understand what he was saying since I wasn't fully able to concentrate on him.

Instead, my attention focused on my new world that was opening around me. Passing by signs in Greek, which looked like symbols to me, reminded me of my parents and me joking about the Greek alphabet looking like ancient Egyptian hieroglyphs. Not being able to understand anything written on signs and buildings as we passed made me feel lost without translations.

Driving through the streets of Thessaloniki was nothing like I had imagined. Prior to my arrival, I must have been picturing something out of a vacation brochure—palm trees and beach chairs with umbrellas along the shore. Instead of the vacation scene that was stuck in my head, what I witnessed was the hustle and bustle of city life. The palm trees and sea were still part of the scenery, but so too were the city busses, smart cars, and BMWs that whizzed by while pedestrians walked along the sidewalks. We passed by coffee shops, restaurants, bars, and ice cream shops. Billboards of local celebrities, cars, and stores lined the streets. As we drove closer to my apartment complex, we drove on a road that overlooked the sea. I was told we were within walking distance from my apartment, and this was a great place to come to enjoy a coffee, ice cream, or a drink in the evening.

The area was called Krini. I had a feeling I was going to spend a lot of time there. On one side of the road, there were the coffee shops, ice cream shops, bars, and restaurants. On the other side was the sea, along with a marina where numerous boats were docked. It was the perfect place to overlook the sea while enjoying your choice of beverage, snack, or meal.

The Greek music playing in the car, the amazing sights of this new foreign city, and the smell and feel of the soft sea breeze gave me a sense of gratitude and peace. This was my first impression of Greece, the amazing country I had heard so much about. Maybe the sense of gratitude and peace was because I was living in the moment, something I've always struggled to do. Enjoying the drive and taking in the scenery, I silently expressed my gratitude to My Guy up above. It was still hard for me to believe all of this was happening. I finally snapped back to reality and began to engage in my coach's conversation.

"This is all so beautiful, I think I'm really going to like it here."

My coach chuckled and replied, "Yes, I believe you will like it here. Greece has that effect on many people. We will teach you the language, and I am sure you will be Greek in no time."

I liked the idea of that.

We finally arrived at the club facilities. We passed by the gym first, which looked small from the outside at first sight. We parked at the base of the soccer stadium, and I followed my coach up the back side of the stadium up to the second level where there were multiple doors alongside the long structure. We stopped halfway along the outdoor balcony and walked into a small room that was all business, with a desk along the far side, a filing cabinet adjacent from the desk, and a few chairs along the wall near the door for visitors to sit. From what I could gather, this was the main office of the club.

There were three women and one man inside, all who seemed to be waiting anxiously to meet me. The woman who stood next to the filing cabinet immediately greeted me with two kisses, one on each cheek, and a big hug. She added something in Greek. Although I couldn't understand what she said, from her tone, gestures, and body language, I gathered she asked about my travels and welcomed me to Greece and to the club.

My coach then formally introduced me to her. Her name was Ms. Rena; she was the president of the club. Ms. Rena had a strong, almost intimidating presence about her. She was a tall, slender woman with olive skin and piercing brown eyes. Her persona was professional, yet pleasant.

Next, I was introduced to Margarita, who was "chief" of the club, if I understood the translation correctly. Margarita was slightly taller than me, about 5-foot-9, with medium-length silvery blonde hair and blue eyes. She looked to be in her late forties. She carried a cigarette in her hand and I could smell her smoky breath as she also gave me two kisses, one on each cheek. After getting two kisses on my cheeks a second time, I figured this must be a cultural greeting, like Americans shaking hands. She also spoke to me in Greek. I replied with a smile and a nod to everything she said.

The next two were Konstantinos, the general manager, and Eleanna, who is the coach of the younger division girls team of the club. Konstantinos had very thin brown hair and a gentle air about him. He reminded me of a giant teddy bear. Eleanna looked to be about my age (twenty-two), maybe a few years older. She had brown hair with fair skin and a contagious laugh. She was very friendly, and I was relieved when she greeted me in English. "Finally," I thought, "someone I can have a conversation with."

Aside from coach Andreas, Eleanna was the only other one who spoke English. She served as the translator for me and the other three once coach Andreas left. I was surprised at our ability to communicate despite the language barrier.

With the introductions concluded, I followed Ms. Rena and the others as they led me to my studio apartment. As we walked across the long balcony that ran across the entire second floor, I was mesmerized by my view of the sea. There were trees lining the foreground, a few white buildings with red rooftops standing behind. Then, out in the distance the vast and spectacular sea with huge ships along the harbor. The sunset glistened over the water, illuminating the entire view in an iridescent glow of orange and hues of soft red.

Ms. Rena unlocked the door to my apartment, held it open, and gestured with her hand to invite me in first. I walked in to see a fairly spacious studio. Along the right side of the room was a small kitchen area with a stove top, microwave oven, sink, dishes and silverware stacked neatly, and a small kitchen table with two chairs. Along the left wall was a tall chest of drawers. Farther along the wall was a desk with a small TV, and in the back corner of the room was a full-sized bed. Adjacent from the bed was another door that led into the bathroom with a sink, toilet, shower, and washing machine.

After thanking everyone for their hospitality and warm welcome, I said goodnight and was left in my apartment alone with my thoughts. After all the anticipation leading up to my arrival and after all the excitement upon my arrival, reality finally set in and knocked me square in the face. Thoughts of uncertainty and doubt slowly dripped, filling my mind to its brim.

"I'm all alone in this foreign country. Did I make a mistake in moving here for eight months? I can barely understand the people here, how am I supposed to communicate? What if my skills aren't good enough and I'm sent back home? I'm going to be such a failure."

What started as an exciting and gratitude-filled day melted into an unsure and fear-stricken night. I stuffed my face in a pillow before the tears fell and the silent sobs escaped my lungs. I realized there would be no turning back.

I slept in tears.

Day 2

The day after my arrival brought relief.

We had the day off. I defined jet lag and exhaustion, the latter from sleep I couldn't get. I was nine hours ahead in time. My body's future and present were confused.

Different place.

Same time.

Weird.

I was wide-eyed awake at four a.m. I turned on the TV and found one of the few English-speaking channels. The picture quality wasn't HD. I had no idea what movie was playing. But I could understand. That mattered. A lot. Somewhere between the lousy TV connection and messaging back and forth with family over the internet, I finally found sleep.

I woke around ten a.m. and began getting ready for the day ahead. A day guaranteed to be equal parts wonder and uncertainty. One of my new teammates, Mando, who lived two doors down, took me to lunch at the square. It's where we met Konstantinos and Eleanna. The square filled every sense with life. Cafés, restaurants, bars, ice-cream shops, clothing, shoe, and jewelry shops lined the square. Every eatery, café, and bar had patio space with tables and chairs under umbrellas. We claimed an empty patio table at one of the restaurants. The waiter greeted us as we settled into our seats.

Eleanna ordered for me since I had no idea how to communicate with the waiter. It took all of one bite – and one swallow – for me to give my first Greek review.

"This sandwich is so good! What is this called so I can order it for myself?"

Eleanna spoke as I was teeth first into the sandwich.

"It is called gyros."

"Yee-ros," I echoed.

She nodded.

"But do not eat too much of it. Gyros are like our fast food. Too much of it is not good for you."

"Well, I think I am in trouble then!"

Their laughter, with me and not at me, felt like home.

After lunch, we returned to the apartments and stayed in Mando's room. We talked about lunch and the team while she made iced coffee (called frappe) for everyone.

My luggage was still sight-seeing all the finest airports in Europe, and I had made the mistake of packing my chargers in the bag I checked-in, instead of tucking them in my carry-on. Lesson learned the hard way, I sighed. My computer and phone were dead from the night-long internet-a-thon with my family. Mando was kind enough to let me borrow her computer to update home.

Sitting on the balcony overlooking the seaport and the amazing new city that would be my home for the next eight months, I felt twinges of excitement and appreciation. But the uncertainty and fear still lurked like a shadow inside me. Outwardly, I was in the company of new friends, watching boats floating through the harbor to parts unknown. I breathed the smell of the sea.

"Why are you worrying?"

Exactly.

Even though that thought sank to the depths of me, I began to realize how much I had been worrying about things out of my control, and even crazier, thinking about the worst possible scenario of things that would never happen. Courage began to lift me to the surface of the here, of the now.

"Trust."

I laughed quietly.

I shook my head.

I looked skyward.

I smiled.

I spoke as silently as the inside of a church on a Tuesday afternoon.

"I trust You."

This balcony, this city, this country . . . I'm not sure how to explain its full effect on me. But the people had the greatest impact. I arrived a stranger. I was greeted as a friend. Within a single day, I felt like a member of the family. It takes only one moment to create friendships I knew would last my lifetime. I will be eternally thankful to have these people with me on this journey and beyond.

Evidently, my luggage had seen enough of Europe's finest terminals and baggage claims. It arrived later that afternoon. I felt like seeing where it had been, but I needed to unpack as much as I could before dinner.

I accompanied Konstantinos and Eleanna to the square. Alex, my assistant coach, and his fiancé, Eleni, joined us. Alex stood around 6-feet tall with dark brown hair and a constant smile. He wore a fashionable pair of glasses. Only his sense of humor surpassed his energy, which appeared boundless. And his laugh was contagious, as I soon discovered. Eleni possessed a gentle spirit to go with gorgeous medium-length brown hair. We were almost eye-to-eye in terms of height, with her slightly taller. Eleni's true depth could not be measured in feet, in inches. That's what drew me to her. It could have been the benevolent nature she had about her. Or, the compassion and kind-heartedness that flowed from her. Whatever it was, I felt a sense of comfort in her presence, almost like a motherly love type of comfort.

Once again, my eyes fully opened to a totally different world as we strolled along the square. It was nine p.m. Children were running and shouting along the open concrete area playing soccer providing the soundtrack to the night's life. I added to the smiles and the laughter.

There was another addition.

Justin Bieber.

Wait.

Justin Bieber?

In Greece?

Go figure.

"What is so funny, young lady?" Alex posed the question.

"I wasn't expecting to hear Justin Bieber music playing out here." Now it was my laughter that was contagious.

Dinner didn't disappoint. Outside. Dimly lit atmosphere. Conversation and laughter filling the air of the crowded patio space. Greek music to perfectly accompany the ambiance of a relaxed and beautiful evening. I sat next to Eleni, who was warm and kind. It was nice to have a conversation with her as her English was great. I believe we would have understood each other even without words.

The only time anyone spoke English was when they spoke directly to me, otherwise everything was in Greek. Sometimes, everyone at the table would get caught up in a conversation, and I would have no idea what anyone was saying. Even so, I found myself laughing along with the group because of everyone's animation and body language. You don't always have to understand the words someone is saying to understand the emotions being expressed.

Our waiter arrived to interrupt the conversations. I was informed he was a fan of the club I was going to play for. He spoke to me in English with a very strong accent. "Aha! So, this is the American we have all been hearing about. Are you a playmaker? A shooter?"

Alex responded first. "She is everything! She is going to do great for us!"

Alex was speaking to the choir.

"I am sure of it. You will see me in the stands screaming for you. As my welcome to Greece and Apollon, your drink is for nothing."

I couldn't equal the waiter's great animation that rode shotgun to his words. "Thank you so much! I look forward to seeing you in the stands, and thank you for the beer on the house."

"On the house? She is crazy! What does that even mean?" It was Alex, pointing to his head, exaggerating the word "crazy." It produced another round of laugher to the table as I attempted to explain "on the house." Explanation concluded, it was Eleni who offered this wise advice.

"I believe next time you just need to say, 'Thank you for the free drink.' "

"I think you're right. And, after thinking about it, the phrase on the house does sound a little absurd, doesn't it?"

"For sure, young lady," Alex replied.

"Well, cheers to on the house!"

I raised my glass to my first drink in Greece. The clinks were all around.

I was already a celebrity and no one had even seen me play. Not my words, theirs. This time the feelings were nerves, unease. Everything returned to feeling foreign. For good reason – it was. I found solace in my solitude, staying quiet for the remainder of the evening as one often does when uncomfortable or out of one's element.

Day 3

It's funny what you notice.

Before my first solo shooting workout, my eyes were drawn to the nets hanging from the rims as I entered the gym. They were wide and fell loosely from the rim. The nets back home get smaller toward the bottom, like a funnel. These nets had the shape of a bucket, hanging stiff from the rim.

My eyes were next drawn to the three-point line. Same arc, yet different. I knew it was a farther distance at the professional level, about twenty-two feet (compared to about twenty feet in college). Nothing I wouldn't be able to handle in time and with lots of practice. I was already living outside my comfort zone, so what's a few more feet? More urgent – and important – I would need to develop an instinct for the new line to know where I would be on the court without constantly checking my feet.

My first workout was frustrating. There, I said it. I was shooting average. I've never set my bar at average. My consistency was not where it should have been, either. But I was sure with a few more days adjusting to all the new stimuli, my shot would find what it temporarily lost—its rhythm.

Workout complete, it was time for lunch—no translator required, as spaghetti and salad arrived at my studio apartment not long after I returned. A quick nap followed before I retraced my way to the gym. This time I wouldn't be playing solo. This time my first team practice was the afternoon's agenda.

There is a scene from the movie *Love & Basketball* where one of the main characters goes to Spain to play professional basketball. The coach is giving a pre-game speech in Spanish and Monica, the main character, has no idea what he is saying, with the exception of understanding her name being said about every few sentences. That is exactly what I felt like in practice. So much Greek, so little—if any—English. Everything was spoken in Greek—corrections, directions, and I didn't know what else. A teammate stopped and translated every once in a while, as did Alex, our assistant coach. Practice moved rapidly, too rapidly to stop and translate all the time. All I could do was mimic my teammates and their actions and trust my basketball instinct to take over and do the rest.

Margarita, Ms. Rena, Eleanna, and Konstantinos made a cameo. I felt the spotlight, and the pressure. Everyone wanted to see what this American could bring to the table. Let's just say I've practiced better. Communication is just about everything in basketball. Not only did I feel like I wasn't on the same page with my teammates and coaches, there were times I felt like we weren't even holding the same book, let alone reading from the same chapter.

Overall, it was difficult and not just on the court. I started to miss my family and home even more. The time difference (nine-plus hours) didn't ease the adjustment. With morning workouts, afternoon practices, and weights in between, it was difficult to find time to connect with family back home.

My initial attack of homesickness floored me.

"What did I get myself into?"

My thoughts, my words, my angst – all are natural. And entirely human as is questioning ourselves when we climb to the precipice of our comfort zone alone and realize we have nowhere to turn but within to find the strength to overcome the discomfort before us. I felt scared. I also felt empowered, if that's possible. There I was. Foreign country. Living alone. No one to lean on. And I just stabbed a switchblade into the balloon that was my comfort zone.

Day 4

I awoke to the sound of children playing.

The laughter and the screams came from an elementary school directly across the small soccer field at the back of my complex. As Mando and I were heading to the gym together for our morning shooting workout, I could hear a man on the intercom talking for several minutes. I turned to Mando.

"What is he saying?"

She didn't need time to listen, only translate. "They are praying. That is how we start off every morning."

That moment really touched me. I thought how different America has become with prayer not being allowed in our schools anymore. And how we can no longer recite the Pledge of Allegiance in the schools because of the phrase, "One Nation, Under God." It's a shame.

I related to these children. To start every morning with prayer is a blessing. From personal experience, I realized how much of an impact it has. As we plant the seed of prayer in children, we are hopeful that it guides them and eventually blossoms into thankfulness as they grow. Even if it is unconscious, I believe it has an effect.

Now, if God will only help me with my shot.

At the gym, we attempted a little over two hundred shots in an hour or so. I still had not adjusted, and my shot was still not where it should be. I knew I was holding myself to a higher standard. I've always been that way. But I was a professional athlete now, so it became an expectation. Every miss inflated my frustration.

My anticipation for practice later that afternoon was coursing through my body. There weren't just butterflies in my stomach. It was the entire zoo. My palms dripped sweat. I was determined to do better, to show my talents and skill set, which were primarily my shooting consistency and range. Arriving at the gym, I was greeted by Coach Andreas.

"Hello, Vera. You look ready to go today."

His demeanor was upbeat. I could sense his excitement. His smile made me feel better. My tension eased. But only a little.

"Hey, Coach. I'm ready to go. I was able to come in this morning and get some shots up. I'm starting to acclimate a little better now, so we'll see how practice goes." I spoke with confidence. I was excited to show what I could do.

"That's very good!" Coach Andreas' accent was strong. I had to listen intently to decipher his English.

"You know, I've been thinking. I know it is hard for you to understand Greek . . ."

I cut him off mid-sentence and blurted my frustration without thinking how it sounded.

"Understand! There is no understanding this foreign language to me. I don't understand a single word. As we say in America, it's all Greek to me!"

I chuckled about that last statement, although Andreas didn't seem to understand the joke. His face was expressionless. I thought my attempt at being funny offended him.

"Way to go, Vera," I thought to myself sarcastically. I could feel a little tension rising in the conversation. I looked away and broke our eye contact, rolling the basketball in my hands from one hand to the other, waiting for him to respond.

"You are right."

I heard compassion in his voice.

"It is hard for me to remember to speak English during practice. I will do my best to speak English more so you can understand what is going on. Maybe you can stand next to Vassiliki during the drills today. She is a very good translator."

"Okay, thank you, Coach."

I hurried away and into the locker room to get changed for practice. Once in practice gear, I re-entered the gym and sought Vassiliki. She sat in the corner with some of my other teammates, talking amongst themselves. As I approached, they quickly became quiet. Human nature being what it is, I immediately thought they must be talking about me. I tried to dismiss my suspicions and started the conversation.

"*Geia sou*," I said as I waved to them. I was doing my best to try and speak their language as I greeted them with a hello.

"*Geia.*"

It was a group reply in unison. I sat next to Vassiliki and began thinking what the best way might be to ask her to serve as my translator. The team continued speaking amongst themselves in Greek, naturally. With fear of interrupting the conversation, I waited patiently for an opportunity to speak to Vassiliki alone so I wouldn't have to ask her in front of everyone.

Vassiliki was one of the friendlier teammates. She was a few years younger than I and was easy to talk to. She was fluent in Greek, English, and sarcasm. Her sense of humor included great animation.

Before I could ask, Coach Andreas called her over. They spoke in Greek, so I tried to act like I wasn't paying attention to their conversation. I tried to keep an eye on them with my peripheral vision. As they spoke,

Vassiliki looked over to me with a smile and nodded her head. I imagined Coach Andreas must be telling her to help me out with the communication aspects during practice. At least, I hoped that was it.

Conversation finished, she ran back to me. "Okay, Vera. I have been told to be your translator during practice. So, whatever you do not understand, you can ask me. Okay?"

"Oh, thank you!" Her friendliness and kindness made me feel better about the practice ahead.

That feeling lasted about one possession, maybe two. Practice was a constant battle between two languages. Not all of my teammates spoke English. So when Coach Andreas communicated in English, there were a few who did not understand. When Coach Andreas gave direction in Greek, I was the outlier. My frustration was now their frustration. It was not met with open arms by all my teammates. Instead, there was the body language, the eye rolls, the whispers each time Coach Andreas spoke English.

Vassiliki did her best to try and explain what Coach Andreas was saying when he switched to Greek. But the translation often got lost in the fast pace of practice.

I didn't complain. The solution to alleviate this issue rested on my shoulders. I needed to learn some phrases in Greek to understand what was being said so English wouldn't have to be spoken for my sake. I had been studying. The disadvantage – Greek is difficult to speak, let alone to understand. The advantage – My Spanish tongue. It allowed me to pronounce words. That would be useful, if I somehow, some way learned the language. I decided to play to my strengths, whatever those turned out to be.

Day 5

IKEA, and Eleanna, and the things we take for granted.

I know what you're thinking. Two girls. Shopping. Dangerous. But my fifth morning was not about wants. It was about needs. Just a few things for my studio apartment. And speaking about my home, it couldn't have been nicer. It lacked for nothing essential and provided the first installment into what I would eventually refer to as my Appreciation Account. Let me explain.

A clothes dryer is a luxury in Greece. I was not living the luxurious life. Nor did I want to. The club bought me a little something I could hang my clothes over to air dry. Being afforded with the luxury of having a dryer my whole life, going without one made me realize what I took for granted every day. No longer. I knew if I only took this one simplistic act of appreciation, this whole experience would be worth every moment moving forward. But I knew so much more was in front of me.

Living in another country, being immersed in a unique culture, and only hearing a foreign language definitely gave me a sense of gratitude. Not only for everything I had back home, but also for the experiences I was getting in this new place. Travel is a great way of bringing you into an awareness of everything you have, instead of focusing on what you don't. Those differences ignited a transformation in my way of thinking and my way of life. Those aren't just words.

Greece doesn't offer a 12-step program for a social media cleanse. It doesn't need to. In its place, Greece offers Greece. Meaningful conversations and the time to enjoy them. Eye contact when speaking one-on-one or in groups. When you are in the presence of someone, all of you is there, present in that moment, without the distracting device held in the palm of your hand, the one buzzing for your undivided attention. It's the moment at hand, not the moment in hand. Being fully immersed—and invested—in the presence of the people around you is liberating in ways I had forgotten once, but hopefully for me, never again.

After IKEA, Eleanna and I joined Eleni and Alex at a café along the sea. The view was breathtaking. There were people swimming in the crystal clear, blueish-white water and tanning along the beach. The blue umbrellas over the café tables along the beach reminded me of a picture in an advertisement for a vacation spot.

Alex reminded me I was actually living here. "What is the name of your coach from college?"

"His name is Coach Kruger."

"Ahhh yes, I know Freddy Kruger!"

"Yes, yes, very scary, just like him."

The words, spoken in English, also were spoken through laughter. It wasn't the only time English and laughter went hand-in-hand in the conversations that ensued. Again, Alex and Eleanna played leading roles.

As we decided to leave, Alex told Eleanna, "Go get the car so we all don't have to walk so far."

Eleanna would have none of that. "No, we will all walk so Vera can see the sea."

Her response caused everyone to repeat, "SEE the SEA." Laughter piggybacked the final sea.

Our gathering was far from over. We decided to eat at a restaurant in Kalamaria, which was near my apartment. I left the ordering to them. The multiple entrées were shared—family style. And I do mean multiple. Not in any particular order, fried octopus, grilled octopus, smoked fish, a type of rice with shrimp, and little fried fish were set in front of us. The fish looked like minnows, about an inch long, and were fried intact. I took the head off as I couldn't quite grasp the concept of eating "fish brains." I tried everything. I wanted to be open to everything Greece offered—food, music, scenery. I never regretted that decision.

Too bad the smiles of the gatherings weren't permanent. Later that evening, I laced my shoes and got ready for practice, which was difficult. Again. We worked a lot of defensive drills, transition and rotation. Attempting to communicate with my teammates on the floor was equal parts frustrating and futile for me. Basketball in general can sometimes be organized chaos, especially on the defensive end. Hearing all the shouts of direction and which man to take, I didn't understand a single word. My teammates' frustrations were simmering as well. They couldn't understand when I shouted, "I have help," or "I go," as I would close out during defensive rotation. It's not that we both weren't trying. They tried their best to teach me Greek basketball terminology, which I was sure I would pick up within the next few days. I had no other choice.

We managed to find some levity in the locker room after practice. A teammate tried to tell me something that sounded like meeting up for coffee. But I'm only guessing.

"I'm sorry, but I don't know what you are trying to say."

"Yeah, me too."

The exchange of broken communication resulted in team laugher. I smiled and walked out of the locker room.

Even in our infancy, I could already sense the positive spirits among my team, coaches, and staff. Everyone was easy to get along with and so welcoming in spite of the tongue twisters. I was happy to count more blessings with so many caring people who added so much to what I had already been given.

Our team was looking to sign a post player. I secretly hoped the team leaders would sign another American. It would make things easier for me, or so I believed. More important, it would be nice to have someone I could speak freely to in English.

Wait and see time, I guess.

Day 6

Swish! Swoosh!
Swish! Swoosh!
Swish! Swoosh!

Those are the sounds of my shooting rhythm, which I heard for the first time one day shy of a week. The sounds are the whipping of the net. I can hear them so strongly in my mind—like the sounds are engrained there. But to transfer the sounds through letters? That's tough.

It didn't matter. The sounds—and my shot—were back in my right hand.

It gets even better. The relationships with my teammates were falling into place, too. I could see they were also trying to reach out more as I was the only foreign player on the team at that point in time.

I had a conversation over Facebook chat with one of my teammates. It was best to communicate that way. She agreed, writing, "It is far easier for me to read and write in English than it is to have an actual conversation." No doubt copy and paste into a translation app helped as well. I was amazed by how many languages most people here can speak. Most speak, or at least understand, English. It was explained to me that in their school system they also learn German, French, Spanish or another language along with English. Even though most of my teammates could speak English, communication on the basketball court is an entirely different matter. There is no time to think about translating what one wants to say from one language to the next. So, my teammates instinctively spoke Greek, and I instinctively spoke English. It was like a dodgeball battle between the two languages.

I thought back to my own personal experiences. After taking Spanish classes for countless years, I am still unable to speak the language. After being immersed in a different language, I see the importance of learning at least one other language. I regretted not taking my Spanish classes as seriously as I should have.

Later that evening after practice ended, I was speaking to Spyridoula, one of my teammates. She was one of the younger girls. Her personality was on the quiet and shy side. She always wore a smile and had a soft and contagious laugh. From the little time I had spent around her, I knew she was a positive person I would enjoy being around. We stood in the lobby of the gym as she asked me a lot of questions. She couldn't really understand why I would travel abroad alone at such a young age.

She looked at me with what I felt was perhaps awe or maybe confusion and said, "I would be too nervous to do what you are doing."

I explained, "After someone graduates from college in the United States, most often the only option to continue playing competitive basketball is to come overseas." I added that it was hard for me to leave my family and friends behind as well as my comfort zone, but it was the sacrifice I made to continue playing basketball. Something I have learned with my experiences in college is the more you step outside of your comfort zone, the more you grow, and the better you become. I believe this to be true in basketball as well as any other facet in life. You simply have to grow. And you grow where you are planted.

She nodded, as though satisfied with my reply, and then with a smile told me, "I will show you the city during the day and my sister will show you the city by night." Night life was always booming and I was excited to see it.

#

The heaviness of practice lightened daily. Coach Andreas did his best with bi-lingual explanations, which still seemed mentally exhausting. I was thankful he was doing all he could to ensure I understood. I appreciated his effort—lots—because another frustration took root.

During my collegiate days at Adams State, I was taught and did countless repetitions to take a big first step past my defender. It's simply part of the game back home. Surprisingly, and to my ultimate frustration, that big first step is considered a travel in Europe. Coach Andreas had me doing extra drills to take a small quick step while taking two dribbles in the place of the one dribble I was so accustomed to. Breaking a four-year habit that had become instinctive would not come easily. I had a feeling I was going to be called for traveling a lot that season, as this big step was something I had learned to do unconsciously. I even imagined my luggage telling me, "and you think I traveled a lot before I got to Greece."

After practice, Eleanna was telling me and some of my teammates the names and colleges of all the import players in Greece. No surprise that I am, of course, the only Division II athlete. Every other player came from a big-time Division I school, which could serve as an intimidation factor. In my mind, however, I saw it as a compliment that filled me with a sense of pride, knowing that I belonged as much as any other import. After all, if I did not believe in myself, how could I expect others to believe in me? Knowing my résumé gave me a sense of pride. Here, it didn't matter what college you played for or what accolades were received in the past – we were all there, same league, same ball, same goal. I just had to go out and play ball.

I was confident. Basketball is basketball in any language. My past prepared me. New country. New teammates. New uniform. New fans. It's what I wanted. It's the reason I'm here. It's my job. And it's so much more. If I played to my abilities, the confidence would grow. When the confidence grew, so too would my sense of belonging and my enjoyment.

It was in my hands.

Then again, was it?

Through His grace, God has given me this amazing experience.

Day 7

Game Day. Finally.

Our pre-season opener. My professional debut. A fitting end to Week One. Ready or not, here . . .

First, I had to get through the day.

I admit I was a little nervous before my first true European competition experience. I slept in a little longer before getting ready for the day ahead before tonight's tip-off. First stop was the square to pick up lunch. After a quick stroll through the square, I returned to my apartment and dined on my balcony overlooking the sea. Mando joined me a few minters later. She came bearing a gift—a frappe. Her company was the perfect distraction, and for an hour or two my nerves were at ease. Once she left, I returned inside. I visualized my performance. I pictured sinking all my shots, making moves to blow by my defenders, and even rehearsed some Greek phrases to try to communicate with my teammates. The anxiousness to play overwhelmed me. Only one thing to do. I was the first player inside the gym, beating the scheduled arrival time by an hour.

An elderly gentleman who worked the gym café greeted me when I arrived. I had met him a couple times before, but never managed to catch his name. He gestured for me to join him inside the small café in the lobby. He handed me an orange juice and some cookies along with a Greek message, which I imagined was wishing me luck for the game that evening. *"Efcharisto,"* I replied, equaling his friendly smile.

The locker room was empty and as quiet as an abandoned gym. It would be at least another half hour before another voice would be heard, coming from either a teammate or a coach. Not wanting to sit and stare at four bare walls in the small room, I took my iPod and walked to the gym. I sat in the bleachers and listened to some upbeat music, the same playlist of songs I would listen to on game days back in college. Mostly Hip-Hop and Pop songs, music with a beat to get my mind ready for the competition.

As I sat, I began visualizing the upcoming game. I imagined feeling and watching the ball releasing effortlessly from my hands and floating through the rim, touching nothing but net. I wish I could say my visualization process was flawless where I imagined nothing but great things unfolding. However, negative images flashed into my thoughts as well. I imagined shooting the ball, and instead of making the shot, the ball clanked off the rim. I wish I could explain why I sometimes "air-balled" my thoughts. But I can't. I hadn't quite mastered the whole visualization process. Or is there such a thing as mastering the process? I wasn't sure. See? Doubts.

Just sitting silently, I felt the nerves palpably. They appeared as beads of sweat on my palms and butterflies fluttering in my stomach. The chess match in my mind continued. It was Black vs White. Once again, it was my move. I was making every shot, playing great defense, pulling down rebounds. I soared through the air. I broke down the full-court press with my dribbling and passing. I was remembering all our plays. I was speaking Greek. Okay, the last sentence I made up. But this positive reinforcement in my own mind helped stem the flow of nerves. I rose and returned to the locker room, which had come alive.

It was the usual locker room environment before a game. I still had my headphones in while I listened to my iPod. There was some light conversation going on amongst my teammates (in Greek, of course) while some of my other teammates also listened to their music with headphones on. Once I changed into my uniform, I made my way to the court to get some form shooting in before our team warm-up started. I needed to move to rid myself of the additional anxious nerves. The team warmed up to Greek music blasting through the speaker system. And then, it was time.

I started. My defensive assignment was one of the opposing team's best players. She had me in inches and in muscles. There were more just like her. Throughout the game, I was always looking up, always getting pushed around. I expected to be one of the smallest guards. I was even considered a small guard back in my college days . . . all 5-foot-8 of me!

My shot was off. Not good. I didn't hit a single three-pointer. Even worse. But aside from a poor shooting performance, I ended the night with twelve points. Not bad for my first professional game, but disappointing to me. I knew I could have played better, should have played better.

There's more to the story. You could say my bad play turned foul, as in foul trouble. I had been told, and had even seen on TV, that European basketball players have a tendency to flop. Just imagine playing defense on an opponent who is dribbling the ball down the court. They start to drive toward the basket. You play defense, and they throw their body into you. With the slightest bit of contact, they flail through the air and scream at the top of their lungs as if they are in extreme pain. Talk about acting. The amount of flopping I witnessed from the opposition was Oscar-worthy. I was in foul trouble—early. Late, too. I wasn't used to either. I took pride in playing defense with my feet and not my hands (thanks to my college coach). I just hoped the acting lessons played out in front of me would serve me later. Sometimes, you have to learn from your new environment, right?

Michael Jordan once did a commercial about how many times he missed last-second shots. Be like Mike? On this night, I was.

Twelve seconds remained. We trailed by one, but we had the ball on the sideline opposite our bench after a timeout. Coach Andreas designed a pick-and-roll. I was the ball handler coming off the pick. I was the final shot. I came off the screen set on the left wing and headed toward the top of the key. My defender became my shadow over the top of the screen. As I caught the ball on the top of the key, I saw the 6-foot-something post player holding her ground as a help-side defender in the lane. I took two dribbles, rose and shot a jumper around the free throw line. My eyes were locked on the rim. I saw the ball rotating through the air with my peripheral vision while still focused on the rim and holding my follow through. The ball hit the back of the rim, the opposing team got the rebound, and after a foul and free throw, we lost by two.

It was bittersweet. I was, of course, gutted I missed the game-winning shot. But I was grateful for the confidence Coach Andreas had in me. He wanted the ball in my hands during a high-pressure situation. These are the moments all competitors play for, and these are the moments I live for. There is something about going into crunch time and having the outcome of the game put into my hands that gives me such a rush. You can't fear those moments; you have to embrace them. They only come once every so often. No one remembers the shots you don't take, so why not give it a go, take the shot. The risk is the reward.

It's easy to speak the words and give advice when it comes to situations like that. But actually embracing the moment and giving it your all, without the fear of failure, is something we should all strive for.

Postgame, Coach Andreas waved me over.

"Vera, don't worry about the game. Everything is still very new to you, and you have to remember this is your first experience playing Euro-basketball. You played good defense, and we just need to keep working on the timing of the offense.

"All will continue to fall into place once you get to know your teammates better. After only four days of practice, you did just fine and have nothing to worry about right now."

Thanks, Coach.

I am my own biggest critic. This I know is a fact. Sometimes, I have to make a conscious effort to be my biggest fan, as well. Someone once told me, "It's possible to simultaneously be a masterpiece and a work in progress." I hope that someone is right.

Thankfully, there was something else for me to digest besides the loss. I went to dinner with Alex, Eleni, Konstantinos, Eleanna, and a few others at a local tavern. It was a great time filled with lots of laughs. As usual, the conversation ping ponged between Greek and English. When the conversation turned to Greek, I was getting better at reading facial and body expressions and could follow along with the feeling of the conversation, even though I wasn't following what was actually being said.

The group then attempted to teach me a Greek word, which I was having trouble pronouncing. Eleanna slowly sounded out the word, and as I tried to repeat it to what I thought was somewhat accurate, the entire group burst into a roar of laughter.

Eleni was always teasing and laughing at my "accent" in a friendly way. I know they all have an accent when speaking English to me, but I've never thought about the accent I have when attempting to speak Greek.

In defeat, I found my victory. Even though basketball was the reason I was in Greece, the relationships I made with these amazing people were the real reason why God had brought me here. God's work is mysterious, and I was excited to see what lessons I would unearth. I had a feeling those lessons would not be learned with a basketball in my hands.

Day 8-9

Another day. Another opponent.

Another loss. In a word, *yuck!*

I was doing my best to stay positive, but the competitor within me seethed. I'm not a poor loser. It's just that I'm not a good loser. Thankfully, I was not left alone with my emotions.

Speaking with my agent and coach after the game, we agreed it would take time for everyone to get into sync. We also talked about a few aspects of my game that needed improvement. I was all in. To me, the feedback and critique showed they wanted to see me succeed and planned to continue investing in me.

After the meeting concluded, Alex and Eleni took me to Plaza Food for dinner. They basically adopted me and became, in essence, my foster parents. They claimed me as their child, which I willingly accepted. We met up with all of the younger players from the club. Apollon Kalamarias, the club I played for, had multiple levels of playing divisions. There is the professional level, where I was employed, which can have up to two foreign players on the roster. There are two more divisions in the club I was aware of. One I assumed was the 18U (under age eighteen) group and another that looked to be around middle school age.

These younger players were at our game, cheering us on. It was great to see the camaraderie and so much support amongst the club. I decided then and there to definitely attend their games as often as I could. I felt like a celebrity around them. All of them giggled and smiled around me while each eagerly awaited their turn to test their English-speaking skills with me. All possessed outgoing personalities and sense of humor, which kept me laughing through the night. Nothing like love to put a loss in perspective.

After we ate, Alex and Eleni showed me downtown. It was amazing, I don't know how else to explain it. We drove along the main streets first and then parked so we could walk around.

There were two main streets filled with shops where you could find pretty much anything and everything, from clothing stores, jewelry stores, high-end fashion stores to cafés, taverns, bars, and my personal favorite, ice cream shops. Most shops stay open late into the night, if not the early morning. As Alex explained to me, you can do anything and get anything anytime you want in Thessaloniki as most shops stay open twenty-four hours. Ice cream any time day or night? I might not ever return home.

Along the sea walk, the shimmer of lights reflected on the glimmering water. The sea always seemed calm and steady. Tonight, a few men fished along the concrete with nothing but a single fishing line. There were a multitude of vendors walking along the streets selling shoes, jewelry, food, wallets, purses, – anything and everything. I also found out the hard way that there was a specific lane for bicycles, which I was unaware of, and almost got *Trek-ed*. You live and you learn in a foreign city, that's for sure.

We stopped for ice cream at a fancy little place, best described as a 5-star establishment, unlike any I'd ever seen. Sorry America, but Greece has you beat in the world of ice cream.

We continued our sea stroll, passing and sometimes stopping to see vendors' hand-made crafts and watercolor paintings. The aroma of fresh-roasted corn on the cob wafted through the smell of the sea. Along the way, we passed the statue of Alexander the Great and the historic White Tower of Thessaloniki. Along the shore were boats jamming with music and flashing with lights. They were floating bars. The scene was straight out of Hollywood, and I was part of the movie.

#

It is written God rested on the seventh day. It is fact I had my first day off on the ninth day. It was much needed. So what do basketball players do on off-days? Watch basketball, of course.

Eleni and I watched a second-division game there in the city. We were joined by a teammate. Later that evening, the entire team scouted a game between two other division-one teams in our league, which we would face later.

We could have replayed what we just witnessed. We didn't. We had something else in the DVD player. It was Konstantinos, starring as the late, great Bruce Lee.

Days before at practice, Konstantinos got into an argument with a man at our practice because the man was being loud. Alex translated to me that Konstantinos told the man he would give him a karate chop, or *"karatia,"* as they say in Greek. Everyone had been making jokes and teasing him for the past few days. Really, who tells someone they are going to give them a karate chop during an argument?

Alex and I planned for the opportune moment to tell him, *"Akous Kostas? KARATIA!"* Which translates to "Kostas, do you hear me? I'm going to give you a karate chop!"

That moment was now.

Once the entire team was outside in the parking lot, I told Konstantinos the rehearsed line. The eruption of laughter was volcanic. Konstantinos couldn't keep a straight face. In mid-laugh he gave me the gesture of slicing his throat with his hand.

On the walk back to my studio apartment, gratitude washed over me like the sea on the shore. I finally felt like part of this team, and I was beginning to embrace their culture and make it my own.

It was hard to fathom all that had taken place in all of nine days. It felt like I had been living this wonderful new life longer. Imagine two strangers, Alex and Eleni, opening not just their home, but their arms and their hearts to me. How does one even begin to repay that unconditional love and kindness? To have a place to go, to have a place to feel so welcomed so that I was not always in my room alone is not something I ever expected.

I felt blessed then. I feel blessed now.

---⊙---

Day 10-11

---⊙---

*It was becoming a life in full, filling not just my days
and nights, but also my heart and soul.*

Practice. Friends. Practice. What could be better?

After the morning shooting workout, I went over to Alex and Eleni's for lunch and frappe. Their apartment was a ten-minute walk from home, and I no longer needed directions or a tour guide. I was finally starting to find my way around the neighborhood. To get there, I walked through Pezodromos square, which was always filled with people at coffee shops, no matter what time of day it was. It's safe to say Greeks are addicted to their coffee. With another seven-and-a-half months ahead of me, I wondered if the love for coffee wouldn't start to grow on me as well.

The team was not at full strength for afternoon practice. With a few girls missing, we focused more on conditioning and agilities. I smiled through most, if not all, of agilities and plyometrics. For those of you not athletically inclined, agility drills are used to train the body to have the ability to move quickly and easily. Plyometric drills, sometimes known as "plyos," are exercises which exert maximum force in short intervals of time. Plyos are used to help increase power and vertical jump.

With that body of work completed, Coach invited me to the mall. We walked around for a while before settling on a quiet café. Ice cream for me, coffee for him—naturally. The hour-long heart-to-heart used the whole alphabet, not just the Xs and Os. I felt free to open up about everything, and I did. Our wants were identical—what's best for the team, what's best for me.

Coach handed the baton—me—to Eleni, who seemed to appear right on cue. She bought me a book and my dinner. She and Alex sure did spoil me, as well as everyone else who was a part of the club. Grateful, blessed, honored. *Merriam Webster's Collegiate Thesaurus*, circa 1988, is 868 pages. It's still not filled with enough words to truly tell how everyone made me feel.

It wasn't just off the court. With Coach making a conscious effort to speak in English, practices became clear and concise. He still took out his frustrations in Greek. Fine by me. I probably didn't want to know what he said anyway.

The skies were the only damper – equal parts gray and wet. They reflected my mood on the days when I couldn't reach any family or friends back home and collected their toll from me in full. My 5 p.m. was their 8 a.m. It got hard to coordinate, and I tried to find something to do to pass the time. After all, even I couldn't spend all day, all night inside a gym.

I started reading the book, *Mind Gym,* by Gary Mack. It was recommended by my former assistant coach. Sports psychology and the way of the mind intrigue me to no end. I worked on my mental game just as much as my physical game daily while at Adams State University. I looked at the professional level as my post-graduate work.

The psychological aspect isn't just a mind game, no pun intended. I relied on it then, I am relying on it now. No matter where life takes me and in which direction it will continue to be a huge factor in whatever continued success I achieve.

I am not the strongest, fastest, quickest, or most skilled player. What got me to this level was my determination and work ethic to be the best I can be in all aspects of my game. I knew if I was going to survive at this level, my mental game would have to set me apart from my competitors.

The next flash of light wasn't one of those *a-ha* moments. It was a streak of lightning, interrupting the darkness that was this night. The brightness illuminated the entire room. It lasted for barely a fraction of a second. Then, monstrous thunder stole its place. I opened the door to my balcony to watch—and to listen. What a show.

Day 12

I couldn't shake the cold.

When it rains in Greece, the coldness that accompanies it soaks your bones. No type of jacket helped. Neither did the layers I wore. Only one thing eventually worked. Sweat.

I caught a break. The rain stopped long enough for me to reach the gym for the morning workout. For the second successive day we first poured ourselves into agilities and plyometrics. One of my favorites is the agility ladder. For those who aren't familiar with an agility ladder, it is made of plastic and rope that resembles a ladder laid on the gym floor. The goal behind the activity is to focus on footwork and to improve quickness and agility. It's one-at-a-time through the "ladder." One foot in each box, two feet in each box, lateral in and out, etc.

Next came the Xs and Os. We were 24 hours away from a friendly game (scrimmage) against Aris. Our timing of offense, while improving, wasn't clockwork. But improvements could be seen, which eliminated some of the daily frustrations with basketball.

After practice, my adventures with Alex and Eleni took us to watch some of Eleni's friends play. They brought with them a piece of my home. On the drive to the game, Alex played some of his favorite American songs. It was our version or carpool karaoke, long before James Corden made it famous on late-night TV. Even a car ride with those two was a great time.

Alex often joked about little things I'd say, especially when we chatted over Facebook. He made fun of the fact I typed "lol"—which most of us know is short for "laugh out loud." Usually, we read each letter individually and say l-o-l, but Alex read it all together as if it were a word. It was hilarious hearing him say, "LOL" as a word when he laughed about something. Translation lost, but not the response. I really did "laugh out loud."

After the karaoke drive and game, The Tavern was our dinner destination. It was 3x5 small but filled with 8x10 life. A man sang and played the accordion, and there were no private conversations as voices were bold and expressive and were heard and enjoyed by all.

My taste buds discovered heaven one dish after another and Alex received the proper kudos. As I explained before, most times in Greece with Alex and Eleni, all the food is placed in the center of the table and everyone shares. It's not a free-for-all, but with food this good, I was ready to box out anyone and everyone if need be. Maybe it was the food, maybe it was the time, maybe it was simply the custom but the atmosphere of The Tavern started to shift. Instead of engaging conversations, everyone started to sing along with the musician and raised their glasses for a toast. Everyone sang. Except me. As much as I wanted, I can't lip-sync Greek. Not yet. It didn't matter. These nights, these memories aren't about me. Not then, not now, not ever.

A woman got up and started dancing. Once she lost herself in full-movement, people threw napkins at her. I wasn't too sure what to make of this custom. Was it a compliment? Was it a complaint?

I turned to Alex.

"Why do they throw napkins at her?"

His instincts were ahead of inquisitiveness.

"Many years ago, the Greeks used to smash plates in taverns. Since we no longer smash plates, we will throw napkins. It is a way to show our appreciation for the person who is singing or dancing. Most of all, it is a way for us to have fun!"

He threw a pile of napkins at the woman and then gave me a stack of napkins.

"Come on, VJ!" He exclaimed, encouraging me to join in.

"The real fun is when we go out to the clubs for *bouzoukia*. There, we throw flower petals on stage for the performer. It is our appreciation for them. We will take you one day. It will be the most fun you will ever have."

"Okay, I will hold you to it," I replied excitedly.

More people got up and joined the woman and they started to do a type of line dance as the rest of The Tavern, including me, clapped to the beat and cheered them on. I instantly learned there is no such thing as late in Greece. As midnight struck, there were still more people coming in to eat and join the party.

The Tavern opened another door to a world in which I was still an infant. Without knowing a single word to the songs being sung, I found myself humming to the tune, clapping to the beat, and becoming a part of the celebration. It amazed me how the power of music can cause complete strangers to come together and dance to the tune of this universal language.

Even I, as an outsider and foreigner, felt I belonged. To feel Greek, must one speak Greek? Not here. Not this night. Smiles and laugher shrink distances and differences. Maybe this is how growth happens. You never see growth happening in the moment. Growth is one of those things that can only be measured in hindsight. It's true, what they say, that life is lived forward but can only be understood backward.

As the night began to approach its end, we stopped at a site along the ancient walls of Thessaloniki on the drive home. Standing on the ancient ruins, I viewed the present in the distance. I was in two places at once, touching stones that have been standing for thousands of years while overlooking the city. The view of the ruins mixed together with the lights of the city were a picture book sprung to life. Not even the snapshots taken captured the brilliance. Inspired by awe, blessed by God. Sometimes the speed of life slows you down to show you the standstill beauty we too often miss.

Day 13

*The streams of the morning sun through my window
woke my senses as the sounds of the school's morning
prayer over the intercom stirred my soul.*

I didn't understand the words, but all of me felt their meaning. It brought me to the realization of how much we, as humans, share universally, no matter where we live, what we look like, what our religion is, or our taste in music. The list is endless. At the end of the day, we are better together than we are alone. The reason? Love.

The levels of love are never-ending. I am constantly living and experiencing new ones as my life continues to unfold. I've never studied love. There is no scalpel in my hand, waiting to dissect and examine love's various aspects or its myriad of levels. I just know what I feel. Hearing the prayer filled my heart with love, causing me to feel joyous and grateful in the moment I was living.

The power of prayer and its effect on people is something I am in the process of trying to learn more about and to understand. How other people pray and how they connect to God is my vision quest. Separate languages, same prayer? I tried connecting God's dots by linking their prayer with my own.

The inner retrospection took a detour. Hard to believe, but I had only been here for almost two weeks. It felt so much longer. In a good way. In the best possible way. My initial days seemed distant, like someone already cut and pasted them into a scrapbook. I was feeling at home. Each day was better than the one before. I was accustomed to the way things worked and snuggled into the hustle and bustle of life in Kalamaria, and more specifically, life as a Greek.

It showed in practice, too. After last night's game, I felt inspired. My feet felt light, my legs explosive. It was one of those days where everything came naturally, and I felt at ease doing it all.

"By the end of the season, you'll be dunking the ball."

That was Coach, always with the right words at the right time.

The crew went to Plaza Food after practice for the usual dinner. The Greeks, however, never live the same day, two days in a row. As we were getting out of the car, I noticed people dancing in the street up ahead of us. They were holding hands and moving in a circle while a woman held a wedding dress. My bewildered thoughts, which I could only imagine led to a puzzled look on my face, led Eleni to explain another Greek tradition. The wedding party will go to the house of the bride the night prior to the wedding and dance with the wedding dress. These days, most learn tradition and culture on YouTube. Today, I was not most. Today, I lived it.

Music serenaded my walk home. I didn't spend time inside. I stood on my balcony, allowing the cool fall breeze to pass over me and through me. I was entranced by the lights of the city and the music playing. I couldn't tell you from which direction the music emanated. It didn't matter. To this day, I'm not really sure where the blessings that pour over my life come from as every day I feel blessed in a unique way. I simply appreciate them, accept them, and give thanks for them.

In a way, the blessings were like the loud music blasting outside my studio apartment that night. I can choose to enjoy the music and accept it with gratitude or consider it burdensome as it replaces the silence of the night. I understand more than ever the attitude you have in life, and on a daily basis, creates a ripple effect to the eventual outcomes of whatever will come. Choosing to listen to the music with ears of gratitude, I was able to fully feel like I was living in the moment. I struggle with living in the now. But during that moment as my mind was at ease, nothing else existed.

Each day began anew, which is exactly what I needed. The daily unknowns ignited a fire and sparked my soul to life. After only two weeks, I already felt like a changed person. I can't explain how the change happened on a day-to-day basis. It just did. But looking back and seeing the progress of growth I gained in such a short amount of time, I was different in one of the best ways a person can be different.

In a word, gratitude.

Day 15

*I would need to live four lifetimes to repay
everything given to me during my time in Greece.*

It wasn't often I had a chance to pull close to even, but today was one of those opportunities.

Weights and practice piggybacked the morning. That opened two doors—an early start to the weekend and the opportunity to accompany Alex and Eleni to watch the club's younger girls play. Alex helps coach that division as well, and I wanted to show my support in any and every way possible. Support is not a cul-de-sac, it's two-way, especially to the younger generation of athletes who look up to you.

As a kid in Las Vegas, New Mexico, I never had an athlete role model I looked up to. As my athletic skills and reputation for my talents as an athlete grew, I knew I wanted to be that inspiration for young athletes, the piece that was missing from my puzzle. Kids need good role models, ones who set the right examples, ones who give them a visible, concrete standard of what they should strive to be, along with a vision of the successes that are in their grasp to attain.

It's hard for me to believe but I've been told that I did become that inspiration to athletes in New Mexico. I packed that part of my past with the hopes of making an impact in my present here in Greece. It's a passion of mine, one of those burning desires God placed in my heart. This lifelong commitment has no roots. It goes where I go.

I spent the rest of the day at Alex and Eleni's apartment, which is where we usually hung out. We cooked homemade pizza and homemade chocolate cake – which was probably the best I have ever tasted. I had an extended basketball conversation with Alex, which turned into us acting out defensive rotation and positioning on guarding a screen in the living room. We recruited Eleni for the demonstration, instructing her to act as a screener, while we acted out the different scenarios that could arise in a game.

Alex was all business. In serious coaching demeanor, he explained the situations and clarified what to do in each. Eleni provided impromptu comedy. She made silly faces and danced while Alex was trying to explain what to do. After a while, Alex simply surrendered.

"Okay, I give up. Let's just eat again. To the kitchen!"

Ah, seconds. We smiled all the way to the pizza.

Greek culture and Hispanic/Northern New Mexico culture are cousins. We both love our food, and many of our best memories are made sitting at the dinner table or in the kitchen.

I think back to the times when I was a small child, sitting in my grandma's kitchen. The strongest memory that comes to mind was helping my mom, aunties, and grandma make tortillas. We gathered around the table as my grandma prepared the dough. I rolled the dough into a small ball and flattened it with a round wooden rolling pin, which we call *bolillos*. My grandma's, mom's, and aunts' tortillas came out perfectly round—always. Mine on the other hand, seemed to take the shape of anything but a circle. Once the dough was flattened out to a circle, we then placed it on a griddle on the stove. Even as I got older, into my middle school and high school years, I have many memories with my family in the kitchen. As mom or grandma prepared dinner, my sisters and I set the table and talked about whatever was going on in our lives at the time. I remember laughter in those moments, the air filled with conversation, and the smell of the foods.

The smells are different in Greece, but the laughter and the love are the same. I found comfort in the similarities of family time spent in the kitchen and dining area. Waiting anxiously for the meals to be prepared, enjoying the meal while everyone was engrossed in the conversation, and simply enjoying the company of those who were there with me in that moment – those are the moments when L-I-F-E is spelled in capital letters. Recalling the fondest recollections from my childhood, it's the simple memories that are as permanent as a tattoo. I know these simple times spent in the kitchen and crowded around a dinner table in Greece will be just as indelible. There were so many times throughout the day that I stopped and gave thanks for being blessed into a new family.

There had been a time when I was doubtful that I was going to find a team to play for overseas. I couldn't find an agent to represent me, much less find a team. Then, the first team I was supposed to sign with didn't come through on its end of the contract. For a while, I began to lose hope. Nothing seemed to be working out. Giving up was only a thought away. I was down to an ounce of faith.

Now, looking back, I understand why all those circumstances and setbacks happened. God orchestrated everything. He placed me with this specific team to be around these particular people. Sometimes what we see as a setback is God really setting us up for something better that He has in mind. I learned on the fly. There would be no midterm, no final. If there were, it would have been this: when it's hardest to trust, that's when we have to trust the most. When it's hardest to pray, that's when we must pray even harder. And when the situation seems impossible, that's when we have to surrender the situation to God and let Him take over.

It's easy to look back when things are going well and see how everything fell into place. No sweat, right? What is hard, and it's something I struggle with to this day, is learning how to trust in the moments of uncertainty, when nothing seems to be going our way.

Day 16

Faith shared.

Our club is not professional only. The athletes come in all sizes, in all ages, with some of the youngest girls having celebrated all of eight birthdays. Old and young, professional and amateur, athletes and proud parents of athletes, together we sat, we stood, we prayed in our gym that had been transformed from a House of Hoops to a Home of Worship for a blessing.

The main religion in Greece is Orthodox. I was raised Catholic, a practice I continue to this day. I didn't know what to expect, but my mind and my heart were open. As the priest stood at an altar placed at center court, he began singing out a blessing. Although I couldn't understand what he said, his actions looked similar to what a Catholic priest does. Holding what appeared to be olive tree branches tied together, he dipped the leaves at the end of the branches into a bowl and sprinkled the crowd with Holy Water, as people instinctively made the sign of the cross over their chests. But not quite like Catholics do.

This practice is something I am accustomed to, although we don't use olive tree branches as a means to sprinkle Holy Water across the congregation. As Catholics, when the Holy Water hits us, we too make the sign of the cross. In Greece, or with the Orthodox religious practices, they make the sign of the cross in the order of the forehead, chest, right shoulder, left shoulder. The direction they make the sign of the cross signifies clothing ourselves in the grace of God. It's like putting on a spiritual robe—we cover ourselves in His grace. The Greeks hold three fingers together while they do this—pointer, middle, and thumb—as a sign of the Holy Trinity. The Father, Son, and the Holy Spirit.

Catholics go in a different order: forehead, chest, left shoulder, right shoulder. This direction signifies tearing off the sheet off the dead body of Jesus when he was raised from the dead. The sign of the cross represents the resurrection of Christ. Catholics use five fingers instead of three. The five fingers represent the five wounds of Christ. Two piercings in His hands, two piercings in His feet, and a piercing in His side.

Instinctively, as I had done for the majority of my twenty-two years of life, I followed the Catholic direction of signing the cross over myself.

I was intrigued to learn the *why* behind the gestures of both practices. I was told Saint John Paul II once said the church needs to learn how to breathe again with both of its lungs—its Eastern one and its Western one. He emphasized how both lungs were necessary in order to provide enough "oxygen" for the spiritual battle going on within each of us.

I enjoyed my chance in getting to learn about the Eastern teachings of God firsthand.

After the priest finished with his blessing, the president of the club and other people held in high regard spoke about the upcoming year. At least that is what my teammates pieced together for me, translating when they could.

With no weights, workouts, or practices scheduled, after the blessing, my agent picked me up from the gym and took me to a café called "My House," one of the many coffee shops in the area of Krini.

Thomas, my agent, is fascinating. He wears multiple hats. And once upon a time, he wore a whistle, the ones coaches do. He understood the game and was able to provide insight and advice in what I needed to do to improve. We talked about my future as a professional basketball player and what I needed to do to help ensure my career would be a success. With Thomas, there are no generalities. He is as specific as one needs.

When I am counting my blessings, it doesn't take long to reach Thomas. One of the first things I admired about him is that he takes pride in placing his athletes on a team where he feels they can succeed. As he told me, "It's not just about sending your player anywhere and getting commission from it, it is knowing that I am putting them in a place where they will succeed and it is a good fit for everyone involved."

When I started my search for an agent a few months before I started my journey, a lot of people told me that it would be hit-or-miss in finding a good agent as many don't really care about the athlete as a person and only want their commission. I definitely know this was not the case with Thomas. It's beyond comforting, knowing he had my best interest in mind and my back at all times.

The best conversations are the ones that make you think, make you feel, the ones that are point-blank. This was one of those conversations. We discussed that I needed to start working harder to become a better all-around player. He told me about some players that were sent home because they weren't living up to expectations and basically got fired. It's scary to think about being sent home based on my ability, or lack thereof. As they say, sometimes fear can serve as a great motivator.

The dialogue got my full and undivided attention. As it should have. His words became my actions each and every time I entered the gym thereafter.

With my head full, it was time to feed the rest of me. Around 3:30 p.m., I was at Alex and Eleni's for lunch. Alex's mom, who I started to call *yiayia* (which means grandma in Greek), made some pork and fried potatoes, which looked and tasted like pork chops. The fried potatoes were cut up in cubes and had a sort of yellow tint. I stayed out of the kitchen, so I'm not sure how the dish was prepared. But I did more than my share in making sure there were no leftovers. I wish I had told *yiayia* that I'm free for dinner anytime. The series *Friends* was playing on the TV, and I was so excited to see an American/English-speaking show. I also should mention *Friends* is my favorite series of all time.

After lunch, Alex headed to one of his many practices, since he coached three teams of three different age groups. Eleni and I went for a walk on Krini, the street with all the cafés next to the sea. We walked by the marina, took some pictures and acted as tourists would, taking in the amazing sights the sea had to offer. I loved the smell of the salt water. It reminded me of all the fishing trips I used to go on with my dad. I hoped that when my parents finally came to visit, my dad and I could go deep sea fishing, which had always been a dream of ours.

I walked in admiration of the sights before me. Grass fields and trees made up the forefront of the landscape all the way to the concrete sidewalk and street of the marina. Walls made of stone out in the water separated different areas of the marina, where the boats were aligned like a white picket fence. The shimmery reflection of the calm sea captured my gaze as the mountains made up the perfect background. After walking for a while, we decided to stop at a café. Coffee for Eleni, ice cream for me. Ice cream is a passion of mine. In Greece, it also became my weakness.

The Greek word for ice cream is *pagoto*. It is the same as the Italian *gelato*. American ice cream is generally served at a colder temperature that makes the scoops hold together. The ice cream is smooth, light textured, and creamy. *Pagoto,* or *gelato*, has a higher proportion of milk in the ingredients. It is churned at a much slower rate, incorporating less air and leaving it denser than ice cream. *Pagoto* is served at a slightly warmer temperature than ice cream, so its texture stays silkier and softer. It's all a personal preference as to which is better, ice cream or *pagoto*. I'm definitely a *pagoto* girl.

Back home, I had just enough time to rest a little, clean a lot and do a load of laundry before Mando's knock had me on the move again.

Mando and I walked to the square to meet Alex and Eleni to watch a soccer game between two local teams. The choice was a small sports bar with tables so close together it looked like people had to turn sideways to squeeze in between. The place was stuffed. Smoke and excited voices filled the air. Alex caught our attention and motioned for us to join them in the only two vacant seats left.

Soccer, or football as they refer to it here, is massive. I was clueless as to its importance and its support. Everyone was in full throat from the first touch to the final whistle. Those decibels amplified when the favorite team was close to scoring a goal or when one of the players flopped. Now I understood where all the acting on the basketball court originated when it came to the flop.

Day 18

*I woke up ready for a morning shooting workout
with Mando.*

We should have called ahead. When we got to the gym, the men's volleyball team was practicing and we found ourselves in a timeout. We took our talents to coffee.

The café we frequented is called The Small, Espresso + Bar. I was informed that most of my teammates went there for coffee or drinks before or after games. Mando said the owner of The Small was our biggest fan and got the crowd going.

"You will see what I mean on Saturday for our game."

I couldn't wait to soak it all in—the sights, and the sounds.

As the waitress came to take our order, she asked in Greek what I wanted. I looked at Mando, told her what I wanted in English and she handled the translation. This was the way it usually worked whenever I ordered something. The waitress again spoke in Greek to Mando.

"Ah, so this is your foreign player; I have heard a lot about her."

I had to laugh during Mando's translation. I kept the teeter-totter translation going. I asked Mando to tell the waitress that I hoped the things she had heard about me were good.

We stayed at The Small for almost two hours. This time, basketball was not the subject. Mando gave me a Greek lesson on common greetings and the proper response to common phrases and questions asked. My pronouncing of certain words produced a domino effect of laughter, starting with Mando and ending with me. I can only imagine what I sounded like to a native Greek attempting to speak their language. Wait! Maybe I don't want to imagine.

The lesson, though, was motivational. I wanted to be able to understand what people were telling me, even if I couldn't respond in Greek. I would feel a lot better not being lost the majority of the time to everything that was said around me. I started to pick up certain phrases and could sometimes understand part of a conversation, but I still found myself more times lost than found.

After the lessons, we headed back to our apartments. I sat out on the balcony enjoying the fresh air while watching the boats in the port out in the distance. I listened to music and took a quick nap to help pass the time.

I went over my usual visualization process and got myself ready for the scrimmage later that evening.

The scrimmage was chaotic, the replay in my mind scrambled. I had about fifteen points, or so I was told. (I don't really keep track of my stats during the game as I find that to be a distraction.) This was our last "friendly game," as they call it, or our last scrimmage. Regular season started in a few days.

After the game, I went to Eleni's. I really believe she should open her own restaurant. Tonight, she made chicken and rice with bell peppers. The rice was similar to Spanish rice, which is made with tomato sauce, and the chicken was prepared whole in the oven. The red bell peppers were oven roasted and had a sweet taste to them. I wasn't starting to get spoiled with her cooking, I was spoiled. She even made dessert: chocolate pudding with biscuits. I had a feeling extra cardio was in my future if I kept up with the amazing food and desserts I couldn't—and wouldn't—say no to. After dinner we watched *Thor.* I was always excited to be able to watch home. And I do mean home. *Thor* is one of many movies filmed in New Mexico.

Hard game. Great food. Surrounded by love. I had felt all this before. Every time I came home.

Day 19

One-on-none.

I knew the gym would be empty. I wanted it that way. Basketball is a team game, an aspect of the sport I love. But I also enjoy being able to spend time on my game alone, mix things up, break the routine. There's just something about an empty gym that brings a different level of focus. The smell of the hardwood floor, ball bouncing with the echo of empty space, and the ability to create any situation within my mind. The change of pace worked. The shooting workout was seamless. I left the gym as I had found it, like a church in silent prayer.

Not long after, I was with Eleni, heading to the mall. I can't precisely describe what I was expecting, since the only malls I was familiar with were the ones in America. But I was thinking different. I thought correctly. Sort of. The solitary difference were the stores—the ones the mall had, the ones I was used to. At this mall, there weren't large corporate retailers. No JC Penny, no Dillard's, no Macy's and so on down the list. The stores in Greece are similar though and range from moderately priced to expensive to "I definitely don't belong in here." The food court also accommodated life in Greece, with coffee shops, Greek food, some Asian food, burger joints, and ice cream shops. If you took me to a foreign mall for the first time and blindfolded me, I would still find the ice cream shop on my first try.

The layout was mall. One large building, housing numerous shops on two levels, with escalators and elevators to and from each floor. The smell of coffee and Greek pastries permeated the air. Part of me was expecting to run into Sarah, Deanna, and Jenna, my sisters, who have been known to stalk a mall or two or three. The thought of them brought a smile.

I bought a Greek-English dialogue book to assist with my learning of the language. It gave me the translation of the word or phrase which I was trying to say in Greek. I still hadn't learned the Greek alphabet and couldn't decipher their letters enough to try reading. Thankfully, the book showed how to pronounce the words with English letters.

After taking the tour through the mall, we sat down to enjoy some coffee. I began reading some phrases from the book to Eleni and some of her friends. Correction. I attempted to read some phrases. Hilarity ensued. First off, the Greek alphabet looked hieroglyphical to me. More like symbols than letters. Thankfully, the book also spelled out the words in English letters, which it referred to as "Greek-lish,"—Greek in English writing. At the very least, I could try and pronounce the words phonetically.

For example:

Hello: Γειά σου (YAH-soo)
How are you?: Τι κανείς (tee-KAH-nis)?
Good morning: Καλημέρα (kah-lee-MER-ah)
Good afternoon/evening: Καλησπέρα (kah-lee-SPER-ah)
Goodnight: Καληνύχτα (kah-lee-NEEKH-tah)
Thank you: Ευχαριστώ (eff-kha-ri-STOE)
My name is . . . : Με λένε (may LEH-neh)
What is your name?: πως σε λένε? (pos-oh LEH-neh)

Language and accents are the buffet of life. They're also DNA, no two are the same. My Greek accent is unique. How so? Well, it seems to elicit laughter with each and every sound, right Eleni? She appeared to be having the time of her life with my attempts. We both were.

We had a late practice, scheduled for 8 p.m. Since the gym was booked the rest of the day, I happily decided to go with Mando to watch a friendly volleyball match between our club and Paok, another club from Thessaloniki. It was a men's match and the tempo was 0-to-60 fast. I played volleyball back in high school and fell in love with the game. My coach, Dawn C'de Baca, told a reporter once that I would have been a better volleyball player in college than basketball. I know her words came from her head as well as her heart. She was the first coach I was willing to run through a wall for. In my own way, I did, playing on a torn calf muscle during my sophomore year in high school. Partly because of my competitive nature and partly due to not wanting to let Coach Dawn down. It takes a special kind of coach to bring out the best in an athlete, and she holds that specialness inside of her.

Some of the kills these guys displayed were incredible. Once the ball hit the floor, the velocity was so great that it bounced up and came close to hitting the ceiling. I enjoyed reminiscing on my own volleyball days and the feeling of getting my own kills and digs once upon a time. It won't be my final match, that's for sure.

Strategy preceded sweat at practice. Coach discussed and diagramed what we needed to work on, based on Paok, our next opponent. After the meeting, we conditioned to exhaustion. My body was ridiculously fatigued at the night's final whistle. I definitely regretted doing my leg workout earlier that day. I left the gym a little after 10 p.m., went for a gyro sandwich at the square, and returned to my apartment. I was asleep before my head dented my pillow.

Day 20

I admit I am a girl of letters—

I love to read—and I was an athlete of all seasons back in high school. Volleyball in the fall, basketball in the winter, track and field and softball in the spring. My high school letterman's jacket would give NASCAR drivers' suits a run for their money. Theirs are sponsorships. Mine are accomplishments.

But I didn't compete for accolades, adornments, or personal achievements. It was the competition itself. I still do this, even when no one else is around.

With the gym yet again occupied, I opted for a run along the sea. I usually felt like Superwoman—sans cape—when I ran here. Training at 7,500 feet throughout college gave me a great head start with my conditioning at sea level. I came upon a paved incline and set a challenge of two times. Two became four. Four became six. It felt good running. Remember? Superpowers, right? I would have continued before remembering a little thing called practice. I stopped. My legs didn't. They began to tighten. I found a bench, propped one leg up and stretched. I repeated the process on the opposite leg. That's when I took a closer look at the bench. Never feeling quite satisfied and always seeking competition, I decided it was perfect for triceps dips and pushups.

I needed a second stretch. I'm glad I did. Had I not, I would not have seen the people swimming in the sea and not have heard the men singing on a bench not far from me. Even when I was least expecting it, Greece always found a way to entertain me.

The bench soon became my favorite sofa. For a long while, I couldn't take my eyes off the sea and imagined the Greek melodies the group of older gentlemen sang were of the sea.

There were three of them, sitting on a bench not far from me. They held in their hands what looked like whiskey bottles, and their attire was casual—pants and t-shirts. They swayed back and forth to the tune, with facial expressions resembling those giving a performance on stage. The passion of their songs showed not only in their voices, but also on their faces. Although their voices were deep, the tune was pleasant. Their inflection rose in pitch on certain syllables and fell on others, like the sea not far from them. I found myself enraptured by their singing, by the performance, and was absentmindedly nodding my head along.

Even if I did not remember this day, I would never forget these moments. This is what God had in mind, to be captivated and living in the moment, and in those moments to be grateful for everything we have.

#

We received our new uniforms after practice. And yes, I was able to get number 4! This has been my unique number since I was in elementary school. I don't think it would be the same if I were wearing a different number out on the court. VJ#4 just has a ring to it.

I ended up at Eleni and Alex's after practice. And no, I wasn't wearing my jersey, even though I secretly wanted to. They also had invited other friends, and we snacked on some cheese and crackers while we watched a soccer match.

Alex told me to have my camera and swimsuit ready for Sunday. At first, the destination was hush-hush. The interrogation didn't take long for him to spill the details. Alex planned to take Eleni and me to a resort up in the mountains, to a small town called Drama. Alex showed me pictures of his and Eleni's previous trip. He also pulled some photos off the internet. It looked like a beautiful town—the views from and of the mountains looked incredible, and that was just from the photo gallery. I couldn't wait to get there. Then again, I was equally as anxious for our game Saturday.

Two days.

Two moments.

I wanted to live both right then.

Day 21

A body doesn't recover on its own.

I wish it did. It takes work. I spent the morning icing my legs, an unpleasant but necessary part of the recovery-and-rest process my body needed after pushing the limits the past few days. Unlike other athletes, basketball players don't taper, and our season opener was one day away.

Basketball isn't all brawn. It's brain, too. It's important to free your mind. I found such liberation at The Small café in Pezodromos square. The team commandeered the outside umbrella-covered tables, the ones with a nice view of the center of the square. Children's laughter and the sound of bouncing soccer balls filled the large concrete slab while children slalomed through with their free spirits and joyous attitudes. The café's music mixed together with the soft sea breeze flowing calmed the mind.

The conversation at the table ebbed and flowed, from Greek, to English, and back to Greek. I was caught in the current, only this time it was more lazy river, less white-water rapids. My teammates' English invited me into the conversation. I appreciated that. A lot. Eventually, they returned to what came naturally, Greek. I couldn't—and didn't—blame them. Unlike before, this time I found myself able to understand certain words being spoken and I followed along as best I could.

My curiosity, desire, and willingness to learn their language captivated me. But it couldn't contain me. After a while, I found myself daydreaming. It's as if the Greek language had lifted me into the breeze and I was in a daze, floating silently away.

Day 22

I waked with confidence.

No nerves. No jitters. Smooth, strong strides. Retracing the steps my soles knew by heart. I'm not exactly sure how many steps it took to reach the gym from my apartment. Maybe one day I'll count. My mind was singular. All thoughts reduced to two words: Game Day!

First stop, the locker room. Next stop, the court. Both were blurs. Sharpness returned during the warmup. My shots fell through the rim with such ease. My legs were coiled, ready for explosion. My body craved for the competition coming up. Playing the three previous friendly games, or scrimmages, worked to my advantage. I knew what to expect. With those games beneath my Nikes, I had a better sense of confidence, while adapting and adjusting to the different style of play.

Back to the locker room. Greek conversations filled the room. Everyone had their own pre-game rituals. Relaxed, I leaned back against the wall and visualized myself knocking down my shots, playing good defense, and pulling down rebounds. I reminded myself that no matter what my offensive game turned out to be, I had full control of my defense and my attitude.

We re-entered to full-throat passion. Duke University's "Cameron Crazies" are well known throughout college basketball and perhaps beyond. Our "student section" was Duke's equal. The section consisted of guys between their late teens and early twenties. They were loud. They were crazy. They were wonderful.

In unison, they chanted and they sang. It sounded like a boy band having to scream their lyrics above the shrieks and screams and shouts of teenage girls. They stayed on beat and pogo-sticked to the cadence of their chant. It sounded very much like a type of fight song. It whisked me back to high school, to college. In America, all schools have their own specific fight songs. I assumed that's what these guys were chanting, the fight song to our club.

Aside from the student section, the turnout was decent. I remember one time specifically I went up for a rebound and got pushed from behind while I was in the air. I hit the floor hard, and when no foul was called, the gym erupted with anger. The crowd exploded with boos of frustration at the ref. Shaking their fists in the air, red-faced and veins popping out of their foreheads, they reminded me of my playing days at West Las Vegas. I come from a two-high school town in Las Vegas, New Mexico, whose fans are passionate and crazy about their teams and notorious for this obsession. I thrived in that environment then. I was hoping I could reach their level now.

This once-upon-a-time story didn't conclude happily-ever-after. Then again, it's not the ending. Yes, we lost. By seven points. But remember, it was the opener and not the finale of the season. The frozen scoreboard was misleading. We were up six points going into the fourth quarter. Our collapse assisted their comeback. My shots were limited in the fourth quarter, our turnovers were not. We committed too many late, which cost us the lead, the victory. It was a decent start to my professional career—fifteen points, nine rebounds, three assists, one steal, one block. I missed a few opportunities to score. It happens. It's basketball.

Neither team went quietly into the good night. After the game, our opponent went to break in the center of the court. The student section took offense, voicing their displeasure first with yelling and then with booing. The railing that separated bleachers from court took the full lean of the agitation, as raised fists pumped the air already filled with shouts.

Part of me expected the verbal to turn physical, especially after an argument broke out between one of my teammates and an opposing player. Bedlam was closing fast on chaos. The anticipation that this could turn into a full-out brawl spiked my adrenaline levels through the roof. Our coaches didn't wait for cooler heads to prevail. Instead, they were pushing us into the locker room as quickly as they could, trying to prevent any further arguments or real fights from ensuing.

One of the coaches finally got hold of my teammate, the one who was arguing, and brought her into the locker room. She entered still shouting over her shoulder into the gym, still arguing. Calm somewhat restored, Andreas, our head coach joined us. He spoke first—naturally, and instinctively, in Greek. I studied his face, his emotions, his body language and demeanor, trying to decipher the meaning of his message. I could sense the disappointment from his tone. And, a little bit of anger still pervaded his emotions. Witnessing many post-game talks after a loss, I was sure this wasn't far off the norm. Talking about what we could have done better that could have affected the outcome of the game, what we must do to improve moving forward, and some challenges to specific individuals on the team.

Of course, this was all me speculating what he was saying, doing my best to translate to myself based on sight, not sound.

After coach finished speaking, I turned to Vassiliki, my trusty translator.

"What was he talking about?"

"Too much to say, and nothing about you. We just need to do better."

Sensing that she didn't want to talk about everything that just happened, I shrugged it all off and started changing out of my uniform. The locker room turned into silent night. As I threw my bag over my shoulder and began walking out of the locker room, Adriana, our post player, patted me on the back.

"Welcome to Greek basketball, Vera."

There was a sly grin on her face as she spoke. I had a feeling what happened wasn't out of the ordinary. I understood how prideful these clubs were and how high the competitive fire was to win in this league.

I walked out of the locker room and took a seat on the bench, waiting for the gym to clear before I returned to my apartment. I sat there for a while reflecting on my mistakes. It's what I've always done and probably will continue to do. I put all losses on my shoulders. I rewound the game in my mind. I pushed play. I saw key points in the game when I could have done something different to change the outcome. I saw my mistakes and made a mental note on what I could do differently if the situation arose again. Visualizing what I could have done that would have created a different result. I pressed stop.

One thing that I have learned throughout my career is how to let a loss or disappointment go, learn from it, and move on. After reflection of the game for about an hour or so, I let go and in preparation of our next opponent, started focusing on some of the tangible things I could do to improve my game and to improve our chances of winning.

Eleni and Alex waited for me. In my tunnel vision, Eleni shone the light, and the darkness of the loss vanished. Giggling, she said, "Andreas was calling out the play, "FIVE, FIVE," and Vera screams, "*PENTE, PENTE!*" I shrugged my shoulders while she laughed, adding, "I thought it was too funny when coach calls the plays in English and you call them out in Greek!"

I couldn't contain my laughter.

"For the record, I can count to ten in Greek," I finally responded. "I will pass for a Greek soon enough."

"Of course you will!"

It was Alex, with the final words before we said our goodbyes and went our separate ways.

Later, Eleni sent me a link from a local site that had sent a reporter to cover the game. Of course, everything was in Greek. I used Google to translate.

"What to see: A group with a history in the category returns after an impressive season in A2 (the second division in Greece). With several young Greeks and a few experienced on the team, we will see some of the best players of the A2 division over the years try to compete in the A1 division. You will see the three Kazantzi sisters who used to play for PAOK in the roster for Apollon and we will see an American player who can do many things on the court.

What we will not see: Large and experienced players. They will lose games due to inexperience. Missing a foreign player underneath the basket where there is lack of solutions.

The Star: Vera Jo Bustos. The graduate from Adams State comes with good references and a player who can do many things for the team. Playing positions from "1" to "4," she can score, rebound, and defend where needed. She will be the benchmark of the Rossoneri. The symbol will allow the Greek women to compete with the talent in the A1 division to provide an even support to Bustos. If so, then Kalamaria can avoid play-out."

After reading the article, I didn't feel like the star of the team. Not after a close loss I could have prevented. I shook the nagging of negative thinking resting on my shoulders and began to talk positively. It's easy to spiral down the nasty funnel of negativity. If I didn't speak words of positivity to myself, my thoughts would control me, get the best of me, and I would suffer two defeats in one night. That's where slumps started for me and where I would start to question my value as a player. I learned that as a player you can't get too low after a loss, nor can you get too high after a win. It was one game. Time to focus on the next.

And besides, all stars need darkness.

Day 23

I awoke a child on Christmas morning.

Or so it felt. My heart was wrapped in excitement. Anticipation opened my eyes, wide. I didn't dare blink.

Alex and Eleni were there, 9 a.m., right on time. Once seat-belted tight, we were off. The rear-view mirror had the day off as it reflected the stadium we left behind. That was the last time we looked back.

"Where are we going?"

It was me, being impatient. As always.

"It's a surprise. Don't worry. You'll love it."

It was Alex, being mysterious. As always.

Can't drive without gas and frappe. I wasn't much of a coffee drinker prior to my arrival to Greece. Frappe addiction took hold early.

I realized our "go" was going to have plenty of "stops."

The first was the "Lion of Amphipolis." It's a lion mounted on an altar. The dull-white stone reflected its age. The statue was initially found in pieces and then restored.

"How old is this statue?" I asked.

"Too old," Alex replied. "It was from the time of Alexander the Great. There are many statues and artifacts from the time of Alexander the Great all over Greece."

Intrigued to absorb everything, I read the inscription at the base of the monument:

MINISTRY OF CULTURE 28TH EPHORATE
OF PREHISTORIC AND CLASSICAL ANTIQUITIES
<LION OF AMPHIPOLIS>

The famous <Lion of Amphipolis> is part of the late 4th century BC funerary sculpture, a monument to martial virtue. It is believed that it was erected in honor of Laomedon from Lesbos, one of Alexander the Great's three greatest admirals, known to have settled at Amphipolis.

It was restored and erected on a conventional base at the spot where it was discovered on the west bank of the river Strymon, near the old bridge. Its discovery is connected with Macedonias contemporary war history: Greek soldiers digging during the Balkan War (1912-1913) found the first pieces of the monument.

With Alexander the Great still in my thoughts, our drive through the countryside of Greece continued. We passed small churches and cotton fields. The cool breeze hitting my face reminded me of countless drives through the mountains back home in New Mexico. The ground was littered with stones and patches of grass between them. We drove through a city named Drama, which Eleni said has the second-best night life next to Thessaloniki. The farther we drove the more altitude we gained as we traveled higher into the mountain. As we snaked the winding road, the views become more amazing with each switchback. From the top of the mountain, I could see the beautiful Greek landscapes off in the distance. The mountainous scenery cascaded into the background of what seemed like a picture from a textbook. I could see the road we drove in on fade away into the mountains, its snake-like form cutting through the trees. The peaks off in the distance flowed into a blue-gray color as the baby-blue sky seemed to kiss their tops.

One turn later, the village was suddenly visible and seemed to mute the American music we were blasting. In the valley with vast mountains bookending both sides, I saw Drama, with the small, red-roofed houses distinct in the distance, from a new angle. The sea was miles away, nowhere to be seen. The Greece I knew was by sea only. Until now. This Greece, these mountains, took away what breath remained by their sheer beauty.

Finally, we arrived at the hotel in the village. Eleni and Alex said hello to the owners who greeted all of us with hugs and "Greek kisses," as I grew to call them. I learned one kiss on each cheek was a proper greeting with someone who was known on a personal level. It's similar to giving a hug in the U.S.—well, at least in the Southwest. I understand cultures are different everywhere.

After our greetings, we decided to go for a walk in the mountain near the hotel. We took a scenic drive near the city to reach our hiking path. I saw children playing in the street, men and women sitting outside on the porches of their homes enjoying each other's company, and some elderly women, who I presumed were walking home from church.

One of the men who worked at the hotel accompanied us as a tour guide. He escorted us to an old military fort that was built inside the mountain. While we drove up the dirt road, the sound of the rocks crunching under the tires brought back memories of driving up the dirt road to Gallinas, a canyon with a small stream located near my hometown.

When we arrived, the man gave us a tour of the fort. Inside, it was pitch black. We each had flashlights to find our way around. Our guide didn't speak English, so every time he said something Alex translated.

The fort was built in the early 1900s and took almost twenty years to complete. According to our guide, it would take four hours to walk through its entirety. There were also tunnels underground, which connected to other forts inside another mountain about three miles away from where we were standing.

"It will take you four hours to see this fort. If you want to see the other one, call a taxi."

Alex's words brought laughter and life in what long ago had been left for dead.

We walked into a little room where a small window let in light from the outside world, and we could see the neighboring country of Bulgaria. There are no borders that distinguish Greece from Bulgaria. The land flows effortlessly from one country to the next. After a couple hours of exploring the fort through the mountain with our flashlights, we decided to head back to the hotel. Sometimes, hunger has priority.

As we made our way to the exit, I became anxious, worrying about our flashlights dying.

"If the lights go out, there is no way we will find our way out of here."

I kept that thought internal. I'm glad I did. The exit appeared, as did the sunlight.

We passed by wild horses, pigs, and cattle on our drive down the mountainside and to the hotel. I loved watching the wild horses. A couple wore halters over their noses. Confused, I asked, "If these horses are wild, why do they wear halters?"

"The children of the village put those on the horses for them to catch and ride them," our guide explained and Alex translated. "They are wild horses in the sense that they have no owner, but they are tame and gentle enough for the children of the village to ride them. They belong to the village."

"Wow, that must be cool to grow up in a small village like this," I replied. "Roam around the countryside with wild animals roaming around with you!"

The car was in complete agreement.

"There are many great ways to live," our guide said. "The small village of the countryside is one of them. It just depends on a person's personality and what he wants out of life."

"Wise words," I thought, wondering where I would eventually settle down and raise my own family.

That night's dinner at the hotel was overshadowed by the wine. It tasted amazing. The bottle label was written in Greek, so I can't recall it by name. But the wine was made by the owners of the hotel. That information is worth remembering.

It was explained to me that this mountain town was more of a winter attraction site. So, during the warmer months, it was a bit dead in terms of tourists wandering through. The hotel, meanwhile, was a two-story, small brick building, best described as cozy, homey. The lounge area featured comfortable couches and love seats facing each other with a coffee table sitting in the center of the space. Back in one corner was a fully stocked bar. Around the corner, past the front desk, the stairway led to the second-floor rooms. There was also a hot tub and sauna located on the first floor. Perfect for those chilly winter months. To the left of the front desk was the dining area. The table was long and rectangular and could comfortably fit a dozen.

Since guests were minimal, the owners joined us for dinner and conversation. It's no longer awkward for me to sit silently amidst Greek conversations. For one, Alex or Eleni always found time to translate without interrupting the flow. For another, I felt welcomed, included. This night, with these new friends, it felt like I was visiting family members I hadn't seen in years, and they were spoiling me with food, wine, conversation and love for the time I had spent away.

After we finished eating, the chef showed us his second passion— photography. His photo album included beautiful pictures ranging from the sunset over the mountaintops to a bee hovering over a flower with brilliant colors. He showed pictures of traditional festivals they have and the traditional attire they wear. I'm not sure which was more enjoyable, the food or the photos.

Next, the "book of experiences" was brought out. It was large, measuring around 12x12. The cover was made of old, brown leather, which exposed its age in the form of stains on the pages and wear on the cover.

"You will be famous in Greece one day, so you should give them your autograph and tell everyone about your experience here," Eleni told me. "They will also want your picture. Picture of our own celebrity!"

As I signed the "book of experiences," the hotel owners and Alex were busy taking pictures of me. I could feel my cheeks redden as the moment unfolded and the feeling of being a "celebrity" in Greece returned.

We moved from dinner table to lounge area, carrying conversation and coffee with us. I substituted body language for Greek, replacing the verbal with visceral. I felt the gist of their anecdotes based off their movements and facial expressions. I found myself laughing at all the appropriate times without knowing why. I suppose body language is a language within itself. So if I can learn that, why am I still struggling with Greek?

The hot tub called. We answered. The ambiance was five-star spa. Dim lights and soft music. A kaleidoscope of constantly changing colors inside the hot tub and a mind, body, soul at peace.

My book of memories is wordless. It's reserved for days like this. It's devoid of the written, the spoken, and of actions.

My book of memories is all about feelings. I will feel this day forever.

Day 24-25

*Ever noticed that life is often described
like amusement parks?*

There are rollercoasters. There are merry-go-rounds. There are lazy rivers. I found a ride to my liking. It's called familiarity. Wake up, work out, go for lunch, read, wait for afternoon practice. It was a routine that fit, but left enough room for life's unexpected detours.

On Monday, while I was going for my lunch with Mando, she had to stop at the bank. I tagged along. To get inside, Mando pressed a button that looked like a doorbell on the side of the door. Once she opened the door, she instructed me to follow her. We were in a small space between two glass doors. In order for the second door to open to get into the bank, we had to close the first door. Once the first door closed, she pressed another button, which unlocked the second door. Were we entering a bank or Greece's CIA?

It was another first for me. I could only imagine how that scene could have turned out had I arrived alone. I pictured myself having a silly moment and not being able to figure out how to get into the bank. In America, people are stuck between a rock and a hard place. In Greece, Vera Jo is stuck between a door and another door.

The bank was set up like a DMV. Once we were inside, we had to take a number and wait our turn. There were numerous chairs lined up in neat rows facing the counters. A machine-like voice would call out the number, which was also flashing above the counter of the teller who waited to assist.

#

There were no detours Tuesday. I finished reading *Mind Gym* by Gary Mack. A new book was in my immediate future. A new player wasn't far behind. I found out earlier we would be getting another American on our team, a post player from the Big South Conference. She would be playing the five position, inside as the post player or "big man." I had high hopes. We needed an inside presence. She would arrive later that week, and the club would take care of all the paperwork needed for her to play Sunday.

I was ready for life's next ride.

Day 26

In a world of Twitter, Instagram, Facebook, instant messaging, had postcards become pay phones?

I was about to find out.

On my way to lunch with Mando, I asked her to help me find a shop that sold postcards. We walked past the square to a side street that was anything but. It, too, was lined with shops. I had been unaware of its existence, but here they were. We walked past ice cream shops, clothing shops, antique shops, tourist shops. After we searched for forty-five minutes, a gentleman who worked at a bookstore told us they did not sell postcards in Kalamaria. We would have to go downtown to find one.

It wasn't a defeat, more of a detour than a dead end. I was able to explore more of the neighborhood of Kalamaria and expand my boundaries. It felt like a Saturday afternoon, people strolling the streets and sitting in the cafés drinking coffee. I didn't quite understand how so many people were out and about on a weekday. Though opposite of home, it's a lifestyle I could get accustomed to.

#

I had another quiet evening. The team ordered me pizza for dinner, which I enjoyed while watching the sunset peer over my balcony. The lights of the city shone over the sea. Over the trees of my backyard, the sky displayed an array of purple, orange, and yellow along the horizon. I tried, but failed, to capture the brilliance of the view I was experiencing with my camera.

No 3x5s, no postcards. It didn't matter. Maybe next time. Then again, when do God's blessings need postage or come in glossy or matte finish? I simply gave thanks and held out hope that one day I would experience a moment like this with my family—the people I loved.

◉

Day 27

◉

My agent Thomas called, inviting me out for a frappe.

The club had provided me with a cell phone. It's simple, yet sufficient for my needs. It's the one I use to communicate with my coaches and agent. But the phone is programmed in Greek, forcing me to memorize what the names translated to in Greek. In the alphabetical game of hide-and-seek, Greek was still hiding, still winning. So I relied on my memory to match the name with the number to identify the caller.

Thomas drove to an awesome restaurant/café on a hill that overlooked the Aegean Sea. As soon as I sat down, I noticed huge white birds floating on the water. My assumption was swans, since those were the only large white birds I was familiar with. Does Greece have swans? I forgot to ask. They glided effortlessly and serenely through the water against a backdrop of boats bobbing ever so slowly.

The talk with Thomas was enjoyable, as always. The conversation covered Xs and Os, present and future, and life. He taught me how to order my own frappe in Greek.

"*Frappe, gl-ee-ko meh ga-la.*"

His enunciation was slow, meticulous. It translated to an iced coffee with sugar and cream. That I could say in English. In Greek, not so much. I struggled. Thomas laughed before helping me with my pronunciation. I was excited to put my Greek skills to the test next time I went out and ordered a coffee without the need of a translator. I'll let you know how it goes.

Thomas dropped me off at the square. On my way to pick up my lunch, a young man walked alongside and engaged me in conversation.

He asked something in Greek. When I looked at him, puzzled, I think my expression gave away that I didn't speak Greek.

He responded to my confusion in English.

"Where are you from?"

"I'm an American, from New Mexico."

He chuckled.

"It has been a long while since I have heard an American accent."

We parted ways, and I went to get lunch. I've never given much thought to the sound of my voice. I sound like . . . me. But what does "me" sound like to others? That thought made me laugh. I was the minority here, and I could only imagine how bizarre I sounded whenever I spoke. I just hoped I sounded cool, like foreign accents sound to me.

I went with Alex and Eleni to Cosmos after practice. We browsed through the shops and then went to eat at TGI Fridays. What's a mall without a Fridays? It was my first time eating at Fridays—ever. How ironic that my first time eating at this American chain restaurant was in a foreign country. I wish I could say I ordered for all of us, but the menus were in Greek. Dang it! So close and yet . . . As much as I was falling in love with Greek cuisine, I have to admit it was nice change.

What didn't change is how Alex and Eleni made me feel each and every time I was with them. They were such a joy to be around. Alex was always joking and teasing me, with the latest being my "blondie times," which I am sure were many.

Turns out it was couples night for me. After dinner, I joined Coach Andreas and Margarita, (not a couple together but the important couple of the club) who were going to the airport to pick up my new American teammate named K. Her flight was delayed, so we waited in the airport restaurant. Margarita was another of my many, many unofficial Greek tutors. We worked on words and phrases. Sadly, I only got the colors orange and green right. Margarita spoke English, but that was around twenty years ago, according to Andreas, who served as our translator. We reversed roles of teacher and student until the plane landed.

After luggage, customs, and the drive, we reached our apartments around 2 a.m. Andreas left me with this message.

"You will be her guide around Kalamaria because you are already like a Greek!"

The city could wait. For me, practice couldn't come soon enough.

Day 28

There are times in life when you can't repay kindness.

When those moments arise, I think about paying it forward. And that's what I attempted to do with my newest teammate.

After I caught some sleep following the late and exciting night, I took K to get some lunch and showed her around the square of Kalamaria, just as I had been shown three weeks earlier. Everyone was excited and eager to meet her. I was confident she would help us. Her strength makes her a presence inside, which is just what we needed. I was certain having her on the floor with us would free me up for more open shots.

Our first practice proved me right. Afterward, Thomas took K and me to get a frappe. I ordered solo.

"Frappe, gl-ee-ko meh ga-la".

The waitress nodded in approval. Thomas applauded my best Greek accent while we both laughed. Thomas is extremely kind-hearted. Our conversations are effortless. He reminded me about positive thinking and offered his help in any way he could.

Thomas dropped us off at the square, and we walked over to Eleni and Alex's apartment. They took us to a nice restaurant where we had a great dinner. Eleni and Alex laughed and joked with me when I tried to teach K my limited Greek vocabulary.

Alex's review came first.

"You are a pro here in Greece already. You are fluent in Greek!"

Obviously, I wasn't within a 3-pointer being fluent in the language. I maybe had twenty words I knew and a handful of phrases I memorized. During the meal, Alex started speaking to me in Greek, knowing that I didn't understand what he was telling me.

"Otee-na-neh," I'd reply.

Translation: "Whatever."

Alex laughed and gave me a high-five, appreciating my humor. The mood was always light and fun with him and Eleni. Life owes us nothing. We owe life everything. I know how to repay kindness and how to pay it forward.

But how do you repay blessings?

Day 29

*There are those who believe if you train the mind
the body will follow.*

I am of that faith. The morning's film and practice was designed to make us think.

Most teams have rituals they follow on the day before a game. Ours was no different. It featured lots of uncontested shooting and highlighted the plays we wanted to run offensively and reviewing the plays we expected our opponents to run, the latter based off the scouting report provided by our coaches. We also received a paper scout to help better understand our opponent. It was basically homework. Our grade would be the scoreboard.

The scouting report broke down individual player tendencies, which plays the team ran, along with baseline out-of-bounds and sideline out-of-bounds plays. It was thorough and familiar. Basketball's language in the way the game is played is universal—thank God.

I kept the day's theme going after practice. I watched *Facing the Giants*. The movie was inspirational, the perfect choice before the big game. The movie was based on God and how His works can change any situation. The movie unlocked a whole new feeling to the meaning of inspiration and motivation inside me.

After the credits, I self-reflected about how intricate God's presence, timing, and plan has been consistent in my life. God definitely circled this date in time for me on my calendar. He had answered my prayers and made my childhood dream of becoming a professional athlete come true. Even with all odds stacked against me, here I was, a day away, preparing for my second professional game in Greece.

What follows inspiration? In my vocabulary, it's ice cream. I found K to be my accomplice. Soon, we were a party of three after we ran into Eleni, who was heading to watch Alex's younger team play.

Flashbacks flooded my mind as I watched. Memories fresh as yesterday. Little girls playing without worry, without fear. Relationships built in victory and in defeat, relationships still standing today. Dreams of high school, of college, and yes, even of pros. Late nights and countless hours in my backyard. Practicing my ball handling, working on my shooting, getting in trouble with mom since I wouldn't come in for dinner because I hadn't finished my workout.

One girl, one ball, one basket. It was those hours, spent alone, that laid the foundation to where I now stand. I couldn't dream myself here. It took work, and no one had to place the hard hat on me. It's the invisible one I still wear to live my dreams.

My past was returning to my present as I thought back to all the days I listened to motivational speakers asking me, "What is your dream?" I leaned back on the bleachers, watching the young girls play with a sense of pride and accomplishment and told myself, "I am living my dream."

"Perfect moments," as I like to call them, happen about as often as I make a round tortilla in my grandma's kitchen. Today, I made a perfect circle.

We all are guilty of falling into the traps of the human mind. Spending too much time thinking of the past, contemplating too much of the future, we seldom live in the present.

Mistakes live in the past. Fear lives in the future. I challenged myself that day to live and play in the moment. That is how I would make the most out of this journey and to honor the friendships and memories I was making.

It was easy to get caught up in being so far away from home and the time change that affected the window of opportunity I had to speak to anyone back home. The culture change and the language barriers were two other traps I fell into. I also slipped into the defeating trenches of negative thinking from time to time. I alone allowed my thoughts to take control of me. I alone focused on everything that was difficult and challenging in front of me, instead of keeping sight of the positive and living in the moment. I alone was being my own worst enemy.

I alone drew the line in the proverbial sand.

On one side:

Live in the moment.

Stack up as many perfect moments as I could during my time in Greece.

Accept the challenging situations for what they were, acknowledge them, and move past them.

After all, isn't life about our perception of our own realities?

I stepped over the line and stood firmly into that side.

Day 30

Game day.

I was looking forward to our first road trip, a 100-mile jaunt to the city of Ptolemaida, which was west of Thessaloniki. Now, if I can only keep my eyes open.

I was not, am not, a morning person. Today was not the exception. We left in the early hours of the morning. I was awake walking to the bus, getting on the bus. That's when the eyes closed. I woke for a few minutes and saw mountains out the window. The rest of the time I saw the inside of my eyelids.

Once we got to the gym, I had to do my best to get my body awake and my mind moving. Looking back, I slept-walked the first half.

I'll end the suspense. We lost. My first half was nothing to email home about. If I kept a SportsCenter not so top ten list, the first half was moving up the charts. I couldn't remember the last time I played so poorly.

There was no time for regret, but there was time for redemption.

I collected myself during halftime and came out with better energy, a more aggressive mindset. I finished with fourteen points and seven rebounds. I wasn't sure about the rest of my stats.

College taught me more than curriculum. It taught me character. It taught me catch-and-release. *Huh?* Let me explain. During my early years at Adams State, I got down on myself and stayed there for hours. Until I realized there was nothing I could do about the past. Live, learn, and move on. Catch-and-release.

I released the bad and took hold of the good, which was the second half. I had a good drive to the basket and scored over the 6-foot-5 post player. I drained crucial jump shots. Defensively, there was a dive for the ball and a steal and a banged knee.

I was a different player after intermission. From half-bad to not-bad, I could accept that, I could build on that. Even so, I again felt responsible for the loss. I know if I had played better in the first half, it would have been a different game and a different outcome. Then again, the past is just stories we tell ourselves.

It was a wide-eyed return. I'll never stop being amazed by the beauty of Greece. For almost two hours I enjoyed vast mountains with a lake at the bottom of a valley and a picturesque landscape. Who gets to visit the sea and the mountains in one day? I do.

I looked at my phone—4 p.m. I had four hours before dinner. I iced my knee while I Skyped with mom. I streamed a movie. The sunset diverted my eyes from the screen. There was fire in the sky.

I walked to Alex and Eleni's. We had chicken and salad. The chicken was prepared in the oven with potatoes. The salad was Greek—tomatoes, cucumbers, and Feta cheese. Alex jokingly calls me the "ultimate eating machine."

I own that title.

What can I say? When it comes to food, I'm willing to try anything and everything once.

Day 31

To the best of my recollection,
Freddy Kruger never did Greece.

Had he, someone else would have written this story. I lived a nightmare—a wet, dark, nightmare. But that's not how the day started.

It began unremarkably. It was a rest day, which was nice as I was able to sleep in. Even though nothing was required, I got to the gym, got some shots up, and got some conditioning on the bike in the weight room.

Now, this is where things started to get interesting. Cue the background horror music. I had plans to go out with some of my teammates and some of the players from the men's team. It had been cold the past couple of days, so I had the heater on. As I was taking a shower to get ready for the evening, I heard a knock on my door. A little startled, I wondered who could possibly be knocking.

Suddenly, the world went black. All power left the room, taking with it my calm and composure and the warmth from the water. I had just put conditioner in my hair so I was trying to get it all out as fast as I could because the temperature of the water reached freezing. I was doing a little dance in the shower. Icicles drummed my back. I've never moved faster.

The power goes out, someone is showering in the dark. This is how an episode of *CSI* starts. I found no humor in that thought. My verbal obscenities proved that. I fumbled to find the shower knob before sifting through the darkness with my hands in search of my towel. With towel wrapped around my freezing body, I continued my blind search for my phone. I found it and managed to turn on the flashlight.

Whew!

As I was dressing, I wondered who had knocked on my door. I tried not to imagine the worst. Instead, I wondered if it was my new American teammate. Perhaps her power might have gone out, too. Thinking it had to be her, worrying about her, and not wanting to be alone in the dark, I set a personal record for getting dressed.

To my surprise, when I exited my room, I discovered I was the only one in the dark, but I set another personal record running to her room.

My knock preceded my questions.

"Hey, are you okay? Did you come knocking on my door a few minutes ago? Did your lights go out?"

Her face was a selfie of confusion.

"Uh, no. I didn't knock on your door and my lights have been working fine. Umm, are YOU okay?"

I explained my episode. That's where the drama ended, but not the mystery. She laughed and joked about me still having some conditioner left in my hair. On my way back to my room, I knocked on my Greek teammate's door.

"Hi, Mando. Umm, just checking to see if your lights went off?"

Her lights were obviously still on. Her expression was puzzlement.

"Everything is fine here, Vera."

I explained what had happened while I was in the shower.

"Ok, I will be right there to see what is happening."

Her response restored a measure of calm. Still, confusion remained.

So, why was my room the only one that lost power? I questioned my predicament while sitting in the dark. Mando arrived with back-up in the human form of Ephrem, the head of security and maintenance man for the complex. He solved the situation without breaking a sweat.

He only spoke Greek. It didn't matter. His mannerisms and gestures were easily read. He pointed to the heater, and to the bathroom and shook his head. His words were fast, loud, direct.

Mando clarified.

"He says that you can't have the heat on at the same time you take a hot shower. He says it is too much for the generator to handle. When you do both, no more power!"

Ugh!

Ephrem walked out of my room. His head was still shaking and his mouth was still muttering in a tone of frustration.

I yelled, "Thank you, Ephrem!"

He kept his back turned, only raising his arm and hand. He never broke stride as he walked toward the room where the generator that powered the complex was.

"I think I got him mad," I told Mando.

"He is fine," she replied. "Don't worry about him."

"Some things you just have to learn the hard way," I said. It made us both laugh.

Ephrem worked his magic. The power was restored in plenty of time for me to finish getting ready.

Our night was an evening best described as now and then. The *now* was the movie. The *then* was the city.

Communication and conversation turned into a game of charades with one of the guys. Well, for me it did. As he tried to think of the right word to say or how to explain something, I shouted out words in anticipation. I had become good at this game. I had to, even though there were times it wasn't necessary.

As I began to spend time with others outside of my teammates, I found the majority of the younger generation had a basic understanding of English. Most within my age-group spoke the language, though it was only the basics. It wasn't their acumen of English I struggled with. It was their accents. Our dialogues remained works in progress.

Soon they would revert back Greek. I suspected it was out of frustration. The incompetence I felt at times was self-defeating. I spoke one language. I had a determination to learn Greek. I owed it to them. I also owed it to me.

A tour of the city completed the night's double-feature. Once more, I was one with the monuments and ancient ruins. If reincarnation exists, I wonder if I had been here before, when the ruins were first erected. My reference point was the movie *Troy*. I imagined the old walls in full form with huge buildings standing before me. I also imagined what other heroes had walked in the very same spot I was now walking. Alexander the Great? Achilles, perhaps?

These ruins awoke a fascination of ancient Greeks and Greek mythology inside me. I was enthralled by the past, by the people, by the possibilities of this place, by everyone who lived before me, by everyone who once stood where I was now standing. I was in two places at once. I was then; I was now.

What a day! It ended where it began, my apartment. I flicked a switch. The lights turned on. I still hadn't solved who knocked on my door. Just to feel safe, I turned on the rest of the lights and took a look around.

———⊙———

Day 32

———⊙———

Most times, I am my own worst nightmare.

Last night, I was my own ROFL meme, *sans* Emoji. Well, to my teammates I was.

ROFL is the acronym for "Rolling On The Floor Laughing." It's used mostly on Twitter, Instagram and everything where depth is TMI, "Too Much Information." It seems my "cold shower in the dark" from the previous night was the talk of the locker room.

A stream of teammates and other friends approached individually and in groups, asking about the incident. After each explanation, the response was the same—doubled-over laughter with bouts of tears in their eyes from laughing so hard.

In between his own guffaws of laughter, Coach Andreas explained to me that not all of Greece is incapable to have the heat on and take a warm shower at the same time. With the way the generator is set up in the apartment complex, it is only our apartments that can't handle the electricity overload with the water heater and the heater going simultaneously. Even I had to laugh it off. Spend enough time around me, and you will encounter a fair share of embarrassing moments. Anything to keep them ROFLing, I guess.

We smiled—and sweated—through a tough practice. Even though we only had one day off, I missed my teammates. They weren't just teammates, they were beginning to feel like family. As were Alex and Eleni, with whom I spent another unforgettable evening. I was glad laughter did its part to bridge the slight language barrier that remained. I was building a bridge from America and Greece, one smile at a time.

————⊙————

Day 33

————⊙————

My family and friends will testify that I can find a workout in a spool of thread.

Luckily, there was a track not far from my front door.

Since our practice wasn't until eight o'clock in the evening, I couldn't just sit and wait. My morning was 400 meters. Then, 800. Then, 1,200. Then, . . . well, you know where this is heading.

I opted for intervals, sprinting the straightaways, jogging the curves. I wasn't working speed or endurance. It was me being me. Doing my best to get the edge over my competition, me trying to be the best I could be. Today, it was intervals. Other days it's extra conditioning, or weight training, or long hours in the gym fine tuning my shooting and overall skills.

Activity is not a synonym for achievement. Not in my dictionary, not in my life. I don't work out to stay busy. I work out to achieve my dreams. Not just the ones that have come true, but also the ones that remain dreams.

Satisfied with the work invested, I grabbed lunch and relaxed at my apartment until practice that evening. Our practice was active, accomplished. A few of my teammates and I took those feelings to TGI Fridays for dinner.

I carried the most excitement. American meal. American restaurant. I splurged. I ordered a steak. My teammates were rookies when it came to eating at the American chain. Only one had been there before. Indecisive expressions revealed their newness to the restaurant and to the menu. I recommended burgers and sandwiches.

As our food came out, one of my teammates took a spoonful of sour cream and downed it in one gulp. Her face turned sour and bright red, and she started making noises and faces. They weren't hilarious to her, but they were to the rest of the table. I lost full control. Tears streamed my face and muscles cramped my stomach from laughing so hard.

"I thought it was yogurt," she said.

Round Two of the laughter, the tears, the cramps. I'm glad it didn't stop there. I noticed my other teammate was eating her sandwich by taking everything apart. She ate the bread first, then the chicken, then the bacon. She ate everything separate.

I gave her new instructions.

"You're supposed to eat it all together! Just smash it down a little bit so you can eat it all in one bite."

I gestured with my hands how to smash down the sandwich. She smashed the remaining half and took a bite.

"AHHH, yes! Much better. It was not so good before. Now, it is good."

I imagined how many times they had laughed at me with some of the things I had done unknowingly with the variances of our cultures. And they should have. I never took offense.

But on this night, the laughter was finally on a different face. Mine.

Day 34

All practices can't be virtual reality.

But there are times, and places, when they should be. Coach Andreas picked this morning to be one of those times.

Andreas had three of us drill game-like shooting situations. It required repetition. It demanded intensity. It rocketed our heart rates. I wiped the sweat, left the accomplishment. Given the option of on-court training verses off-court training, I would ball all day as a means of getting in shape, staying in shape.

The day proved too real the rest of the way.

I had an invitation from Thomas and Dimitrius, an agent friend of his, to meet for coffee after practice. I had a surprise for them.

Quite proud of my ability to learn some of the language in simple greetings and ordering my own coffee, I didn't skip a beat when the waitress came up and asked us what we would like to drink.

"*Frappe metrio meh gala,*" I replied, asking for an iced coffee with sugar, not too sweet.

Thomas clapped his hands and said, "Bravo, Vera," applauding me for ordering my coffee in Greek.

Dimitrius chimed, "Yes. Very good. Your accent is very close to Greek. It seems like you could have been born here."

"Thank you for the compliment," I replied. My face challenged the sun, beam for beam.

I wasn't leading the race to learn the language. Then again, I wasn't so far back that I would never catch up. My learning stride was quickening and I was thankful someone noticed.

Thomas presented his upgraded diagnosis of my game—where I was, where I still need to go, what I need to do to get there. He is someone I rely on to tell me not what I want to hear, rather what I need to hear. I thanked him for that and could have thanked him for so much more, including the fact that we never part without smiles and jokes.

I wish the day would have stayed that way. Midway through the afternoon, my stomach started acting up and I felt sick. I had a good practice but didn't feel very well. It was during those times that I missed being home. I missed having mom there to tend to me and make me feel better. There was something about my body feeling sick that made my heart homesick as well.

Neither my body nor my heart improved the following morning. It had been a while since I had stopped and realized how much I missed home. Now, there was no stopping it. I had my moments of solitude when I would sit in that studio apartment and wrestle with my homesickness in the late hours of the night.

At times, I asked, "What did I get myself into?" as I thought about how far away I was from home. There was no such thing as just hopping in a car and getting home quick, like I did so many times in college. That was out of the question.

The darkness of the reality of where I was closed around me like the lid on the top of the box. I was inside. Outside were the words:

Fragile! Handle with Care!

Day 36

*Whatever had lodged in my stomach had receded
in the day before, and so did my homesickness.*

I took it as a positive sign, waking up anxious and excited in anticipation of tonight's game. The opponent was tough. That was a certainty. We needed a win. I needed to play better. The two went hand-in-hand. Well, in my mind they did.

Physically, I couldn't be more prepared. All the prep work had been done. So, I focused on the mental side. I visualized my shots falling easily. Staying on balance, elbow in tight, wrist snapping with a perfect follow through, listening for the sounds of the ball passing through the net—*swish*. I visualized myself getting defensive stops and soaring through the air, pulling down rebounds. I visualized slicing through the defense into the heart of the paint to attract multiple defenders, and once those defenders were locked in on me, I'd pass the ball to an open teammate for a layup. I imagined as many aspects and positive scenarios of the game as I could.

Through my experiences and studies, I've learned that I have to control my thoughts, or I would let them control me. I have the tendency to focus on the negative. We all do. It's called the negativity bias. But what does that get me, if not more negativity? Where does it get me? Not where I want to go. Thoughts create our actions, and actions develop our habits.

I wanted to become a person of positivity, radiating joy and a personality people were drawn to. Creating my own path of positivity and success on the basketball court and in my life, I chose to focus on best-case scenarios. Visualizing what I wanted to see happen and expecting it to happen. When we learn to expect the best and hold ourselves accountable to that level of expectancy, a new mindset comes into play. Knowing I had the ability to control my mentality, the only person who could beat me was me. We tend to get what we focus on. Our thoughts have more power over us than any outside influence. Negative thoughts, self-doubt, and fear are our worst enemies.

My mind was ready. The game, though, was still hours away.

I invited Eleni for coffee, though I opted for *prazino chai* (green tea). Since I needed lunch, Eleni came along to help me order. We stopped at Goody's, the Greek version of McDonald's. It's fast food, featuring burgers, spaghetti and chicken. It even has a gyro sandwich on its menu. We ordered our food to go. A nap was my dessert.

The scoreboard favored the opponent, but it wasn't what I would call a total loss. Well, not in terms of our play on the court. I tried to do my part, finishing with eighteen points and draining 4-of-5 from the three-point line, which is a good percentage.

It was tough to get a shot off. I was being face-guarded and struggled to get open without many screens. Frustration seeped into my mind. I never lost complete composure, but it slipped through my fingers from time to time. Without the mental discipline and constant work on my mentality, I would have checked out and allowed my frustration to consume me. It's happened plenty of times in the past before I decided enough was enough and started working on my mentality.

I couldn't do anything about the physical. None of us could. I finished with multiple bruises on my arms, legs and torso. I was upset we lost. That part of me will never change. But I took pride in overcoming the frustration I felt. I took a red pen to my performance afterward, circling the failures and mistakes, and making side notes on how I could change the outcome of the next game with what I had learned.

I went for my second scoop of Goody's for postgame. This time, K joined me. We were starving and couldn't wait to eat. Ordering proved a challenge. None of the employees spoke English. It became a game of point-and-nod. The woman who took our order pointed to the pictures on the menu and looked up to see if we agreed or disagreed. You could dine-in or do a walking drive-by. We grabbed plates and silverware.

When we finished we didn't know what to do with our plates. We didn't see any place for us to put them and didn't want to be disrespectful and leave them on the table for someone to clean up after us, if that was not customary. We noticed some young girls sitting across the lobby and decided to ask them what we should do.

"Do any of you speak English?" K asked after approaching them.

One of the girls made eye contact with K and made a hand gesture that implied she somewhat spoke English.

"What do we do with our trays? Do we leave them on the counter, or do the employees here pick them up for us once we leave?"

K's excitement was short-lived. So, too, was the girl's.

The young girl got scared and ran to grab one of her friends to help her communicate with K. Her friend resisted. For some reason, terror replaced indecisiveness on their faces. Sensing their fear, we walked away from them and back to our table. An employee from the restaurant must have been watching. He came and took our trays.

We left the restaurant in a rush, laughing most of the way back to our apartments, astonished about what just happened. That was the first time anyone seemed afraid of me. Learning the language would keep this from being a repeat performance.

I was wondering if I should share this story with Alex and Eleni as I was walking to their apartment when something else got my attention. I noticed lots of white tents surrounding the square with young children dancing in the center to music blasting from a speaker system. It seemed to be a celebration of sorts. I stopped and observed from a distance. I listened for only a couple minutes as I knew Alex, Eleni and Coach Andreas were waiting on me.

I'm not sure I even made it all the way inside the car before we struck out and headed to a local tavern.

Before the food arrived, Alex had something he wanted to say.

"You are the best player I have ever coached in terms of character. That is a better compliment than saying you are the best basketball player in all of Greece. No one can ever say that you are a bad person. You are a good basketball player, of course. What makes you great is your character. Everyone wants a player like you around."

I couldn't reply.

His words made my night.

Imagine being a person others wanted to be around, a person who brought others joy from their mere presence.

I couldn't.

Until now.

It stopped me in my tracks. It got me reflecting about what I was doing with my life and the type of person I want to be. It got me thinking about how I could better serve others and take the focus off myself. Only a life serving others is truly a life worth living. That's a life of significance, a life I want to live.

Still mostly speechless when we arrived at TGI Fridays, I listened to Alex, Eleni, and Andreas began telling me about Christmas in Thessaloniki.

Alex provided this description, "The city is beautiful. It is filled with Christmas lights. The city glows during the night."

He put photos to words, showing me pictures from past years of how the city looked with all the decorations. Alex switched to Greek and Andreas started laughing. Both explained that the people from Thessaloniki have a distinct "accent" in comparison to other Greeks in different cities and regions of the country.

Alex began exaggerating the accent when he spoke. I parroted. I laughed at his exaggeration, and they laughed at my pronunciation.

I took it as a positive sign.

Day 37

Before I arrived here, the only thing I pictured were
the baby blue waters and the white sandy beaches.

I never imagined Greece was just as beautiful up in the mountains as well.

It is, as I learned for a second time.

Eleni and Alex drove K and me to Agia (Saint) Anastasia. It's a monastery located in the mountains. The drive along the countryside was breathtaking. Rolling green hills with olive trees lined the pastures. Wildflowers illuminated the landscape, and a light breeze carried the sweet scent of the fresh mountainous air. The weather was a bit overcast and somewhat chilly. I found the coolness refreshing.

We walked, talked, clicked as we circled the exterior of the church, which provided a great vantage point of the surrounding mountains. In the forefront, the tall trees grabbed my attention. Off in the distance, the peaks rose higher and higher, as if each were in competition to see which could be the first to reach the skyline. I glimpsed a winding road cutting through the mountains and could only sometimes see it through the thickness of the trees.

We pocketed our cameras and phones before entering as videos and photos were forbidden.

"It is a sign of respect not to take any pictures inside," Eleni explained. "Anyway, being fully present serves as the best memory you will have!"

I snapped shots of the church's beauty with my eyes, a blink for every click. My heart would be my portfolio. Photos fade. Memories, too. Not these. These will be archived, bright and vivid and moving in my soul.

The first relic I came across was a huge gold portrait of the Virgin Mary. It looked like it was made of aluminum or some type of metal that was sculpted in fine detail to show an expression of compassion on her face. I stared into eyes that look too real. Her shawl and crown appeared to be made of real gold shimmering in the dim lighting. There was a small hole at the bottom of the portrait where you could add an offering. I watched as Eleni put some coins into the small opening and muttered something in Greek under her breath. I added my own offering.

As I moved forward, a warm sensation ran through my body. There were lots of large framed pictures of Saints and the Virgin Mary hanging on the walls. I could smell the scent of wax burning, which reminded me of a Catholic chapel. As I walked in farther, I saw a station where you could light candles for prayer. There were single wooden chairs, which looked to be from a different century, lined up along the walls. You could see their age by the look of the tattered wood. Everything seemed an antique and priceless. The chandeliers were magnificent, old and yet pristine. Their lights were dim and yet illuminated the crosses and relics hanging on the walls.

We were careful not to disturb a baptism. I watched as the priest placed his hand on the children's foreheads and blessed them with a smile on his face. The priest was donned in a white gown lined with gold.

As we moved quietly away from the ceremony, Eleni filled in the historical blanks.

"There is a small piece of the cross that Jesus was crucified on here in this church," she said, pointing to the room across from us. She moved her hand in the direction of the burnt walls. I noticed that most of the walls were charred from fire damage.

"Back when the Greeks were slaves to Turkey, they would come into our lands and burn our churches," Eleni said. "Some of the churches have been restored. Most of the old churches that you will go to will have some burn marks on the walls."

I wasn't just seeing history, I was hearing it. I felt in awe of the historic stories that were so meaningful to the history of Greece and its traditions and beliefs. As I continued to embrace what was before me, I realized this easily could be a Catholic chapel full of antiques and history. It made me think about my family and how much they would enjoy the chance to see this for themselves, especially my mom and grandparents. In moments like these, I wished I could show my loved ones what I was seeing through my own eyes. Not only did I feel a serene sense of being closer with my loved ones—I seemed to be closer with other faiths, too. If I could feel the same sense of warmth in a church of a different religion, I questioned if religion really mattered. As long as you believe in God, is there much of a difference? Is one religion superior to another? As my heart moved and my soul danced, I understood that religion serves as the vehicle that brings me closer to Him. Not the source. Religion is man-made and I am God-made. I walked out, touching not the ground but enlightenment.

The adventure continued at a village called Agios Prodromos, where we ate lunch at a tavern. The table quickly filled with gyros, souvlaki, Greek salad, and a few others I forget the names of. I wasn't eating my way through Greece one meal at a time, though it does look like it from time to time.

I was falling for Greece, falling hard, falling fast. We fit. People noticed. Some commented how much I was like them, how I could pass for a Greek, which I always took as a compliment. Other times, I heard I could pass for a Spaniard, or Italian, and that I look European, not American.

Everything was foreign and yet everything felt ordinary, if that is even possible. I believed I was destined to come here, to live here, to learn about life here. Alex and Eleni are not only great people and remarkable friends, they were the best teachers on the subject of life. I can't remember them ever being stressed over the little things and things outside of their control. Every day was positive. Every day was joyous. How did they do it? Before I left Greece, I was going to find out.

Maybe the first clue came on the drive home in Alex's story, a story of a joyous fisherman and a fisherman who never seemed to have enough.

"You know the differences between being joyful and stressed?" Alex asked. "The wealthy dream is that of constant work and stress, while the joyful dream is that of enjoyment and peace. I will tell you a story that I heard. While it may not be true, I think it serves to get the point across of what people want out of their life. There is no right or wrong, but each person must decide for themselves what they want."

Eager to hear what he was about to share, I leaned forward in my seat as much as the seatbelt would allow.

"There was an elderly fisherman lying on the beach after his day of work was over," Alex continued. "Satisfied with his work he put in for the day, he sat underneath a tree while he listened to the waves and prayed with gratitude. His small fishing boat was anchored on the shore with his catch of the day, freshly gutted and ready to sell. He made his living off the sea and made just enough to feed himself and his family and to live comfortably each month. With the understanding that the sea would always provide, he was never stressed or worried about the fear of lack.

"Off in the distance, he could see a large ship approaching the dock. It wasn't a ship he had ever seen before, and he knew it wasn't local. He continued watching from a distance as he saw many men exit the ship. He then saw one man who seemed to be in charge, giving orders to the others. As this man walked off the ship, he noticed the old fisherman laying on the beach and took an interest in him and the small fishing boat that floated alongside him. He made his way over to the man, and they began talking.

"The young man introduced himself and said that he was from a different country, working on expanding his business into the European countries to be a global business. The old fisherman listened to the young fisherman talk about his successes he had accomplished in his young life as he continued to brag about himself.

"Then the young man offered the old fisherman a job to work for him and his company. He told the fisherman that he could make him wealthy beyond his wildest dreams. 'You can own an entire fleet of ships for yourself and then retire in the future and lay on the beach for the rest of your days!'

"The old fisherman replied, 'What does it look like I'm doing now? I don't need to own an entire fleet of fishing boats to enjoy life. I have the luxury of sitting on this beach every day after a meaningful day of work. I have all I need, young man. I have lived my days and seen the greed take over many of my friends. If I have any advice for you, it would be to slow down and enjoy life. Don't get so caught up with the luxuries of what the future has in store for you that you forget to live for today. Tomorrow may never come. Enjoy what life brings you today, in this moment, for you only get it once. There will always be opportunity to make money. Time, however, can never be gained once it's lost. You only die once. You live every day.'"

Words without wisdom are meaningless. Alex spoke with wisdom, as did Eleni. Their words mean everything.

I sat back and let that story sink into my mind for the ride's entirety. Even if the story wasn't true, the lesson it brought was true enough for me. I vowed to myself then and there that I would never allow the pursuit of money to rule my life.

Day 40

Blood, sweat, tears.

That's what coaches expect, if not demand, from players, isn't it?

I have experience with sweat and tears. But the blood part? Not so much. Well, not before today. But once more, I am putting ball before basket.

It was coffee and conversation, and not a bloody collision that got the day started, as K and I met our agent, Thomas. He took us to a shopping center with a little café in the back overlooking the sea. It was an unusually crowded scene with a part of the work force on strike.

"Why are all these people on strike?" I asked.

"Because they have not gotten paid," Thomas said. "So, they are on strike and not going to work until they get paid."

The Greek government had been going through some financial trouble. This was one of the first times I had seen the impact of those problems in person and the people's response. I prayed for the people, and for Greece, to find the best possible resolution.

We found a place to sit and ordered our coffee. Thomas saved the pleasantries for later. He reiterated our last conversation about the state of my game before reinforcing an even more important point. This season, I was also auditioning for next season. That reminder remained constant.

"You are very fortunate to have a job and you need to do your best to make the most of it," he said to me and to K. "The list of women waiting to get the chance to play professionally overseas is very lengthy while most of them will never get the opportunity."

I nodded before I spoke. "Thank you for giving me this opportunity to prove myself and for giving me a chance to come out here and show everyone what I can do."

His pat on the back was brief.

"You have done well so far. I know I made the right choice in representing you. Even so, we need to continue to get better if you want to have a long and successful professional career."

He's right.

The state of my game he talked about was improving my one-on-one game, which was nothing new, as Coach Kruger used to tell me the same thing in college. To adapt to the European game, he suggested I study some

Euro-players. Watch how they attack the defense once they come off an on-ball screen. He even suggested learning how to flop a little more. That one made me laugh.

We took the scenic route along the sea back to our apartments. I enjoyed the drive; the baby blue waters of the Aegean Sea transcended my being. Thomas was correct. I was fortunate to be given the opportunity to play professionally in Greece, which is one of the most beautiful places on Earth.

What he didn't add was fortune favors the brave. I planned on being a force in our scrimmage later that night. But not in the way it turned out.

The game was against another team in Thessaloniki. Our opponent was from a smaller division, so it did not count on our record for the "cup," or league my team played in. Our opponent didn't view it that way.

Have you ever played pick-up in your backyard against your younger siblings who would do anything to beat you? If you have, then know what type of game we were in for.

The game was scrappy. No surprise there. Basketball is, after all, a contact sport. What it's not supposed to be is a blood sport. There is no gentle way to put this, so I won't.

I broke a girl's nose.

In my defense, I don't believe it was my fault. But I'll let others be the judge and jury. Here's what happened. I was on a fast break with only one defender to beat in front of me. She stood, stationary, and I crossed over right in front of her. As I began to take my first explosion step past her, she reached in for the steal. Simultaneously, I lowered my shoulder to protect the ball. Since I was lower, I was able to explode past her to the rim. Before that happened there was a moment of impact. My shoulder met her nose. It was head-on. It was full-force. It was ka-BOOM.

The whistled sounded. The official signaled. Blocking, defense. No one was paying attention to the call. How could they? Her nose was badly busted. Blood gushed over her face, hands, jersey, the court. My shoulder had a small cut. I added to the blood lost. The clean-up took a while. She would not return. I played on. With my competitive nature and adrenaline coursing through my system, I didn't have much sympathy for her in the moment. You can call me cold. I didn't know truth had a temperature.

Post-game was a different story. I felt compassion for her injury and apologized to her, even though it was an accident. I didn't have to. I wanted to. Once I began talking to her, I realized she didn't speak English. It didn't seem as though she comprehended much of what I said, but I think she understood I was apologizing. She touched my shoulder and nodded as she said something in Greek. I didn't understand what she said, but with her expression, mannerisms, and body language, I got the impression she was telling me it was okay.

Accidents and injuries happen on the court. It's part of the game. Still, I never want anyone to get hurt, especially from something I was part of. If I could have prevented it, I would have. I take great pride in how I was taught the game, how I play the game.

Day 41-42

Call it the power of two.

Salt and pepper. Soap and water. Washer and dryer.

Laundry took longer without the power of a dryer, and clean clothes became a priority in preparation for the trip to Athens. When I looked at the day ahead, all minutes seemed accounted for. I lifted weights in the afternoon. On my own. I opted for quality, not quantity. Soreness was not what I wanted to feel when we next took the court.

After lifting, I went straight to film and then straight to practice, with no stops in between. The film was from our game against Esperides. It was one day old. Coach was editor and director. He showed us what we did right and wrong in certain situations throughout the game. Here's the review: Our defense still needed a lot of work, that was for sure.

Film is one of those teachers of the game that is fully transparent. It was great to study ourselves as a team and see where we could improve as well as to see the things we did right. Sometimes you want to watch with hands covering eyes, especially when it's you making the mistake. I took it like a pro. It's the only way I know how to grow as a player, as a teammate, as a person.

The non-stop pace resumed the following morning. Practice was scheduled for noon, hours earlier than usual. Still in sweats, I grabbed lunch. Then it was shower, pack, walk to the bus for the ride to Athens. The team chartered a 737 on wheels, which was great, since that would be our seat for the next seven hours.

My head never hit a pillow. Instead, a talk-a-thon took place for the majority of the trip. Sadly, I was not all talk. I had lost my voice. That didn't deter Alex and his allies from pouncing on the opportunity to have a whole lot of fun. My voice cracked and squeaked when I tried to speak. That didn't stop them. If they could have, they would have had me perform solo karaoke the length of the drive.

Fortunately for me, there were others with plenty to say, all worth listening to.

The trip felt different from what I was used to in college. On road trips during my days at Adams State, everyone was quiet on the bus. Listening to our music, sleeping, or talking quietly with the person beside us. It was a "business trip," and we acted accordingly and professionally.

On this trip, even though it was business, everyone was talking and enjoying each other's company. It was one big conversation amongst the entire team. When Greek music played, the bus turned into a choir with nearly everyone singing. I caught on to some of the words and mimicked what I heard, my voice squeaking and cracking every so often.

As we neared Athens, I sat next to Spyridoula, who was drawing a portrait of Hugh Laurie, famous for his medical show *House,* for another one of our teammates. I was fascinated with her talent and ability to freely draw a person in such fine detail.

Once we arrived, we checked into the hotel, unloaded our bags, and found dinner waiting for us in one of the hotel's meeting spaces. We were catered to like royalty by the hotel staff. Dinner was set up buffet style, with beef and pork cuts, along with a pasta that resembled spaghetti. Fruits and vegetables also were part of the feast.

After we finished eating, a few of us walked to the Athens Mall. One of my teammates told me that it is the largest mall in Greece. From the outside, the massive building was lit up with windows appropriate for such a large structure. The light coming from the mall seemed to illuminate the adjacent two blocks that surrounded the structure. As we got closer, I could see the Olympic Stadium in the distance. It was even more remarkable, with two large wavy poles extending overtop. The roof looked to be made of solar panels or reflective material of some kind. It illuminated the color of a deep-sea blue, one that matched the sea during the day. Underneath the roof were the stadium seats, with the outside being built of concrete. Spectacular best described the exterior. I could only imagine what the view was like from inside.

By the time we reached the mall, the majority of the shops were closed. We made our way to the second floor food court, which of course remained open. We beelined for ice cream before retracing our way to the hotel.

We returned to a team-lobby talk. The conversation was entirely in Greek, and Vassiliki acted as my translator. I watched as intently as I listened. Body language was my second interpreter. People acted their dialogue as they spoke. It improved my comprehension of what was being said. Body language wasn't something I previously noticed, or counted as a form of communication. But it quickly became my personal Google Translate.

In some ways, I bonded more in seven hours than I had in 42 days. I felt I knew everyone a little bit deeper. These moments are when—and how—teams build trust. Getting to know someone outside of the basketball court, or any kind of work setting, is the best way to knock down the walls we put up. We get to see peoples' interests, strengths, weaknesses, and most importantly, their vulnerabilities.

I couldn't wait for the day when my Greek voice matched my Greek eyes.

Day 43

The day didn't start frustratingly,
but it sure ended that way.

The best-laid plans unrolled before me like a red carpet. Breakfast with a couple teammates—coffee for them, *prazino chai* (green tea) for me—followed by quality time in the lobby with a few of my teammates, as well as Margarita, Alex, Andreas, and Konstantinos. I'm always intrigued listening to them talk, watching their body language closely, gauging the tone of their voices. The tiny words I recognized instilled inside me a sense of belonging. Not just to the conversation, but also in their lives.

Lunch preceded a film session on Ano Liosia, that afternoon's opponent. It didn't allow much down time with tip-off scheduled for 4 p.m. I began pre-game.

Enter, Ano Liosia.

Enter, frustration

Exit, us.

We lost. Again.

I stacked the full weight of the losses on top of the frustration I already was shouldering. Stats don't lie. Only ten points, a few rebounds, steals, assists and a single block. It was underwhelming, to say the least. But only one stat line matters and that stat line included all of one letter, "L."

It was a "what," "where," "why" long ride home to Thessaloniki.

What could I be doing more to help us win?

Where were the areas I needed to most improve?

Why is my shooting so inconsistent?

I didn't need to ask the "who." I was the who.

Day 44

I defined exhaustion.

Physical. Mental. Emotional. I needed this off day. I also needed *Friends*. The enormously popular television sitcom was my feel-good, go-to LOL, long before LOL went viral. I watched a few episodes online in hopes of finding relaxation and rejuvenation, and most important, laughter.

The long trip to Athens drained me, from fatigued legs to fragile mind. My mentality and mindset felt the full effect from the losses. As an athlete, it's not easy admitting the toll losing takes and the slumps teams face during any particular season. Few seasons are ever close to perfection, even championship seasons.

We tend to brush everything under the rug and respond to reporters' questions in clichés, in coach-speak. We never pull back the curtain. We never invite anyone inside. We can't show our weaknesses and vulnerabilities as an athlete. We have to stay tough. Those are the facts and the fallacy.

I was slip-and-sliding into one of those slumps, questioning my own abilities as an athlete, thinking to myself about what I needed to do to put my team on top and finally taste victory. Before I knew it, my *Friends* left me, replaced by doubts and negativity. I felt the need to leave, too. I did, leaving my apartment with no plan in place. It didn't matter. A fresh way of thinking needed fresh air.

The weather replicated my mood. Or maybe it was the other way around. The sky was dark, overcast. The temperature measured cold. A favorite reporter of mine told me a story once about how he didn't see the beautiful sunsets of New Mexico, but how he felt them. He would drive into the mountains until he found a view of the west. He'd sit and wait for the sun to set. When it started, he closed his eyes. He said anyone can see the colors of the sunset, but not many have felt them. He said if you close your eyes, you can feel the hot from the color red, the warmth from the colors orange and yellow. When the sun dipped lower into the horizon, you could feel the coolness of the colors blue and green. When the sun was a sliver, you felt the color purple. And when the sun disappeared, you felt the cold of the color black.

I missed seeing the sun. I ran and walked along the beach. Maybe I took it for granted that this is how Greece is all the time. But it wasn't always sunshine and paradise.

I walked over to the gym (where else, right?) to find a basketball game in the younger division already in progress. I sat in the stands alone and watched their unbridled joy. No pressure, no stress, just squeaks, and scrunchies, and smiles. It helped me see the bigger picture. Not everything needs to be so serious.

I was getting paid to play the game I loved. I was living in a beautiful foreign country. It was God's gift to me and I planned on honoring that gift the only way I knew how, by giving everything I had in every practice, in every game save nothing. I put the losses on me. I put the stress on me. I drove myself crazy. And where had it gotten me? I had to stop. I had to take a step back before I could move forward. If I wasn't enjoying myself, if I wasn't happy, if I wasn't having fun, I wouldn't be the player I was brought here to be. But more importantly, I would be squandering away one of the greatest opportunities ever presented to me. It's ironic how much we stand in our own way sometimes. I wondered how many times I had held myself back from growth. How many times I had failed to identify the stunted development.

It's true. You have to love yourself before you can love others. I love basketball. I love Greece. I love the people I've met, the teammates I have. I just needed to remember to leave a piece of my heart for myself.

Day 45

If.

How could a word so small loom so large? It's not the word, it's what follows it.

"If only I had worked harder."

That lingering thought was the thread and I was the eye of the needle. It poked at me. Over, and over, and over. I knew what it would fashion *if* it ever got through.

I had no regrets about the work I put in physically. But that's a semicolon, not a period; I felt there was always more I could do, that perhaps a couple pieces to this quilt of my life experiences I was stitching had unraveled, and I hadn't noticed.

I tried to work it out, not just in the figurative sense. I got some conditioning in on the bike and lifted weights in the morning, which was a great start. I hoped my well-worn sports psychology books I began re-reading would help me right all the wrong out of my current mindset.

One of the hardest things I've found with professional basketball is the discipline you have to have within yourself in order to be successful. In high school and college, there are so many people to push you and motivate you to be your absolute best. With pro ball, you need to have that self-discipline to replicate.

It required effort. Without having team weights, or film, or whatever it was, it was way too easy to say, "I'll get into the gym later," or "I'll just condition a little harder tomorrow." The trap door into complacency is like quicksand—once in, hard to get out. Everyone has their own definition of what makes a champion. I believe a champion is someone who gives their all when there is no one watching them, whether it's six in the morning or eleven in the evening.

Sure, you need the skill set to be one of the best. But it has to take more. Every player in the WNBA and NBA is skilled. So, what separates the superstar from the player who sits in the final chair on the bench? I believe it's the mindset—one of consistency and persistence of discipline to do what needs to be done, day-in and day-out, regardless—this is what shapes elite athletes.

I am not an elite athlete by any means. But I believe I know what it takes to reach that level. And those skills can be learned by everyone, not just the elite. It is a study I am passionate about. Someday I hope to open the business of teaching this high performing level of mental toughness to others.

#

The coaches built practice around conditioning and plyometrics today. Basketball drills were minimal. Basketballs were like TVs on honeymoons—not necessary. The day wasn't basketball-free. After practice, I watched Alex coach another one of his teams from Thessaloniki. I think there should be bumper stickers that read, "Honk, if Alex coaches your team!" Or at the very least, slip me some programs so I can start memorizing names and faces.

It's not that I don't know where he finds the time. I don't know how he finds the energy to coach all the teams he does. And yet, he still finds time for me afterward.

After the game, we took in some sightseeing for my benefit. We drove to a suburb of Thessaloniki, called Thermi. It wasn't far from Kalamaria, the neighborhood of Thessaloniki where I lived.

The architecture captured my undivided attention. A church towered over the rest of the little town, not just marking its territory, but making its presence known. The body of the church was built with white brick. The roof was dim red, faded by years of sunlight. The church stood guard over what looked like a skate park illuminated with blue lights. A concrete walkway outlined the grass with a cul-de-sac leading the skaters in and out.

It's a scene I'd only seen in magazines. Even with one thousand words I couldn't appropriately describe what I was seeing. The lights of the businesses and cafés that surrounded it created an upbeat atmosphere to the whole scene, as if musical notes were floating through the air.

We walked around the park for a bit, got some ice cream, and enjoyed the view.

This time, there would be no *If only*.

Day 46-49

A metronome had become the soundtrack to the automaton life I created through unthinking repetition.

The monotonous routine consisted of waking up, getting my weight-lifting and shooting workout done in the mornings, followed by lunch, and practice in the evenings. At least a hamster on a wheel has proper sense to know when enough is enough.

The weather wasn't helping. Sweatpants and sweatshirts replaced shorts and t-shirts. Shoes replaced sandals. With the cold now the daily forecast, I wasn't anxious to get out and about and explore. Also MIA were my usual beach walks that helped ease my mind and encouraged me out of my apartment.

Routines can be either beneficial or problematic with each side resting evenly like the scales of justice. When we get too comfortable in our patterns, we stop growing and get complacent. Nothing new is learned. We basically checked our brains at the door. That tilts the scales to the negative side. But routines performed in a positive manner, with purpose and precision, allow us to hone habits and sharpen skills.

I was learning how to balance the imaginative against the mundane. I never struggled staying in rhythm to the routine of discipline, in waking up every morning and getting my workout in the weight room and the gym before my day even started. The challenge for me was finding the right production after lunch and before practice.

In what ways could I better myself during this time instead of becoming lazy and wasting my time just sitting around? There was only so much I could do physically. If I pushed harder, I knew I would injure myself from overtraining. Instead, I lifted books.

I started reading more on sports psychology to see if it was possible to train my mind as much as I trained my body. I brought baggage. None, it turned out, was essential. You don't need luggage in the here, in the now. And yet, here I was, hands full, carrying the guilt of always thinking about the next thing coming up. And of daydreaming what it would be like to be back home, and what I would do after I stopped playing basketball, and worrying about what my career path would be when my playing days were over.

Worry.
Anxiety.
Fear.
Future.
I packed them. I carried them. *Carpe Mañana.* Seize tomorrow.

Really, what is so hard about living moment to moment? How much happier would I be? How much more appreciative would I be of who and what was in front of me at the time and making the most of right here and right now? Time passes quick enough. I realize that. And yet, I struggle not knowing what to do with my time now that I am free.

We think about free time when we are busy, and when we have free time, we think of what it is we need to accomplish next, hence, being busy again. We reminisce of old memories and daydream about moments to come. Don't get me wrong, I think this is great to do once in a while. But every day? I didn't always do what was good for me. But I was trying.

Focusing on the moment is one of life's most simple, yet most profound, secrets. How much more of ourselves and our lives would we master if we first learned how to be present in the moment? Those who understand the power of time and who learn to live in the moment will also balance life. It all starts with where your attention falls. What I don't accomplish today can't get me to where I want to be tomorrow.

Today must be the priority. After all, I am giving one day of my life for it.

———⊙———

Day 50

———⊙———

Athinaikos is to Greek women's basketball
what UConn is to women's college basketball,
the New England Patriots are to the NFL,
Rafa Nadal is to the French Open.

From what I was hearing, Athinaikos is one of the best teams in all of Europe—*Sigh!*—and was on an eighty-game winning streak—*Gulp!* I would be lying if I said I wasn't a tad intimidated. It's a feeling I can recall from memory.

It's hard to erase all doubt. But opportunities allow us to replace a bad memory with a good one. Opportunities give us the chance to overcome fear and play courageously against superior opponents. Courage cannot exist without fear. Intimidation, though, is a façade fear places before us. It's illusion. It's fabricated. It lingers, but seldom lasts. I welcomed the challenge to play this Greek super team.

I just wish I could have played incognito.

"You are one of the foreign players, right?" It was one of the Athinkaikos players. She stopped me mid-stride, halfway between locker room and court.

"Yes, I am," I answered. I knew where I was heading, but not the conversation.

"Are you Greek-American? We have been hearing that Apollon has a Greek-American on their team. I heard that you are from Greece but grew up in the United States."

She spoke with curiosity, the words friendly.

I corrected her assumption. "That is funny. A lot of people seem to think that I am a Greek," I said. "No, I am not from Greece, but I take it as a compliment that so many people think so!"

"As you should," she said when her laughter ended. "You look like a Greek. *Kali tixe.*"

Her final two words translated to "good luck." I felt she meant it. Turns out, we would need it.

We weren't half-bad. Really.

We never trailed by more than ten points before intermission. They won halftime. They started the second half with a full-court press. It disrupted our rhythm and distanced us even further from victory. Barely a couple minutes into the third quarter, I looked up at the scoreboard in shock to realize we were down by twenty.

What?

When?

Where?

How?

It was hard to believe. The score never got closer. We ended up losing by more than twenty points. Still, it didn't feel like we got blown out. We stood Nike-to-Nike against one of the best Europe had to offer and we didn't bow, we didn't back down. It showed. No one affiliated with the club was disappointed with our efforts and exuded excitement about the way we fought.

We shared those emotions. We could learn from this. We could build on this. We lost the eventual war, but won a few battles along the way. The payout wasn't about tonight, but down the road. And it wasn't specifically about the elusive "W," but about the "B." We were all starting to believe in ourselves.

As always, I believed I could play better. As a team, though, there were few similarities to the squad that took the court a week prior. There wasn't one area where we took a step back and stayed there. Hopefully, this would be our starting point moving forward. I just needed to do my part.

I still couldn't feel my shot. You ever sit on a foot for so long that when you finally pull it out and try to put weight on it, you can't? That was my shot. It frustrated me. This time, it wouldn't bury the rest of my game. I put the words I had been studying into practice. I stayed positive. I blinked away each negative thought. I wiped dry each bead of frustration. I helped my team in whatever I could to the best of my physical abilities. I left sweat at both ends of the court. But deep down, I knew I was due for a breakout shooting performance soon. When I say breakout, I mean the kind of shooting performance where time seems to slow. I can sense what the defense is going to do before it does. My shot is effortless. Flow. In the zone. I know it's not something I could force. I was confident the zone would come. It always had in the past.

The final stat sheet showed fifteen points, five rebounds, three assists, and three steals. I read one more line, the one at the bottom, the one that showed who won, who lost. It's the only line that matters, the one line I have yet to help change.

I blinked at the negative thought I knew was coming next. It didn't go away.

Day 51

Albert Einstein's reach exceeded E=MC2.

The physicist saw beyond numbers. He saw humanity. He believed a life lived for others was a life worthwhile.

The value of my life increased exponentially when the general manager asked if I would speak and demonstrate some basketball drills with the youth group affiliated with the club. I was told the young children wanted to meet the "American" of the team. I couldn't say, "yes," fast enough.

Unexpected gifts are the best gifts. I didn't know what I was walking into. I didn't care. To work with young athletes is a gift. I entered the gym and found two coaches and a teenage girl talking under the basket.

One of the coaches was Giannis Politis. Back in his day, Coach Politis was one of the best basketball players in Greece. It's true. And yet, both asked for my assistance. They wanted me to work one-on-one with the girl and provide feedback.

We started with dribbling and shooting. The communication between the two of us was shaky, and I wasn't sure if she understood everything I was trying to teach. We reached the apex of that barrier when I tried to explain the step-back move, where the offensive player attacks the basket, then steps back quickly to create space from their defender in order to get a shot off. When trying to teach someone a new move, one's words are superior to actions in the explanation process. Coach Politis provided the assist required, stepping in from time to time to translate my instructions. Actions finally broke through. She mimicked by body moves and language to near perfection.

The lessons were just getting started. After the individual lesson, I made my way into a different gym. It was small and smelled of old wood. It wasn't quite a relic, but it was well on its way. It would have fit nicely in the movie *Hoosiers*.

I entered unbridled chaos. I used my whole face to smile. Elementary-aged children filled the court, scribbling invisible lines with no rhyme, no reason. They weren't dribbling basketballs as much as they were chasing them. I loved every second of it.

Soon, though, I caught some eyes, then a few more. It was more glance, less stare. I was not the center of attention, chase the basketball was. But the mood and the movements slowly changed. Some huddled into small groups and whispered amongst themselves as their eyes were fixed on me. To others, I remained invisible. Until Coach Politis called all the children to center court and asked them to sit down.

Once he had their attention, he introduced me. All eyes were on me. Athletes sitting. Parents standing against the wall. I wished I knew what he was saying, but he spoke entirely in Greek. When he finished, I stepped forward. I kept my message brief. I paused after every sentence or two, so Coach Politis could translate. Once finished, it was time to have a ball. Or, go get one, so we could start our dribbling drills. They didn't hesitate once Coach Politis translated.

This was not the day for complex. I tried to mix fun into the basic fundamentals of dribbling. As I moved from child to child, I made sure to make eye contact. I gave the universally known "thumbs up." I added a smile.

I couldn't have asked for a better group. I returned their energy, their enthusiasm. And I was just as curious about them as they were of me, a foreign player on their favorite team. I knew I was someone they looked up to because of the uniform I wore, and I could see a sense of wonder and interest in their eyes when they looked at me.

Well, some of them. The others looked away as fast as they could, a little embarrassed, I suppose. Both made my heart smile. I could see myself in their shoes when I was their age, looking up to some professional basketball player, knowing that is exactly what I wanted to become when I got older. In that moment, I was their dream, and they were mine, and both were real.

When the ball-handling drills concluded, Coach Politis began speaking to the children again. This time, another coach stood next to me.

"I will translate what he is saying for you."

Coach Politis spoke to them, about me. Here are his words, in English.

"Let's thank Vera for coming to work with you today."

The young children and parents applauded.

He continued, "I encourage all of you to come watch her play this season. She is a great player and fun to watch. She is a great shooter. I am sure she will make a three-pointer for you and point to you in the crowd as she runs past you. She will come back and help you again later this year."

More applause erupted from the children. My face blushed.

Coach Politis concluded. "Anyone who would like to take pictures with Vera make a line against the wall."

It took all of four seconds before the children formed a line against the wall. I felt overwhelmed, watching them sprint to be first in line and fight for their spot. I also felt envious. Why couldn't I have their quickness?

It was a kaleidoscope of emotions turning inside me, each more beautiful than the next. They had me feeling like a celebrity. And I can't remember the last time I smiled so much or felt so much love and gratitude.

After we finished with all the individual and group photos, I said my goodbyes in English, and they said their goodbyes in Greek. But it wasn't really goodbye, it was, "until next time."

Next time turned into this time. Before I left, a young girl ran up to me, spoke in Greek, and gave me a shirt from the club, followed by a big hug and an even bigger smile. I hugged back with my arms and with my heart.

I couldn't wait to share my morning with Eleni and K, who I met for coffee. They shared my enthusiasm. We decided to watch our men's team play, and I returned to the gym. Upon my entering, some of the parents and kids recognized me from that morning. They greeted me with the "Greek kiss" and began talking to Eleni.

Eleni waited until they had left to translate.

"They said you were great with their children and that they really look up to you. They are looking forward to coming to watch you play."

First, they made my day. Now, they made my night.

The men's game was peas-in-a-pod close and edge-of-a-seat exciting. The game ended victoriously for our club. The fans carried those high spirits into the parking lot, laughing, talking, and smoking their cigarettes. The night's entertainment was a good choice by Eleni. I'd seen some of the players from the men's team at our games. It was nice to repay that support.

#

In Greece, the night is forever young.

K and I joined Alex, Eleni, Margarita and one of her friends for dinner. The tavern was cozy and decorated like an old grocery store with lots of canned foods stocked on shelving against the walls in small groupings. Also on display were large silver buckets, ones that used to hold milk and oil. The shelved canned foods and the wine and beer bottles ran the length of the wall all the way up to the ceiling. The atmosphere was loud and full of energy as it always is no matter where we went. We ordered white wine and different dishes of fish that we shared family style.

Spontaneous, exciting, fulfilling, and impactful are just a few of the adjectives that described this day. I couldn't wait for my next "teaching assignment" with those children. Not just teaching them, but also learning from them—and not just the Greek language.

Perhaps coaching is my destiny when my playing days are finished. With the fun I had teaching the children, I was fond of the idea. If that was my path, I knew it would be a worthwhile life.

Day 52

I would cut the cord.

I would work without a net. For better, for worse, I was going to make the most of my latest day off. This was the day I would explore my city.

Alone.

Just not right now. First, I needed to work out. Business before pleasure.

A challenging weight set left my body feeling good and somewhat shaky. I couldn't stop there. Knowing I had to keep my conditioning up, I intensified the cardio on the bike. Exhausted, there was one more thing to do, make my way to the gym for my shooting workout. To my surprise, the gym was occupied with young kids. I stayed for a while, in part to watch, in part to recover. I accomplished two out of three goals, not bad.

The shower rejuvenated me. It was time. No more excuses. No more crutches. I took a taxi for the first time in Thessaloniki.

Usually, I caught a ride with Alex or one of my teammates whenever I went anywhere. This was my first venture getting somewhere on my own. If a baby sparrow can leave a nest, I can leave my apartment. I got into the cab and said, "To downtown." The driver spoke no English. Somehow he understood where I wanted to go. He gave me a "thumbs up" and we were off.

I walked around the main square near the Electra Palace Hotel. I sat down at a café and ordered myself a coffee and a sandwich. The early afternoon came with a light breeze that smelled of the sea I could see just beyond the square. The busy streets were filled with cars zooming by and pedestrians briskly walking across the street at the stoplights. Around me, I could hear distant chatter of Greek, but nothing I could comprehend. Numerous pigeons filled the stone floors, picking up the crumbs people dropped. I sat satisfied for more than an hour, absorbing the sights and smells in silence.

I resumed my sightseeing, window shopping along the busy streets. The shops had their prime items in the windows, tempting to lure the customers inside. If I had been in the shopping mood and if I had had more than a few Euros on me, I'm sure I would have taken the bait. Not long after, the sun was starting to set over the sea, another picture waiting to be snapped. I ran into K and some other friends from the club and we walked back to the Electra Palace Hotel. We clicked selfies and sat at a café, this time drinking hot chocolate.

This was neither the time, nor the place to sit the rest of this day out. We moved on, this time to Pizza Hut, a rare reminder of home. The restaurant had Wi-Fi, which was high on the list of things you can't live without. I always got excited when I could connect to the internet in places other than my apartment. The internet was a lifeline home, an umbilical cord to my family. The internet connection in my apartment had been on life-support the last few nights. It was slower than a three-toed sloth escaping a freezer. I found myself taking advantage of restaurants and cafés that offered Wi-Fi.

Since I passed "taxi," I double-dog-dared myself to return home by bus. What could possibly go wrong? All I needed was to get from Point A to Point B. It can't be that hard, can it?

I stayed cool. I stayed calm. I stayed close enough behind someone so I could mimic their movements. She walked on. I walked on. She fed coins to a kiosk-looking machine, pressed a button, watched the ticket pop up like a jack-in-the-box, grabbed it and headed down the aisle.

"Easy enough," I thought.

I can't blame amnesia. I wish I could, but I knew exactly where I was. So why did I think the kiosk would be written in any other language than Greek? I was facing a multiple-choice test in Greek. Different buttons showed different prices. I randomly chose low. I was hoping I was right. I also was hoping this would be graded on the curve. I counted my coins carefully. I slid in what I thought was the right amount. Euros, the currency used here, is Greek to me, too.

With the kiosk fed, I pressed the button. A ticket appeared. I tore it and found a seat toward the back. I'd done it. At least, I thought I had. After a couple stops, a man in a uniform boarded the bus and announced something in Greek. I sat clueless. I looked around to see the other passengers' reactions. The man across the aisle from me reached into his pocket and pulled out his ticket stub. The officer was simply checking all the passengers to make sure they had their tickets. As he inspected each of us, he stamped our tickets. Once finished, he waited for the next stop and walked off.

I focused on the surroundings every time the bus stopped. I knew where to get off, I just didn't know when. Finally, I recognized my neighborhood. I made it back safe and sound. I couldn't wait to do it again.

The city of Thessaloniki was growing on me. As was my self-reliance.

---◆---

Day 53

---◆---

*". . . But we're talking about **practice** man.*

What are we talking about? **Practice?** *We're talking about **practice**, man. We're talking about **practice**. We're talking about **practice**. We ain't talking about the game. We're talking about **practice**, man . . . we're talking about **practice** man, we're not even talking about the game . . . the actual game, when it matters . . . We're talking about **practice** ..."*

Allen Iverson's infamous rant looped through my thoughts. The Philadelphia 76ers Hall of Fame guard said the word "practice" twenty-two times in a 30-minute press conference back in 2002.

So why were his words in my thoughts? When I arrived at the gym this morning, I reached for the door; the men's volleyball team already had unlocked it. So I watched practice. Not a game, practice. I watched for forty-five minutes.

"I really have to get myself a gym schedule," I thought.

I passed the time as productively as possible. Since I was able to connect to the Wi-Fi in the gym, I connected to the Google translate app to hopefully add to my Greek vocabulary.

Have you ever thought about that fact that we talk more to our phones than we do in them? And that we want them to talk back? I only bring this up because as I was studying I sometimes pressed the icon that looked like a robot, which pronounced the word in a robotic-sounding female voice. Apparently, the volume wasn't set on low. A few of the volleyball players heard the weird-sounding female voice coming from my phone and looked my way. They saved their weird look for me. I had no doubt they heard me talking to my phone under my breath, as I attempted to recite the new Greek word over and over under my breath.

"Great," I thought. "They all probably think I'm a bizarre foreigner who talks to herself." I didn't switch to whisper as I continued. My self-improvement took precedence.

After the team left and the only nets remaining hung from the rims, I began my shooting warm-up. The volleyball coach walked over and started rebounding for me.

"Bustos, yes?"

"Yes, sir."

It was our first eye contact. He introduced himself as Coach something or other, I didn't catch his Greek last name and didn't ask immediately. I just called him Coach.

"I have come to a few of the women's games to watch you play. You are nice shooter. I like this style of play."

He imitated shooting an imaginary basketball as he described my shooting.

"Thank you. I'm happy to hear that you have been able to come watch us play. Thank you for the compliments to my game. I think every player appreciates when someone enjoys watching them play."

Coach turned teacher.

"Yes, of course. We are a form of entertainment, after all. Especially in the professional leagues."

He had me thinking and speaking.

"I guess I never thought of myself as an entertainer of the crowd. That's a different way to look at it."

It made me laugh. I wasn't alone.

"Yes. The best entertainers, or the best athletes, ignite the passion of the crowd and gain the hearts of the fans. That's how they become so popular."

I nodded in agreement. He went on with his commentary, I went on with my shooting, he went on with his rebounding.

"You know, many years ago when Peja Stojakovic used to play for a club here in Thessaloniki, I used to rebound for him, too. I am smart who I choose to rebound for though. Good shooters like Peja and you don't make me move very far. It is nice to only have to get the ball out of the net."

Stojakovic used to play for PAOK, another club in Thessaloniki. He was drafted fourteenth overall by the Sacramento Kings in the 1996 NBA draft. He played for a few other NBA teams throughout his career and won an NBA championship in 2011 with the Dallas Mavericks.

As Coach finished comparing my shooting skills to the likeness of Stojakovic, I realized that I had probably made more than fifteen three-pointers in a row. In that moment, I got into my own head with this realization and shanked the next shot as it ricocheted off the rim. I ran to retrieve the rebound.

It took a while for me to respond.

"Comparing me to a great European player like Stojakovic is a great compliment. Hopefully, I can be remembered as a great player like he is."

Coach thought I already was.

"I believe you are known as a great player to many people who know you. There are many great players in the world, many great players here in Europe, too. You just haven't gained your popularity with the crowds yet. First, you must believe you are one of the best before you can become one of the best. If you continue to play this game long enough, you will realize your popularity. You are already known here in Kalamaria."

Coach continued to share stories of his own coaching experiences and moments he spent with Stojakovic. I loved listening to his trip down memory lane.

After thirty minutes or so of shooting, I noticed some of the guys from the men's team entering. Was I the only one without a schedule? This time, I wasn't interrupting. In fact, I was extended an invitation to join them for their workout. I accepted, but not before thanking Coach.

"Pleasure meeting you, Bustos."

He departed with a wave.

"Thank you for the talk, Coach."

I headed in the opposite direction.

I was eager to see how another team trained. The session started with plyometric box jumps followed by free throws in between the sets of jumps. No two jumps were alike. We did single leg, double leg, medicine ball jumps, and pivot work into the jump along with some other variations. I enjoyed the change of pace of working out with the men's team. After we finished with box jumps, I asked if they had an agility ladder. One of the guys ran to the back closet and pulled out the ladder. I led the group with the ladder drills that I knew, and then followed when some of the guys threw in their favorites.

My tank hadn't reached "E," but I was done. Or so I thought. I sat down and started to stretch and thought about my lunch choices. But I received a better offer, the chance to play three-on-three. Trying to keep up with their quickness and athleticism was a challenge. I had to be crafty just to get a shot off against the bigger, stronger, faster guys.

Here's something most people don't know. The top women's basketball teams in the NCAA scrimmage against men. Some do it daily. It's not against the rules because those teams are playing against male students enrolled in school. It's not just pick-up guys. A lot of programs hold tryouts to hand-pick the practice players they feel will best prepare them for their opponents, for their season.

Why do they do it? To get better. You have to play stronger competition to improve. And that is exactly what I was doing, trying to raise the level of my game. Playing one-on-one or three-on-three with the guys would help me develop my one-on-one game, and defending them was another way for me to learn different moves to apply to my own game. In one instance, when I was guarding one of the guys, he did some kind of jab step sequence that made me jump in the opposite direction he went. He blew by me and easily scored a layup.

Without shame, I stopped the game and asked, "Can you break down that move and show me what you did really quick?" He laughed and showed me the move he used to beat me. Slowing each step down, he made me understand I had to be a student of the game and learn from others. I continued to guard him for the next few possessions, and he continued to beat me easily with his footwork and ability to get me off balance. I asked one of the guys on my team to switch so I could guard someone else, again without shame.

My next opponent proceeded to drain mid-range jump shots and three-pointers over me with ease. As I guarded him, I studied his movements and change of speed to be able to get open and get his shots off so effortlessly. I couldn't manage to defend him either. I was down to my last option. It wasn't my best decision of the day. This time, the huge muscle man bulldozed his way to the rim and even dunked over me at one point.

Lesson learned. Thanks, guys. I think.

We took a water break. I called for a substitute. I was humiliated, but not in a negative way. Competitors are ruthless. They didn't care that I was a female going up against them, and I appreciated their willingness to go all out against me. It allowed me to be a student of the game.

I stayed and watched from the sideline, taking mental notes on the guy who blew past me with his quickness and footwork and on the guy who created so much space to get his shot off. At the next water break, I asked the big guy if he had a strength plan he was following that he would be willing to share.

After he shared with me and realizing that I had been in the gym for nearly four hours, I had to tell the guys that I was done for the day. I only had two hours to get my lunch, eat, and be ready for weights and practice.

The morning took its toll. I wasn't able to lift as heavy as I would have liked but I pushed my body as best I could. Practice was a marathon of running. My legs were fatigued, but felt good at the same time. Sounds contradictory, I know, but if you are an athlete, you understand what I am talking about. It is a great feeling to be able to push your body—and mind—to the limits where growth coincides.

After practice, I knew I hadn't seen the last of the gym for the day. I hustled home, showered, returned, this time to watch our younger girls play. The majority of my teammates and coach were there as well. We just about yelled and cheered our throats hoarse. My imitations of the Greek shouts brought laughter, but not tears.

"Your accent is so much funnier when you shout," Stella said.

Even I laughed at that one.

The game tipped off at ten. That's p.m. By the end, I was struggling to stay awake, to stay energized. My teammates noticed.

"Vera, you are missing the game. Stop sleeping."

I couldn't identify the voice. Maybe it wasn't just one teammate teasing me. Maybe they all took turns. I somehow made it to the end.

The girls from Apollon won by two points on a pair of free throws with only a few seconds remaining. Here, if you win, you get a pink slip of paper. Eleanna, the head coach of the young girls and one of the managers for our team showed me the pink slip.

"Hopefully, you will get one of these soon," Eleanna said.

"Me, too," I said.

She was talking about the game. Not practice. The game.

Thanks, AI.

Day 54

It was a beautiful day.

The sun shone and it was warmer than usual. It was a good feeling to soak up the sunlight while everyone back home in New Mexico was in a blizzard. I had seen pictures on social media.

I went to shoot again in the morning and had the gym to myself. I played some music on my phone so the gym wasn't so quiet. Afterwards, I went for a walk around the square.

Some of the shops already had their Christmas decorations and ornaments out. The ornaments were about the same as you would find back in the states, decorative lights, and lots of saints that symbolized the Greek orthodox religion.

I walked around with a frappe as I window shopped and enjoyed the day. I tried to find something that would symbolize Christmas in Greece, something I could take back home with me as a souvenir. I came up empty. And disappointed. Walking back to my apartment, a thought occurred to me.

"Spending time in the moment and creating a memory serves as one of the best souvenirs we can have for ourselves. Simple moments create the most treasured memories."

I put ink to journal, thought to paper.

Hellen Keller was right. The best and most beautiful things in the world cannot be seen or even touched—they must be felt with the heart.

Day 55

I awoke to another beautiful day.

The sun was out, the weather was warm. This was not the time to spend indoors, so I didn't. I found myself on the square and at one of my usual cafés, The Small.

"Frappe, please?"

I brought with me, *Leading with the Heart,* a book written by Mike Krzyzweski, the head coach of Duke men's basketball. My agent Thomas had given it to me. I sat and read under warm sunlight for a little over an hour. I could have stayed there all day and would have, had it not been for something called practice.

It was a sweaty interlude and served as the bridge I took that connected book to birthday. I knew the walk would take me to one of my favorite places, Alex and Eleni's apartment.

Mando and I had been invited to celebrate Eleni's belated birthday. I had written her a note in Greek, with the help of Google translate. When it comes to Greek handwriting, Alex and Eleni were the judges.

"It looks like a ten-year-old wrote this note!" Alex joked. "You need to work on your Greek handwriting."

I had no defense. But I had a reply.

"Yes, well, I will need to get better at practicing to draw these shapes that you call your alphabet!"

Alex high-fived me.

It had been a while since I had spent time with them in their apartment. I felt the missing piece fall into place. I looked at the completion. It looked—and felt—like home.

---⊙---

Day 56

---⊙---

Here's the basketball 4-1-1 on Vera Jo Bustos:

She never met a shot she didn't like, she never met a shot she didn't take, she never met a shot she couldn't make. These were actual words I read from an opposing scout that fell into my hands in college.

Dunking excluded, of course.

Yes, I am a shooter. Made in the USA. I am take-it, make-it or take-it again. I am if your shot is off, keep shooting until it's back on. I miss more shots than I make. Everyone does. Doesn't matter. One of the greatest feelings in the world is when you can't miss, don't miss.

I can't remember the last time my shot was as unstoppable as an avalanche. I know it hasn't been since I arrived, fifty-five full days ago. I also know it hasn't been from a lack of practice. I hoist more than five hundred shots a day. Today, was no different.

Part of the men's team was already in the midst of its shooting workout when I arrived. An invitation was extended and accepted. Almost immediately, something was different. It was my shot. It felt good. Most important, it was on target. I knocked in shot after shot after shot. Ten, eleven, twelve in a row, hearing nothing but the sound of the net—S*woosh*!

Nothing beats that feeling. It's a testament to the culmination of years and years I spent perfecting my shot. It feels good knowing my hard work is paying off and it's proof that work ethic and effort are the foundation of my reality exceeding any dreams.

After all, that's the reason I was in Greece. I was here to knock down shots!

I thanked the guys for including me before heading out for lunch. The street was devoid of the usual hustle and bustle, except for an elderly man. I enjoy acknowledging people and was taught the importance of being polite and greeting someone as you pass, even if it's with a simple smile.

"Kalispera," I said. It means good afternoon. He made eye contact with me, stopped in his tracks and erupted in conversation. I wasn't prepared for the volcanic speed at which he was speaking, the words flowing so quickly that I couldn't decipher a single one.

In an instant, I felt so uncomfortable and a little embarrassed with the situation. I looked at him, my face frozen in blank stare. I prayed for a pause, so I wouldn't interrupt. He must have been asking me questions because he stopped abruptly, waiting for a response.

"Signome. Den katalaveno," I said. It means, sorry, I don't understand. He grunted disappointment.

"Ah ok," he said. He waved, gave a slight smile, and walked on past me.

I was eager to engage in a conversation as I had been practicing my Greek. But I had not anticipated the speed of potential responses and had not rehearsed what to do if that situation arose, like it just did. I was dazed before I could clear my confusion and reply. It was a missed opportunity. The disappointment was evenly divvied, each taking half.

We would be returning to Athens for our next game. I stayed after practice to talk to Alex about how I could help my team more and about the state of my game. There was plenty of anxiety to go around. We all wanted to snip the losing string and hold the pink slip that was eluding us.

It wasn't an opportunity I wanted to waste. I was determined more than ever to stay true to who I was, to give what I always gave—my best shot.

Day 57-58

My phone is not surgically attached to my hands.

At least, I don't think it is. Others might disagree. Yes, I like to stay "connected." Yes, I kneel at the altars of unlimited data and free Wi-Fi. Look around. There are billions just like me. Still, I can live without it. At least, I hope I can.

I was up early, ready to board the charter bus for the long drive to Athens. Our previous trip took seven hours. This one was scheduled to last eight. Not sure why, but it was. Did I mention there would be no cell service for what amounts to one-third of a full day? If I hadn't, it's probably because I didn't want to think about it. I knew I would survive without the world wide web.

I promised myself I would be productive, to draw a line through as many items on my to-do list that didn't require internet access. It's never a long list. Then again, it never stops growing. I found self-fulfillment in the fact that I finished reading *Leading with the Heart*, which got me in the right frame of mind for the game. It was a great book. I compare good books to good movies. Once is never enough.

We stayed at the same hotel from our initial trip. We re-lived the past, walking to the mall for ice cream. This time, we didn't linger. We were tired; we needed to unwind. I closed the door to my hotel room for the night. I slipped my earbuds in and went through my visualization process until it was time for sleep.

#

No alarm clocks were set. This was not an early-morning type of day. Game days seldom are. Even though none of us had been behind the wheel, the drive took a lot out of us. It always amazes me how tiring travel is, especially since all you do is sit the whole time. I was last to reach the breakfast buffet where most of my teammates were already eating. They had saved me a seat. I set my coffee and breakfast on the table in front of it.

Every ride to every game is a sight-seeing tour for me. It's one of the perks I never thought of when I signed my first professional contract. Athens is amazing everywhere I looked. The city was bigger than Thessaloniki. More crowded, too. The narrowness of the side streets made it difficult for our large charter bus to squeeze through our route to the gym, sort of like trying to fit into skinny jeans. The residential areas we passed through were crowded. The apartment complexes climbed ten stories. On the balconies that overlooked the streets, I saw clothes hanging on lines and blowing in the light breeze. It reminded me of the way queens wave. Cars lined the curbs on both sides. They were parked bumper-to-bumper. If there was an Olympic sport for extreme parallel parking, the Greeks would win the gold, silver, and bronze medal.

My sight-seeing ended in front of a gym, which was home of the Greek club Panionios.

With a sense of urgency, I donned my uniform and hurried to the court. I wanted a few extra minutes of shooting before we started our pre-game warmup. It took all of one shot to realize this could be the break-out game I'd been waiting for.

The game was four quarters of tug-of-war with neither team ever holding a decisive advantage. We were down three, seconds to go. We were in a time out.

Coach drew a play, black marker on white clipboard. It was designed for me to come off a flare screen. On the board it was all Xs and Os and squiggly lines. So what was the play, in words, not symbols? A flare screen is set with the screeners back to the corner where the baseline and sideline intersect. The shooter comes off the screen in the direction of the baseline along the three-point line and shoots a three-pointer.

I was ready.

I was willing.

I was unable to get the ball.

Here's how it unfolded.

The official handed the ball to my teammate to inbound. *One thousand one, one thousand two, one thousand three, one thousand four* ticked off unofficially, leaving my teammate a second to inbound before a violation would be whistled. She beat the clock.

I didn't need to peek at the Panionios clipboard to know what I was facing. She literally stood right in front of me, eyeball to eyeball. Their plan was to deny me the ball, and if that failed, to defend the three-point line as if the game was on the line, which it was.

I stepped as if I was going to cut to the basket to allow myself to have a good angle coming back the opposite way to rub shoulders off my teammate coming off the flare screen. I got myself open for about a second, enough time for me to catch and shoot with my quick release. I turned my head over my left shoulder to look for the pass, anticipating that it should be in the air. As I looked back, my teammate was having a hard time dribbling past her defender. The window closed as rapidly as it opened. Her only option was a contested three-point shot. Panionios rebounded the miss. We fouled. The clock froze. Two seconds remained. Panionios converted the two free throws for the final separation.

My emotions were stirred, not shaken. I felt I played well. I remember only missing two shots on my way to twenty-two points. I also had four assists, four steals, three blocks, and three rebounds. All were reasons to smile. And maybe I should have smiled more. But I didn't. I hold myself accountable after a loss. I took the brunt of the blame and slung it over my shoulders like a backpack. I didn't need to see inside. And besides, I couldn't. My eyes were already fixated by what was to come. Our team was improving. As was I.

I traced my sudden growth spurt to a couple days ago, when the men invited me for three-on-three. Studying the footwork and change of speed of each player I faced proved beneficial. I also incorporated the jab move I learned. I took pride in my abilities to transfer practice into performance.

It was time to board the bus. Goodbye, Athens. So long, internet. Hello, journal.

I can't remember when I first started putting thoughts to pen and pen to paper. It seems like I've been doing it for as long as I can remember. I've never been hesitant to record my journey. But I felt somewhat reluctant about whether or not this was something I should write about. But they were my thoughts at the moment and I didn't see the harm in letting people know what they were.

Thoughts of being blessed always cross my mind first and foremost. Beyond that, the fascinating mystery of the world we live in. Many times, we tend to be guilty of getting caught up in our own life and focusing on the small and sometimes insignificant problems at hand. We fail to appreciate what we have.

God has blessed each and every one of us with talents. I, specifically, was blessed with a certain amount of athleticism and desire. It is because of these talents and because of the values instilled in me by my family that I am where I am today. I believe I am as normal as the person next to me. Motivation and desire deep in my heart are what sets me apart and takes me places I could only dream of. Everything goes hand in hand. God blesses me with these gifts, so how can I serve the world with what was provided to me?

I'm not famous, nor do I have the platform to reach thousands of people. What I realized, though, is that basketball is the foundation and the platform I was given to help others around me. How would I lead? We can all serve God, and basketball was the path I was given to lead in His name. I knew I would not be able to change thousands of lives, though I was secretly hoping that someday I would, but everyone has heard that to impact one life in a positive way throughout your lifetime is a life well-spent. I reminded myself to be kinder than necessary because everyone is always facing some sort of struggle, and I told myself that I would always have the power, and the choice, to make a difference in someone's life, regardless of how small that difference would be.

We hadn't won a game. I had never started the season 0-6 and as a matter of record I had never lost six games in a row. I was facing the unfamiliar territory of being on a losing team. Even so, did I wish I was playing for a different team?

Not a chance.

I chose to make the best of the situation and be appreciative of the great things that were happening in my life. I am, and always will be, a work in progress to make a difference wherever I go. I could only hope that I could impact the lives of the people around me in Greece as much as they made a difference in my life.

Our record reflected our basketball reality. That's it. I firmly believed I was still winning in life. I was 0-6 at what I did professionally. Personally, I was undefeated in the relationships I made and the joy I encountered.

My effort wouldn't change. My attitude wouldn't change. My goals wouldn't change. This process would be part of the progress. I would learn from each situation. I would continue to find ways to shine a light on my teammates and coaches.

I am under construction, please excuse the mess.

I slowly dozed off to sleep.

Day 59

*I didn't need The Book of Genesis to tell me
I needed to take a day off.*

The gospel came from my body, which spoke both loudly and clearly. I was fortunate that nothing was scheduled in terms of shooting, weights, or practice.

I stood on heavy legs, weighted down by fatigue. My quad muscle was rock-solid to the touch and as tight as a recently tuned piano string. I relaxed throughout much of the day before watching the younger girls of Apollon play against Paok.

God had His seventh day. I finally allowed myself to have mine.

We can all agree that broccoli is good for us. But I don't always order it when I see it on the menu. It's not different when it comes to living. We tend to entangle ourselves in the daily grind that is the web of life. We think we should be working our tails off, going all out, all the time. I not only see that point of view, but most days I live it. There is something favorable to say about persistent discipline and grind mentality, cornerstones needed to build success in any endeavor worth pursuing. Then again, it isn't the catch-all, be-all.

I'm learning that rest is of equal value when it comes not just to the body, but to the mind. Rest allows our muscles to recover, to grow stronger. Rest allows our minds to recharge and refocus, and at times recalibrate our perspective on certain situations that have challenged us in the past.

Hard work is the foundation we stand on to achieve greatness. And I promise, it's not going to crumble if you lie down and relax on it every once in a while.

Day 60

The day off did its job, and then some.

I couldn't wait to start my day, to start my week. My mind was worry-free as I joined my agent for coffee in the morning hours.

We went to a nice café near the sea. It was a relaxing conversation. Familiar, too. We both wanted what was best for me and my playing time in the Greek League. His insights injected new ideas in where and how I could improve. But it wasn't just about the here and now. Thoughts of the future were always on his mind since he was already building me up to sign a contract for the following season. I appreciated him holding me accountable and challenging me. I needed both.

A note greeted me at the front door of my apartment. A package was waiting for me in the office. Huh, I wasn't expecting anything. I strolled to the office, one step anxious, the other step surprise. The secretary at the front desk greeted me in Greek, and I responded in Greek. Her words accelerated zero-to-sixty in her native tongue. I couldn't keep up. Instead, I nodded and smiled, pretending I understood as the package went from her hands to mine. I thanked her as I walked out the door.

I didn't need to read the return address to instantly recognize the handwriting on the package. It was from Mom. I rushed back to my apartment.

I was a child.

It was 6 a.m. Christmas morning.

At 6:01, I was fingers deep into red and green chile beef jerky.

"YES!!!!"

My favorite snack triggered a full scream.

I was suffering chile withdrawals from my beloved home state of New Mexico. If you spell chili with an "i" at the end, then you don't fully understand what I am talking about. Perhaps a trip to the Land of Enchantment will clue you in on my excitement. It was such an awesome feeling to receive mail from home and made me feel closer to what is the biggest part of me. The taste of the chile had me reminiscing on times spent in the kitchen over dinner with my family. It's incredible how tasting a certain type of food can transport you back into a specific place and time.

#

The rest of the day was spent on fast-forward, and no, I didn't eat all the jerky in one sitting, in case you were wondering.

After weights and practice, I spent the rest of the evening talking to my family, alternating Facebook and Skype. The well of emotions surfaced, then overflowed with homesickness. Thoughts of missing out on my sisters' volleyball matches, spending time with my extended family, grandparents, and parents had me awash with loneliness. I was used to being away from home, having lived in Colorado—a decent car ride from home—for the previous four years, so the thoughts of missing out on family events and moments wasn't new. The difference was knowing that I couldn't hop in the car whenever I wanted to drive back home. Distance was the one obstacle I couldn't change.

In pursuit of following one dream, I knew a sacrifice somewhere else would take place. Here I was, living out my dream of playing professional basketball, and my thoughts were on what it would be like to be back home.

I am *here*.

They are *there*.

And *there* doesn't know how lucky it is.

It's interesting how the mind works in that way. Or maybe it was just my mind. My mind always seemed to want to be somewhere else. When I was back home, all I could think about was what it would be like to be living in Greece. How amazing it must be to live in a foreign country as beautiful as Greece.

Now, while I was living in this beautiful country, I couldn't help wondering about everything I was missing out on at home. Why was that? Why couldn't I be joyous and grateful in these moments? Why was I thinking about a place I couldn't be?

I suppose that's where the phrase *"the grass is always greener on the other side"* comes from. We think of other things we could be doing, other places we could be spending our time, and how much better it could be than the current situation we are in.

Some of life's lessons require a study hall. This was one such subject. Sometimes I believe my life should be surrounded by orange barrels. There is always work that needs to be done.

I acknowledged the fact that I missed my family and that I was homesick. But the work here was far from finished. And I never leave anything undone.

Day 61-63

*If it's true that a storm follows the calm,
perhaps I should have braced myself.*

But aside from practice, weights, shooting workouts and the occasional visits to Alex and Eleni's apartment, nothing ominous was brewing.

Yes, the weather was cold. And yes, I was more indoors than out. But I found an efficient—and effective—stride that worked for me when it came to the routine of workouts. In the free time I had, I found myself wanting to go back to my apartment to rest.

Yes, I knew what was ahead. But it was not a storm. It was Paok, tomorrow night's opponent. Paok is one of the well-known clubs of Thessaloniki. I know one victory does not make a season. But it would be a start, and who knows what would follow?

Day 64

I yelled myself into this world at 12:03 in the morning.

I was too young to recall, but I was told much later in life that I arrived alone.

Turns out, I had a twin.

We looked nothing alike. We spoke different languages. But for four quarters and one overtime, we were conjoined at the Nike. Where I went, she went. I half-expected her to be next to me during time outs and halftime. If my shadow had been there, she would have gotten jealous.

It wasn't my idea to be a Doublemint twin. It was Paok's, our opponent for the evening. The scouting report was designed to deny me the ball. Most teams are satisfied when they limit my shots. Paok wasn't one of those teams; they didn't want me even touching the ball.

I did my best to set screens to open opportunities for my teammates. Since my defender was playing lock-on defense and never left my side, every screen I set ended up being a double screen, which gave a better opportunity for my teammate to get open. Being denied so much in college, I wasn't surprised by this game plan. However, I was surprised at their efficiency in enacting it.

The game plan worked—Paok's, not ours. I ended with a season-low four points and Paok ended with an overtime victory.

My teammates picked up the scoring slack. I scrapped for rebounds, grabbing eleven. I also got emotional post-game. It was guilt, written by my own hands. Guilt from losing, guilt from being so close to winning, guilt from scoring all of four points. I felt I could have done more to help the team win.

The cracks in my spirit were visible, split open from the burden of blame that I stuffed inside me, loss by loss by loss. The cruel, negative self-talk wiped clean all other thoughts and left in its place questions about my skills, my talent level. The voice of reason was not even an echo. Instead, I heard:

"Everything you're doing is wrong. You're not good enough. You're not producing enough."

That wasn't the worst. I hate admitting this, but I eventually started to place blame on the others. I felt myself being sucked into that dark wormhole of negative thoughts. No light for guidance. No rope to grasp. I knew I had to reach out for help.

I knew who would reach back.

Day 65

The sadness in my eyes matched the sorrow in my heart.

Last night's overtime loss hurt. A lot. Way more than the previous six. I was down and the count was *nine*.

I got up and out of bed. Eventually. But I stayed in my apartment most of the day. Sure, my body was somewhat sore. But it was mind, my sense of self that needed . . . I'm not sure exactly what it needed, but I knew there was only one place to look.

Skype.

I connected with my family, specifically mom and dad. I needed that lifeline, the one marked "self-confidence." It was Dad who tossed it to me. He has this laugh that will either make you crack up laughing or make you want to roll your eyes at him when you aren't in the best of moods. He helped me remember all the times I dealt with adversity in my past and still managed to come out of those situations successful. He reminded me to stay positive and to make the best of the situation. Control what you can, and don't dwell on what you can't. He also reminded me to return to my "sweet spot" on the floor. Free throw line first. Then top of the key. When in doubt, he always reminded me to find my shot and confidence there.

It's true that, "a father holds his daughter's hand for a short while, but he holds her heart forever."

Thanks, Dad, for always holding my heart when I am too far away for you to hold my hand. You, too, Mom.

I also caught up with my sisters and their lives. Being the oldest, and even being thousands of miles away, I still try to watch over them and be the best sister I can be. My family has been, and forever will be, my greatest blessing.

I felt myself smiling for the first time in a while.

Day 66

The day felt as quiet as snow falling at midnight, except for the overtime loss, which echoed inside me still.

I started going through some of my sports psychology notes and reading some of the books I had in an attempt to put that loss behind me once and for all. I fixated on the concept of confidence from my PGC Basketball notes since I felt mine slipping away.

Confidence boils down to two sources—preparation and mindset/ mentality. The more prepared you are, the more confidence that preparation brings. This, I knew from experience. The more I practice free throws, the more confident I am when I step up to the free throw line. This form of preparation is limitless and not restrictive to athletics. Whether it's playing a musical instrument, studying for a test, learning to cook, anything you want to become good at you must first put in the time to become confident in that particular skill.

Your mindset is what you think about yourself. In a word, it's self-esteem. It was my Achilles' heel. My preparation wasn't the problem, it was my mentality. Way too often, I allowed negative thoughts to take over. I put those thoughts into words, and those words became my actions. My mindset was the windshield, my preparation was the bug. I lost every one of those head-ons.

My problem wasn't just what I was thinking about. My problem was also what I thought of myself. A mind believes everything it's told. Instead of believing that I had within me the ability to score and play at this level, I allowed my mind to convince me that I wasn't good enough, that I didn't belong. I learned the hard way that your mindset negates all the preparation and practice you put into your craft when you allow it.

Preparation + Mindset = Confidence. Looking at some of the all-time great athletes, I realized what set them apart from everyone else was their mindset. At the lower levels of competition, your skill level and athleticism can set you apart. In the pros, most are nearly indistinguishable when it comes to innate talent and learned skills. What the greats possess is that inner confidence and mentality of superiority they have about themselves. They believe so much in themselves they don't let anyone or anything bring them down.

My thoughts drove behavior, and my behavior affected the performance of my game and almost everything else I did in life. The way I thought determined the way I felt. The way I felt regulated the way I acted. The way I acted controlled the way I trained. The way I trained dictated how I performed.

Muhammed Ali proclaimed himself "The Greatest." He believed it. Others did, too. Ali also understood not everyone was the best at what they did. He had a message for them. Basically, for those who weren't the best, believe that you still are. Some would say fake it, till you make it. I say believe it, till you make it. If I wanted to be the best I first had to believe that I was. Then work like crazy to make that belief a reality.

That thought resonated inside me. Now that I was playing at this new level, my belief system had to change accordingly. I was putting in the time to fine-tune my physical skills, and I was also spending time studying my psyche and psychology books. What I was failing to do was putting those actions into actual games. My talent and skills got me here. They wouldn't keep me here. I needed to upgrade my mentality and become a student of my own mindset.

Self-worth would be my starting point moving forward.

Day 67

The older you get, the more goodbyes you say.

This morning, I had to say goodbye to K. She was leaving, returning to the United States for personal reasons.

No one put out a press release like they do back home when a player leaves the team. It was a quiet goodbye from all sides. All I could do was wish her all the best at our sad goodbye. I wondered if our paths would ever cross again.

The club wasted no time in signing her replacement, filling her spot that same day with another American. I didn't live in fear. Then again, the thought of being cut crossed my mind. Fear motivates some, paralyzes others. As for me, I have found it more beneficial to be running toward something than running away from it.

Running away from my fear of being cut wouldn't get me to where I wanted to be. I chose to focus on what I was running toward, the goal of being the best basketball player I could be. I couldn't control what the club owners thought of my game. But I could give them every reason *not* to cut me.

In hindsight, I needed to experience seeing a teammate leave, not because she wanted to, because she was no longer wanted, or needed. The incident proved to be a great mentality shift and raised the level of awareness inside me. I have control over one thing and only one thing—me.

Later that evening, I met Denise, the newest member of the team. She had been playing in Europe the past six years and brought great experience. I was eager to pick her brain and learn some tricks of the trade from her. She possessed what I lacked—longevity.

Her résumé was impressive. So, too, was her personality. We hit it off instantly. She measured 6-foot and had silky, ebony skin. She had a dimple in her left cheek that illuminated her smile. Hope gushed inside me. We needed to turn this season around quickly if we wanted to remain playing in the first division.

After welcoming the newest member to our basketball family, I spent the rest of the evening reconnecting with my first family. My sister, Sarah, took her laptop to my grandparents' house so we could Skype. It was the first time I had seen them in more than two months.

When I saw their faces on the screen, the joy simply overwhelmed me. Until that moment, I never realized that a smile and tears could be that close. I couldn't tell you which was wider, their smiles or the excitement in the voices. They asked about Greece. I wanted to hear about home.

A sudden bolt of irony struck me during the visit. Time seems to stand still and fly by all at once. I was getting homesick more often while the countdown to my flight back home was at a standstill. Time wouldn't budge one way or the other. And while being away, I realized how much I was missing. Missing my sisters grow and mature in their own ways. Missing other precious moments replayed over Skype for my benefit. It caused twinges of jealousy because they were making memories that didn't include me.

"One more month," I told myself. One more month before I was able to go home and see my family. I couldn't wait.

Then again, I could.

Day 68

*Practice was our version of D-Day,
as in familiarize Denise with our playbook.*

Intensity followed instruction. The sense of urgency during the workout was high and rose to a level that hadn't been seen in a while. The energy was contagious.

Following practice, Denise and I had a date with Thomas, who was there to welcome her to the city. Denise was Thomas' latest client. I knew she would be in good hands. Thomas is a great agent, but a better friend.

I ordered my coffee in Greek and had a basic dialogue with the waiter. He was familiar with me since I went to that café often and applauded my ability to hold a conversation. He told me he would be right back with my frappe.

Denise and Thomas were engaged in their own discussion, one I remembered Thomas and I having a few months before when I first arrived. It focused on expectations of play and what Denise needed to do to ensure an extended future in Greece. The sea distracted my eyes, while my mind diverted my attention.

"I could never get tired of this," I thought.

It wasn't just the view, or the coffee, or the smell of the salty water from the breeze that cooled what the heaters we were sitting next to had just warmed. It was the people.

I carried those feelings to Alex and Eleni's apartment. We ate pizza and ice cream. Alex and Konstantinos battled on PlayStation. Like books, all days have endings. I was determined to keep this one open for as long as I could.

---⊙---

Day 69-70

---⊙---

Me: Siri, show me a map of my comfort zone.

Siri: *Silence.*

Me: Siri, will you please show me a map of my comfort zone?

Siri: *Silence.*

Me: Siri, . . .

Siri: *I heard you the first two times. Life begins at the end of your comfort zone.*

Comfort zones, ones you can map and have boundaries, don't exist. Except in the space between a left ear and the right one. It's all in our heads. Yet, that is the neighborhood in which we choose to live, next door to routine. Monotony lives across the street.

As much as I hate to admit, my mailbox is planted deep. Here's my daily planner of late: breakfast, walking to get my lunch, walking to the gym for practice. I can't say I am losing myself in my routine when I am walking it blindfolded.

Someone once told me to never let time fade the excitement and blessing of an opportunity. If I don't change soon, my world will be the dullest shade of gray. The seeds of routine poison me when I allow the monotony to grow. I constantly clear a path that pushes the constraints of my comfort zone and challenge myself in new ways. The days I don't, I become bored, complacent.

Obviously, consistency matters in athletics, when it comes to workouts and regimens. Even then, workouts must be changed every now and again. If not, it becomes the same old routine, no matter how dedicated you are. I imagine I'm not the only one sitting in this particular classroom.

When I didn't have too much going on, like the past two days, I still did my best to add change. I explored a different neighborhood, a fresh coffee shop, a new restaurant. I engaged strangers in my beginner's level Greek. I was tired of living the same day two days in a row.

And I did one more thing, the best thing, actually. I invited Denise to go explore with me. We walked around Krini on Thursday and stayed in around the square on Friday. It's a lot easier to explore and be adventurous when there are two of us, even in the cold weather.

Who needs a Siri, or an Alexa? I don't. I had Denise.

Day 71

Alice had her wonderland.

I had Denise, and a bus, and downtown. Let the adventure begin.

Denise was full of surprises, one of which was her connection to the Aris men's basketball game. Aris is another club in Thessaloniki. Denise has a good friend who plays on the team. They met during one of her previous overseas stops. He left two complimentary tickets to tonight's game in our names.

We left an hour early, thinking that would give us plenty of time. Our best-laid plans detoured unintentionally. We knew we had to take the number five bus to get to the center of the city, which is where the Aris basketball gym is located. We boarded the number five. That's as far as the good got. We boarded the one heading in the opposite direction of downtown.

Oops!

We were now twenty minutes behind schedule. We arrived at the stop where we knew we had to exit, but once back on foot, our sense of direction was set on lost. No big deal, right? Cell phone. Google Map. Gym. We would be there within minutes and before tip-off.

Yes, I had a cell phone. I could make calls. I could text. I could do nothing more. It was an old-school flip phone. There was nothing smart about it. Next option was old-school. We stopped and asked people if they knew where the gym was. Some used their fingers to point in this direction and that. Others used their fingers to scratch their heads. And others didn't even bother to raise a finger, probably because they didn't speak English.

Through either ESP or ESPN, we finally found the gym, hurried through the ticket counter, and found our seats. The gym was comparable to those found on most college campuses in America. It looked like it could fit between fifteen and twenty thousand fans. My guess is we joined 9,998 others who, no doubt, arrived on time.

We were a quarter behind. No, really. We sat when the second quarter started. The crowd's passion was in full voice when we joined the choir. There is no pause button when it comes to the Greeks. And no mute button, either. I can't recall a single second of silence, which is the way all games should be.

The only noise heard above the voices was the pounding of two large drums in the corner of the arena. They sounded like the drums from the movies when armies were getting ready to go to war. The fans chanted to the rhythm of the beat. If Aris was in a basketball war, it was not fighting alone. The atmosphere was intoxicating.

In the middle of this symphony of support, my phone buzzed. It was a text from a Vassiliki, my teammate. The text said for me to keep smiling because she could see me on TV. Only later were the empty blanks filled. A cameraman found Denise and me in the crowd and zoomed in on us while the announcer explained that we were the American foreign players for Apollon Kalamarias. There's more to the story. The game had been broadcast throughout Greece. My first national exposure was in a foreign land.

I showed Denise the text message. She started laughing.

"Well, at least one of us wasn't caught picking our nose or something. We would never hear the end of that."

She laughed, nodding in full agreement.

Denise cheered on her buddy and I found another player from Aris who I began to cheer for. Dan Mavraides. He was "also" Greek-American. Even the Euro-basket website had my nationality tagged as "Greek," which was pointed out to me by an Aris fan.

"Do you know Mavraides? You are both Greek and both from America."

It was the same fan who pointed out my nationality on the website of professional basketball in Europe.

Intrigued by this *other* Greek-American, I watched his game closely and quickly became a fan.

We spent the rest of the game trying to stay in sync with the beat.

The bus ride home was uneventful. I didn't mind.

Day 73

We all have ample definitions of simple pleasures.

Coffee and conversation with Thomas was one of mine. Since there was no rush to this particular day, I lounged for most of the morning inside my apartment.

Thomas arrived as scheduled and we decided on Krini for our C&C. The view of the sea from that part of the city never gets old. Enjoying my morning frappe with this view also defined simple pleasures. Our conversation steered clear of basketball for the most part. I was glad. Talking about life in general was enough.

Later that evening, Denise and I wanted a bus do-over, again setting downtown as our destination. The ride was devoid of detours and delays, even though we were not on any time schedule.

We played tourists, hit up my favorite ice cream spot and walked along the sea. The cool breeze and cold ice cream chilled our bodies in stereo. Neither stopped us from enjoying the moment. I loved how alive downtown always was with people shopping, eating, drinking their coffee.

It was people watching at its best.

Simple.

Pleasurable.

---⊙---

Day 74-75

---⊙---

The word charades is playful.

As it should be. It is, after all, a game. Charades can be helpful, as well. Especially when you are trying to communicate in two languages, neither of you is bi-lingual, and you feel as though you are separated by the Great Wall of China.

Of course, you wouldn't want to use charades if you were having an audience with the Pope, if you were dealing with the KGB in Moscow at 3 a.m., or if you were visiting a doctor in a foreign country and someone was pantomiming the act of sticking you with a needle.

The normality of the past two days halted on Wednesday when Sophia (my teammate) and I headed downtown for a physical therapy session so I could receive treatment on my left leg. My leg had been giving me a few problems, so the team made an appointment with someone it referred to as the "team doctor."

The appointment was more than a little challenging. The doctor broke English. I garbled Greek. Even hand gestures proved futile. It wasn't until the doctor asked Sophia to join us and act as translator did the message get through. I pointed out the problem. Sophia relayed the message. The doctor looked at her, then me, then her, again.

"Uh huh."

"Humm."

Those were the exact sounds the doctor muttered. She resumed speaking Greek to Sophia. It was a little unsettling knowing they were talking about me without my understanding.

When they finished, I asked for the translation.

"She was trying to decide which kind of treatment she wants to do with you," Sophia answered. "She decided she will start with the . . ."

My teammate searched for the proper word. When she couldn't come up with one, that's when and where she broke out the gesture of poking me with something.

"I believe it is a needle?" she finally said, questioning her choice.

"A needle?" I replied. The shock lasted but a couple seconds. That's how long it took for me to realize what she was talking about.

"Oh, you mean acupuncture?" I asked.

"Yes, I believe that is what you say for it," she answered. "Who knows though? Good luck in there."

She giggled herself out the door.

"I'm glad you can get some laughter out of my discomfort!" It was half-yell, half-laugh.

The doctor instructed me to sit down on the table. I did so with a little apprehension, still not knowing what was about to come next and her inability to communicate efficiently what she was about to do.

I tried to relax. She began moving my leg around and prodding in certain areas. I told her which areas hurt and what caused the worst aggravation.

"I begin," she muttered through a thick accent while using her hand to gesture for me to sit still.

She went to the back and returned with some needles. I had received acupuncture before, so I had experience being a human voodoo doll. She poked needles into and all along my leg. Once she had finished placing them, she said, "Okay, no move." She made a gesture with her hands informing me she was going into the other room and said something in Greek. I assumed she was telling me that she would be right back.

I sat with the needles in my leg for about ten minutes. I did my best to relax. She returned and removed the needles, and then escorted me back out to the lobby where Sophia was waiting.

She met my eyes with a smile and teased, "Oh good, you are alive."

"You are full of jokes today, aren't you?" I replied.

Ice cream makes everything better. That was our first—and only—stop on the way back to my apartment. The drive took us through a part of town I had never seen before. I saw old ruins from the old city and sculptures carved into the walls of an old arch, both of which created intrigue and mystique in my mind.

I could only imagine what the city must have looked like hundreds of years ago.

Day 76

*My Wi-Fi connection was the technological
equivalent of a Leatherback sea turtle on its back,
its legs dog paddling air.*

In other words, there was no quick fix. I couldn't just flip it over. Or in this case, turn it on and off. I'd been there. I'd done that. The best solution was to keep my distance. So I did.

Not being "connected" was bothersome, and not just for the obvious. I realized how much I depended on it to do anything in my apartment. I used it to communicate with others via social media, to watch TV on my computer (since the TV I had in my room mostly had Greek-speaking channels), and just to scroll through the internet to stay informed about what was going on in the world on a day-to-day basis.

But there are two worlds—cyber and real. With the first being inaccessible, I opted for the other. I decided today would be a good day to venture into the Kalamaria neighborhoods I had yet to explore.

I discovered a type of flea market that stretched the length of the street. The vendors' stands lined both sides of the block along the sidewalks with little separation between them. Shoppers used the middle of the street as the two-lane walkway. Some vendors sold fruits and vegetables, others sold nuts and seeds. The morning's seafood catch was available as were freshly cut flowers. A couple vendors sold gadgets, a couple more sold toys for kids.

I brought back memories but no merchandise. And photos, of course. I stayed away from the internet until after practice. But I couldn't stay away for good. It was Thanksgiving Day back home in the States. I had a Skype date with my family. It was an opportunity to see everyone—and I do mean everyone—for the holiday. It's tradition that the extended family on my mother's side gets together at my parents' house for the day. There are usually more than thirty people in my house, but the number keeps growing as all the families keep expanding.

Anxious, I grabbed my computer, praying for the best. If the worst happened, I had a backup plan of going over to Alex and Eleni's and using their internet. Plan A worked. The Skype ringtone sounded. I knew who would answer.

"Hi, my honey!"

"Hello, mother!"

She took her phone around the house, showing the screen to every family member. Each got their own "Hello." I'm extremely blessed to have the family dynamic I do. I'm grateful to have such a strong relationship with not only my immediate family, but also my extended family of aunts, uncles, grandparents, and cousins. Twenty minutes later, I was finally back with my mom, talking one-on-one.

That was my fifth year being away from home over Thanksgiving. Playing college basketball at Adams State, we always played in a tournament during that final week in November, so I never had the opportunity to go home over those four years I played there. Year five, I was even farther away in Greece, and I didn't even have any turkey to eat to celebrate the day!

The connection lasted long enough for me to spend quality time with the majority of my family. I was thankful for that. I just wish it had lasted longer. Then again, I always wished it would last longer. There was more to it than just a lost internet connection. Missing out on special moments like that with the family made me miss home. Being an athlete away from home and family over holidays is one of the hardest things I dealt with.

That night, I created a countdown for my Christmas departure. It was worked into my contract that the club would pay for my roundtrip flight home to spend Christmas with my family. It helped alleviate some of the homesickness, but not all.

Lost moments are never found.

Day 77

I finally solved buses.

Uh . . . why did the applause die down so quickly? Haven't you been reading? Come on people, stand up and cheer. That doesn't mean my travails with words that start with the letter "B" are over. Well, not this day, that's for sure.

First, the good "B."

I caught a bus downtown for another therapy session for my leg. By this point, I was used to the public transportation system. I bought my ticket upon boarding and made my way toward the back to find a seat. The closer the bus got to downtown, the more packed it got. By the time we reached my stop, it was standing-room only. I was constantly checking where my phone and wallet were, you know, just in case a pickpocket or thief singled me out. Yes, my imagination goes unchecked far too often.

Familiar with the directions where I needed to go for my therapy session, I exited the bus and walked to the therapist's office. This was the same therapist who didn't speak English very well, and without Sophia with me this time to serve as my translator, I was a bit apprehensive about the communication process between us.

Now, the bad "B."

The building was in the heart of downtown. Like most buildings there, you need special access to get in. A set of buttons, each written in Greek, are by the outside door. The buttons coincide with the business, office, or residence inside. You push the button, the person answers and buzzes you in. That is, if you push the right button.

Yes, I flunked the button test. Don't laugh. It wasn't exactly funny in real time. Looking at the names and buttons, I felt a moment of panic come over me. I was starting to learn the language a little bit, and could read some things. But these words were handwritten and looked to be in some form of cursive. I had no idea which button belonged to my doctor.

I spent five minutes studying each word next to each button. This wasn't the SATs. There was no letter "C." I was in fear of being late so I picked one and pressed.

Click.

I heard the ringing on the other end.

Click.

A female voice followed.

"*Geia sou,*" which means hello.

"Um, this is Vera, here for therapy."

Silence.

Click.

"Okay," I thought, "apparently, that wasn't the correct one."

I pushed three more buttons. I heard three more clicks. One was memorable, though, because I believed I was told off in Greek. Hey, click happens.

I was perspiring anxiousness, wrong button by wrong button. Being illiterate in this country was awful. And being made to feel like I was a pest felt even worse. It gave me greater compassion for all foreigners who struggle to speak, read and write the language of their adopted country.

I persevered.

Click.

"Ahhh, Vera, I wait for you!"

It was my therapist.

"I found you!" I replied.

There was a loud buzz as the door was unlocked from the inside. I opened it as fast as I could and walked into the building. Once I got inside, my memory guided me to the third-floor room. I was aware of the adrenaline flowing through my system from the discomfort of the experience I had just gone through.

My therapist greeted me in the waiting room. She machine gunned her Greek while using her arms for special effects. I understood exactly zero of her words. Still, I nodded and smiled. My make-believe act that I was following every word didn't last. She appeared to be asking me a question. I shoulder-shrugged my reply. That, she understood. She laughed, shook her head. Her arms gestured for me to follow her into the back room.

A magnetic machine awaited me. It's used to help with the energy and the blood flow of the injury. That was explained to me in broken English by one of the assistants, who was helping the lead therapist with my session.

The machine was big, and loud, and had a hose attached to it, sort of like one of those vacuums at car washes. At the end of the hose was a type of magnetic end that resembled a shower head. The end was cold.

The therapist ran the end over the injured area of my leg. Every time, I almost jumped off the table from the level of discomfort I was suddenly in. I had no idea how this machine was supposed to be helping, but with the amount of pain I was in, I was ready to try anything, withstand everything.

I needed to heal. And fast. For my team's sake as much as for my own. We were still searching for our first victory, and I could feel the pressure mounting, because I was holding it, square on my shoulders.

Day 78

"WE WON!" Apollon 64 – Aris 56.

No. it's not April Fool's Day. And no, this is not a joke. It actually happened.

"WE GOT OUR FIRST WIN!"

Wow, that felt really good to say.

"WE GOT OUR FIRST WIN!"

Okay, I'll calm down now. But only for now. After seven successive losses to start the season, we finally broke through. We beat Aris, which is another team from Thessaloniki. Denise played a great game, scoring seventeen points and grabbing twelve rebounds. My Greek teammates played amazing, Vassiliki drained numerous three's and Spyridoula and Stella played great defense. I finished with eighteen points and seven boards. The victory was inclusive. It was total-team. It had to be for us to get the job done.

As elated as I was on a personal level (after all, it was my first professional victory), I was over the moon for my teammates, coaches, and other people associated with the team. It was smiles all around.

Coach Andreas waved a pink slip which indicated victory in his hand toward the team. Eleanna showed me what the pink slip looked like and what it meant a few weeks back, so I understood the significance of what otherwise would have been an insignificant piece of pink paper being waved around.

If this were a movie, seeing the pink slip of paper being waved triumphantly would have been the final scene before the screen faded to black. But this was real. And my lasting image is of Coach Andreas, whose exuberance put the final shine on this one moment.

Day 79

I walked, ate, slept, awoke on Cloud Nine.

And I'm okay with that. After suffering through a record low of emotions and confidence, I would surf this high until the wave reached the sand. Yes, one win felt that good.

Win or lose, I'm usually the type to let a game go quickly, like water slipping through a fist. But not this time. This one, I would savor longer. This one, I wanted to share.

I didn't realize the time when I walked down the outdoor corridor of the stadium down to Denise's room and knocked on her door. She answered half-asleep. I woke her up.

"*Kalimera!*" I said, the volume of my voice resting between shout and yell.

She laughed.

"Geez, Vera, are you turning Greek on me now too? Please, speak to me in English; you're the only person I can understand here."

My agreement was signed in laughter. It had started to become habit for me to greet people in Greek.

"You want to head down to the square and get something for lunch and a coffee?" I asked. "I don't want to stay cooped up in my room this morning."

It turns out, neither did Denise.

"Sure. Just give me ten minutes and I'll be ready."

We walked to the square and settled into one of the local cafés. I ordered what they call "toast." It's what we call a grilled-cheese sandwich. I also got my usual frappe. For two hours, we sat, ate, replayed last night's game. It wasn't an entirely pat-ourselves-on-the-back dialogue. We talked a lot about ways in which we could play even better. We also read some articles that had published online about our win. Hey, there's nothing wrong with others patting you on the back.

After the café, we caught a ride to the Paok gym to watch the women play Kronos. Denise's college friend was playing on the men's team, so we went to hang out with him. Inside, I met J.R. Giddens.

For the New Mexico faithful, I'm sure you know who he is. For those who don't, he used to play for the University of New Mexico and then got drafted by the Boston Celtics in the NBA. He stayed in the league for a while, and was now playing in Greece for Paok.

J.R. and I spent the second half talking all things New Mexico and basketball. We thought it was ironic how we both came from New Mexico and met for the first time in Greece. J.R. claims New Mexico as his home. The Paok men were playing the following day, so Denise and I made plans to be there.

Unless the jersey reads UConn, Tennessee, Notre Dame, Oregon or New Mexico, you can guess the size of the crowd for the women's game. Area codes change, attendance does not. It was exciting basketball. More people should have been there. I knew it would be different for the Paok men. It was. The crowd's passion equaled the teams' play.

The night was just beginning. Thomas, our agent, took Denise and me to eat gyros and ice cream. We followed with a walk along the sea. The lights illuminated the pathway, and their shimmer sparkled atop the water. It smelled better than it looked. Then again, maybe it was just me.

My hands felt the full effect of eating ice cream while walking in the cold. Who eats ice cream in the winter? This girl. I hardly pass on ice cream. The conditions shortened our walk. It's a good thing as my nose, ears and hands were chilled bone-deep. Thessaloniki is a gorgeous city, but I can live without the cold.

We had Thomas drop us at Bennigans, the Paok players' hangout. Bennigans is where the players had their contract for their daily meals. We met J.R. and Denise's buddy. As we walked in, we noticed a few American players from Aris, the other local club.

Apparently, Denise and I had been in the dark about the hangout for the American players in the city. We made friends rather quickly with the American players from Aris, both the men and women, and ended up going back to their apartment. We played cards and talked about our experiences in college. We shared some of the emotions and feelings we had of Greece and what it was like to play overseas.

An American enclave in Greece? Who knew? I didn't. Guess it's true, it really is a small world. At that moment, it was also a Cloud Nine world.

—⊙—

Day 80-82

—⊙—

The rhythm of my routine slowed to where it had been,
a pattern of comfort and consistency, a life that fit my
stride perfectly, a truth of who I was, where I was.

And still, there was room for the unexpected.

One morning, a few of my teammates and I went to Eleni's. The informal invitation said coffee. Eleni surprised us with cream pies. The croissant-like pastry was flaky, buttery, melt-in-your-mouth yummy. The cream filling was its own deliciousness. Her coffee, I can't forget her coffee, was café-quality incredible. Maybe I need to start skipping my favorite cafés and just come here every day. I know I wouldn't be coming alone. It wasn't the croissants and coffee that made this special, it was Eleni.

Aside from that morning, my daily routine was assembly line consistent: wake up, eat breakfast, shooting workout, go for a walk to get my lunch, lift, hang out in my apartment waiting on practice, practice, and then back to my room. Everything was in solid working order, including my thoughts, which suddenly had a subtle new theme. Why does our mind focus on negativity over positivity?

"How could I have any negative thoughts come across my mind right then when I was currently living out my dream, playing professional basketball in the beautiful country of Greece?"

I was no deer in the road. There were no headlights approaching head-on. And yet, I stopped my tracks, frozen in mid-thought. It took a while to think things thoroughly through.

It's truly amazing how quickly we forget the "nuggets" in our lives. The blessings that have been afforded to us. What once was nothing more than a dream becomes a blessing once that dream comes to fruition. It turns into the source of an insurmountable excitement and highlight of our lives. However, with time, the excitement flickers like a light bulb down to its final watts. Negativity grows when light fades to darkness.

That had been my journey for more days than I care to admit. I had let negativity consume my thoughts and drag me down a staircase that was bottomless. Now, when negativity knocks me down, I believe I am strong enough to stand up, smile and say, "Not this time."

My view moving forward was to see life with a positive and loving attitude and to be grateful for all that's placed in my path. My daily routine, the one I once thought of as boring, I now saw as a blessing, one I finally dreamed into life. And before the next dream replaced this one, I was going to squeeze every moment of life out of it while it happened. My actions moving forward were the promise I made to my words.

I made a note to stay true to myself. But what is true? It depends on where you look. And how you look. Do we see true with our eyes? Or do we feel true with our hearts. We are taught the five senses—touch, taste, see, hear, feel—as children. We learn to laugh on our own. When it comes to love, the world's true wonder, all five senses are required—as well as a lifetime.

What is true to me, and for me, might not be what is true to you. And that's okay. We all need to be our true selves. As for me, I realized I don't need to travel far to have wonderful experiences. I can appreciate the ordinary and simple as much as the magical and extraordinary in my life.

I would look for the nuggets, golden or otherwise. And if I fell into negativity's trap, I would do what I should have done the first time.

I would stay true.

Day 83

I woke up in a postcard.

Well, not literally. But it was one of those December days all countries photograph and print, a must-have for all travelers to mail with the words, "Wish you were here!" written on the back. I found those four words to be a lie. If you wish I were here, why didn't you invite me in the first place?

I can't ever remember enjoying such a warm morning in December, certainly never one growing up in the American Southwest. The sun was in full shine and the birds were in full chirp. It had "great day" written in every direction.

Denise and I met Thomas for coffee. We spoke basketball from all angles, starting with individual and ending with team. The better I performed this year meant the better contract I would receive next year. The bigger the contract financially for me also meant a bigger paycheck for Thomas. Aside from the money, I know Thomas wanted to see me perform at my best, much like any coach. The script didn't change when Thomas shifted his attention to Denise.

I took full advantage of the beautiful weather when we returned to our apartments. I walked around the neighborhood of Kalamaria for over an hour. Once I reached the sea, I sat and watched boats and birds bobbing in the water. I turned my head and marveled at the sight of downtown Thessaloniki in the distance. Something so ordinary to one person can be extraordinary to another. I was remembering my thoughts from the day before and did what I promised. I collected this nugget, appreciated this moment.

I imagined that some of the native people of Greece would view their country as ordinary. But as a foreigner, I was forever captivated and mesmerized by the gifts of the moments this country offered. Most days I was where my feet were planted as opposed to having one foot in the past, one foot in the future.

It was true that Greece's present was struggling through a financial crisis. It was also true this country and its people were rich in so many other ways. You just had to pay attention. But we live in a bottom-line society. Well, in America we do.

I believe there are people who are so poor in their lives that money *is* all they have. Yes, you read that sentence correctly. If all you seek and all you have, is money, then you are missing, not just the meaning of life, but life itself.

Look around. Find the beauty. It's here, there, everywhere. It's not hard to spot. Find the beauty in where you are and in those with you. Let life be the reason you are living. Collect moments, not things. Inside the tiniest of seashells is the sound of the entire ocean.

It took a while for me to reach this place. I'm not speaking of Greece, but the place that lives inside me, the place of appreciation for my blessings and the gratefulness for my life. The ironic part is that I had to travel across the ocean, thousands of miles away from home, to discover and embrace my complete self.

Greece is my ocean.

I am its seashell.

Greece will live inside me forever.

Day 84

With this being our third trip to Athens,
I believe I could have driven the bus and gotten us
to our destination without GPS Siri.

That is, if I could have stayed awake for the eight hours it took for us to get there.

The one-way highway commute was direct, but it was never non-stop. Tolls replaced red lights. Here, they are pay as you go, unlike the states, where a camera takes a picture of your license plate and then mails you a bill. Here, drivers had to stop and pay the fee to an attendant in the small booth. Lines formed.

The drive was divvied three ways—one part Jay-Z, one part real *zzzz's*, one part sight-seeing. I awoke to different scenery each and every time, from green pastures with olive vines growing in perfect rows, to the Aegean Sea, to small cities that featured shops off the side of the road. It was the usual lineup of cafés, taverns, tourist shops, and small markets. They held my attention all the way until my eyelids closed.

Once in Athens, I could have played the role of the person who stands in the front of a tour bus, microphone in hand.

"These narrow streets are as old as the Acropolis of Athens."

Then a bit later, *"On your left, the ten-story buildings are apartments. And yes, people of Athens prefer to hang their laundry on lines outside their homes."*

Even though it had been a couple weeks since we were last here, I swear I recognized some of the clothes hanging from our previous visit. What looked fresh were the plants and flowers hanging off the balconies.

The déjà vu continued through check-in. Konstantinos went ahead of the team to talk to the front-desk clerk. After several minutes of interaction, and who knows what they said, the clerk gave him a big envelope with all our room keys inside. He walked over to where we stood as a group and started calling off names. Once the keys were distributed, Konstantinos spoke to us. After he finished, I sidled next to Vassiliki, my trusty translator, for the details.

"Dinner will be at the twentieth hour, and then we will watch some film on our opponent tomorrow," she said. "Konstantinos said he is still making arrangements for breakfast and will give us that information later this evening."

"Okay. Thank you," I said. Vassiliki and Alex were my language lifesavers.

The majority of the team and I spent just enough time in our rooms to drop the bags before reconvening in the lobby until dinner. I took a seat and observed more with my eyes than with my ears since the conversation was Greek. I used body language, facial expressions and hand gestures to glean the gist of the dialogue and the reactions of those listening to the speaker. All were enough for me to laugh with my teammates.

Dinner didn't vary from before, either. The starting lineup: pork steak, pasta with marinara sauce, which was similar to spaghetti in looks but not taste, potatoes, and vegetables. Watching film on our opponent was the nightcap. Coach narrated in Greek. With no subtitles, I made mental notes on their tendencies, strengths and weaknesses.

It was time for sleep.

"*Kalinixta.*"

Goodnight.

Day 85

The day started with the innocence of a child's heart.

Team breakfast. The spread was fruit, thinly sliced deli meats, eggs, croissants and pastries, spread out end to end. It tasted as good as it looked. My plate was fruit, eggs, and a couple of stuffed croissants. My beverage was coffee.

The Parthenon was the main attraction on the drive to the gym. It was out in the distance, but it was close enough to see the structure clearly. The Parthenon is a former temple on the Athenian Acropolis. It was dedicated to the goddess Athena, who the people of Athens considered their patron. Its construction started in 447 BC, and here it is, still standing today.

Maybe I should have taken it as portend that this day was going to be lasting, but not for all the right reasons.

We lost to Kronos by four points. I didn't play well. Again. I got frustrated. Again. I tried to stay positive, but failed. Again. I knew what was coming next. Again. I knew I couldn't stop it. Again.

I was used to being the high scorer, the best player on the court. I wasn't used to this. It wasn't that I was in over my head in terms of the competition. It was that I no longer believed in myself as I once did. In the past, when I faced any challenge I wouldn't sigh, "Why me?" I would scream, "Try me!" I had lost my voice, and I was losing my way.

It's not that I didn't know what needed to be done. I did. I knew I had to work on my one-on-one game. I needed to find another way to score, a way of getting to the rim when my shot wasn't falling. I knew I had to develop another element to my game. Easy to say, hard to accomplish in the midst of the basketball season. The physical work I could do. I've done it before. I wasn't the most-recruited player coming out of high school.

I know there is no room for dreams if your head is full of fears. For me, the deepest angst was being cut and sent home before the season concluded.

The self-limiting beliefs and doubts slowly crawled into my mind after that performance. Again. I started to question if I belonged. Again. It was a constant battle within my mind, the negativity pulling one direction, the positivity holding on for dear life. Again.

Is the flow of human nature coincidence, or do we control the current? I ask because mine seems to flow toward the pool of negativity, filling my mind with doubts until I'm submerged in depression. The struggle isn't in just reaching the surface, but staying there and inhaling the positive, exhaling the negative.

I wish I had left it all in the locker room. I didn't. It rode inside me for the next eight hours. I tried to sleep. I couldn't. It's hard to sleep over the sound of your own thoughts. The scenario went like this: thinking, debating, doubting, overcoming, challenging, and then finding the positive. It repeated itself mile by mile. We finally arrived in Thessaloniki. It was two in the morning.

I wish I had left it all on the bus. I didn't. Back in my room, I watched some RMAC games. That was the conference I played in at Adams State. It was fun to watch and listen to the Adams State game and hear my upbeat former broadcaster, Bryant Johnson, on the air. Watching Adams State run its plays flooded me with memories, and I floated back in time to the good old days when I used to wear the green ASU jersey with the number 4 on my back.

I reminisced on my ability to drain threes against any opponent I faced and to dominate on the floor. I wanted to make sure my memories weren't revisionist. I called up one of my highlight films. It showed me who I was and who I still am. I was thankful for the reminder.

I exhausted myself to sleep. This last thing I saw was the clock. It read 5:00 a.m.

Day 86

I ached—mind, body, soul.

I was the cause. I lived the effect. Rest helped the symptoms, but couldn't provide the cure. Neither could I. Well, not at this moment. The best I could do was get out of my own head for a while and get out of my apartment.

I sought solace in the lives of others. I sat at a café alone, observing the commotion in the square. There were kids running by without cares, women walking past with shopping bags stuffed beyond full, men sitting at adjacent tables smoking their cigarettes. A young mother pushed a baby stroller through a labyrinth of children who were playing with their dog.

I knew nothing of their lives and they knew nothing of my struggles. But they looked and sounded happy. That's what I needed to see, needed to hear, and most important, needed to feel. I needed to feel happy.

I ran into Denise before I reached home. She was heading in the same direction, carrying a bag of food in one hand.

"Vera, I've been looking for you all morning. I tried messaging you and knocking on your door, but I couldn't find you."

Her voice carried concern.

"Sorry, I realized I had left my phone when I was already at the square and didn't feel like turning back for it. I didn't think I was going to be gone that long."

She smiled in the way that only she could. "It's cool. I just wanted to see if you wanted to go watch the Aris men play in a few hours?"

Ah, another distraction. Exactly what I needed.

"Sure thing. I'll meet you out front in an hour, and we will head over."

We walked to the bus stop, chuckling to ourselves about the last experience we had with the bus and with us trying to find the Aris arena. This time, we knew which bus to take and which direction we were supposed to be going. We even beat the game's tip-off. Can you imagine that?

It's a good thing we did. The gym was packed. Not just with people, but with passion. The crowd chanted as one and was in crazed unison over a call the official made, a call that displeased them greatly, shall we say. The drummers were there, too. They provided the beat for the chants. Was this basketball or *Braveheart?* My heart was pumping adrenaline, and I wasn't even in uniform. I so wanted to perform on this stage before this crowd. Just once.

The game was good-to-the-last-shot. I was glad to be there. Evidently, so was one of the TV cameras. Apparently, Denise and I were becoming off-the-court regulars. This time, I did see the camera turn in our direction. I looked directly into the lens, smiled, and waved.

"I could get used to this little celebrity feeling."

That thought made me smile. And in that moment, I ached a little less.

Day 89

I was packing for Christmas break.

Thankfully, it was not for good. And yet, I kept looking for more room. Not in my suitcases, but in my heart.

Yes, I skipped ahead a few days. Those hours were spent mostly with Alex and Eleni. It was hard leaving them. They had become my Greek parents, my Greek family. They opened their door, their arms, and their hearts from the day we met and in unspoken words said I could stay as long as I wanted.

I needed Kleenex then. I need Kleenex now. The moisture on Eleni's cheeks was not sweat. Her tears did not fall alone at our airport goodbye.

We arrived for my flight a little early. It meant everything to sit and talk over coffee. Margarita appeared a few minutes later. She, too, wanted to see me off and wished me a safe journey home.

You know the sound your phone makes when you send an email. That sound was my time spent in Greece so far. *Whooooooooosh!* It felt that sudden. And soon I would be gone.

I walked away, passed through security toward Gate 06. My flight took me from Thessaloniki to Munich, from Munich to Chicago, from Chicago to Albuquerque. And finally, to Las Vegas (NM), which is a two-hour drive home.

Victor Hugo wrote, "He who does not weep does not see."

Yes, I was crying. I've seen so much.

And, I can't wait to see even more.

PART II

Day 1

*In twenty-plus hours, I lifted off in Albuquerque
and landed in Athens.*

That's the one in Greece, not the one in Georgia. I felt the travel, but not the trepidation, since that was my second time crossing the Atlantic and changing continents. Vera Jo Bustos, world traveler? I wouldn't go that far. But I didn't need to act like I hadn't been there before because I had. This time, no acting was needed.

The longest flight was from Washington, D.C. to Munich, Germany. It was a pleasant eight hours. No, really, it was. As the boarding process finished, the middle seat next to me remained vacant. I had a couple international flights under my please-fasten-your seat belt, where I sat constrained in a small space with strangers next to me who pushed the boundaries of my personal space and caused a different kind of discomfort. Having this kind of space on the flight was the first win of the new year.

"Yes," I murmured with a slight fist pump.

I thought the celebration was subtle enough to go unnoticed. It wasn't. My excitement caught the attention of the gentleman sitting in the aisle seat. We made eye contact. I nodded a slight smirk.

"What a nerd."

It was a thought to myself, about myself.

"Now this guy probably thinks he's sitting next to a crazy person."

I laughed at myself over my thoughts and my slight embarrassment. I put in my earbuds and perused through the selection of movies on the screen embedded into the seat in front of me. I needed a game plan of which movies I would watch for the flight's entirety. As of January of 2012, the hit movies of 2011 were offered on board. *Fast Five*, *Hugo*, and *Midnight in Paris* made the cut for my initial selections.

As the plane touched down in Munich, I inhaled the anxiety of the past, recalling my previous experience in a German airport on my initial trip to Greece. This time, it was only one breath. I didn't fall into the same trap of straying away from the crowd and figuring things out on my own. I walked with the crowd off the plane, turned where they turned, and followed their speedy pace, which seemed to be a race as to who could get to customs the fastest.

Signs titled "Non-Euro Passports" began to come into view, and Olympic speed-walking emerged out of nowhere. My competitive instincts kicked in. I needed to beat the guy who walked next to me. I did, though there was no "Yes," shouted and no fist pump. I'm a quick learner. Well, in some areas I am.

Going through customs was a breeze. I celebrated internally for not getting lost like my rookie-self did the first time. For me, traveling alone internationally is still nerve-racking to a degree. But as I got closer to Athens, confidence colored over the apprehension until it could no longer be seen.

The flight from Munich to Athens felt hiccup quick. Since there are no seats with the luggage, I said a silent prayer that mine was below me.

Yes, it's true. Some prayers go unanswered. But this couldn't happen to me twice, could it? Bag by bag shot from darkness onto the carousel, and I watched as the other passengers found theirs.

Are you kidding me? Not aga— . . .

My bag made it to Athens.

Only hitting a game-winning shot would have felt better in this moment. With no lost luggage report to file, I exited the airport and walked toward a line of taxis. I put my hand up to the driver, indicating that I needed a ride. He waved his hand to me with the gesture to keep walking toward him.

"Hello, do you speak English?"

"Not so good."

"I need to go here."

I pointed to the screen on the phone, which showed the Facebook message from Alex that included the name and address of the hotel. He read the name and gave me a "thumbs up" while replying in Greek. The bag was loaded into the truck as I climbed into the back seat.

My face was nose-first to the window, much like my initial car ride when I first landed in Thessaloniki. I eyeballed the sights of Athens as we squeezed through the narrow streets. The high-rise buildings seemed almost on top of the streets we passed through. They were over-crowded with cars parked on the sides and pedestrians crossed in all directions. We passed by a small park that was fenced off from the craziness of the city. Inside, I saw kids playing soccer. They zoomed back and forth, oblivious to the busyness of the city.

We arrived at the hotel where the driver unloaded my luggage. He grabbed my suitcase from the handle, and instantly, the handle snapped from the weight of my belongings. I sensed his horror, thinking it was his fault.

"It's all right, don't worry about it."

Yes, I was agitated, but I spoke with calm. After all, no one was to blame. He apologized and followed me inside to the front desk. The driver and clerk spoke Greek. About what, I have no clue. About who, well, that was easy enough. The who was standing next to them. Knowing you are the topic of the conversation and not fully understanding what was being said was not always the best of feelings.

The hotel clerk opened one of her drawers and counted euros, then handed the cash to the driver. Once the driver left, the hotel attendant said, "Your team manager made arrangements for the hotel to pay your driver, no need to worry. You are covered, Miss Bustos."

"Thank you!" I replied with a smile.

I took the elevator to my room and received a Facebook message from Alex.

"Geia sou, Vera. Hope your trip was good. We will see you at the hotel in 7 hours. Get some rest."

I exhaled relief. I could use sleep. Jet lag wasn't the lone concern. Our season resumed tomorrow. I called my mom to let her know I arrived safely. Next, I called the pillow and slept for four hours.

I was the welcoming committee when the team arrived. I hadn't seen them in a few weeks because I flew home for Christmas break. The reunion was cheek kisses all around, the cultural greeting I happily adopted.

We caught up over dinner. Seeing them, listening to them, being a part of them re-energized me. I couldn't wait to take the court.

Day 2

Remember the ankle-weight fad?

Where you wore ankle weights all day to strengthen your legs? And when you removed them you felt like you could dunk? Well, I awoke to legs feeling like they were weighted at the ankles, the calves, the knees, the quads. Each leg felt like I was carrying an additional hundred pounds. And unfortunately for me, there were no straps to remove them.

The travel toll came to collect and I couldn't tell it, "The check's in the mail." Stretching helped. Maybe breakfast would, too. We needed every advantage since we were facing Esperides, the second-ranked team in the league.

What I didn't mention about the night before was the changes the team underwent in the past three weeks. We would take the court five players short. A couple Greek teammates decided they would not return to the team while others couldn't make the trip to Athens. In addition, Denise did not return to the team.

There was a change in our coaches as well. Coach Andreas had also parted with the club and Alex was promoted to head coach. He brought in his own playbook. With no practice to learn the offensive sets and defensive strategies, I was left to play more on instincts than instructions.

Over lunch, Alex did his best to explain our new offense and defense with the use of a dry erase board. With the language barrier, it was much easier to follow the drawing of a play versus him telling me what I should be doing.

The working lunch lasted only an hour. I returned to my room to rest and to prepare. My legs weren't the only things weighed down.

#

I lived a four-quarter nightmare. When I wasn't running in place, I moved in slow-motion. Or so it felt. My mind was on Mars, my body was on Venus, and I was on the bench having fouled out.

I was gutted. But not before being shredded. I couldn't stay in front of anyone defensively, while offensively, the basket looked smaller than ever. Our opponent was ruthless, as it should have been. We got crushed. I never played worse.

My body wasn't ready. My mind wasn't prepared. Whenever I hear the word failure, this is the flashback. This is the point where I would start playing the blame game. Here, let me show you how it used to work. I would blame travel, then lethargy, then jet lag. My lack of quickness in comparison to my opponents. I could go on. But why? Next would come the anger, disbelief, and guilt.

It was a dreary start to the long bus ride back to Thessaloniki. After a couple hours of beating myself up mentally, I wrote down all my negative thoughts and self-limiting beliefs I felt. I needed a way to unload all those unhealthy, dead-weight feelings.

Then, I stopped. I started a new list of the ten things I did well. It's an exercise I learned from Dena Evans when I attended Point Guard College as a sophomore in high school. I'm not sure how long it took me to find a top ten. Let's just say it took a while to push through the murk and muck of negativity each time I found a positive and brought it out in the open. The last two positives I wrote on the list were that my shoes didn't come untied and my jersey stayed tucked in. I'm not kidding. I had to come up with something just to get to ten.

The more good I unearthed, the more I unveiled a different-looking picture. Yes, I *felt* like a failure, but that didn't mean I *was* a failure. Choosing to say "I failed to play to the best of my ability in that game," versus "I am a failure." I had to separate the game and *feeling of failure* from believing *failure was my identity*. There's a big difference. In that moment, I hired myself as a coach and fired myself as a critic. A critic tells you the negative things that happened during your performance. A good coach gives constructive feedback to help you "fail forward."

Sir Winston Churchill put it another way: "Success is stumbling from failure to failure with no loss of enthusiasm."

My top ten helped restore my enthusiasm and reminded me of my love for the game, not the outcome. I remembered I wasn't perfect, and I was travel-weary, and it was totally unfair to set the bar impossibly high under those circumstances. I wasn't excusing my performance. But it was done, in the past, history. Yes, I was tempted to throw in the towel. And yes, some failures sting a lot more than others. But no matter the hurt, you have the courage inside you to get up and try one more time. Always try one more time.

I wouldn't look back. I wasn't going that way. At the end of my journal entry, I jotted down how excited I was to get back to Thessaloniki and see one of my favorite people in Greece—Eleni.

Day 3

*When people talk about seeing the big picture,
most don't realize there are two views.*

One is how you see the world. That view is most common. The other is how the world sees you. I experienced both when I least expected.

I decided to *really* live the "off" in our scheduled day off. I wanted to make sure my body was adjusted from the jet lag. That meant no shooting workout, no cardio workout, no weight workout. My basketball life was switched off. Or so I thought.

I didn't leave the warmth of my bed until ten that morning. Once I was able to brave the cold weather, I went to the neighborhood market to get some cereal and milk. Before I returned home, I ducked inside a café for a cappuccino.

"*Kalimera*, Vera! Good to see you again. We are happy you are back in Greece."

The voice was from one of a group of fans of Apollon club.

"*Evcharisto!*" I replied, thanking them in Greek. "*Emai Ellinida* (I am Greek), so I am happy to be back in Greece!"

Their laughter effused from one of two potential sources. Either they were happy with my response, or my accent was just too humorous for containment.

"Yes, yes. You are for sure one of us. I will be at your next game cheering you on."

It was spoken through laughter as we were parting.

"I will look for you in the stands. See you next weekend."

For some reason, I shouted the last part.

In an interaction that later proved to be much needed, I saw two views—mine and theirs. What I hadn't realized is I had already established myself as a known basketball star in my little neighborhood of Kalamaria. The people knew who I was. But what seemed to matter more to them was my character. The fact that I took the time to talk with them, even though the language barrier still made it tough to communicate at times, made me a favorite.

I remembered my conversation with the volleyball coach a few months back. He told me as athletes we were entertainers, and the best performers knew how to win their way into the people's hearts. I had cracked the secret to that—acknowledge people.

People will always remember how you made them feel. It doesn't take much to acknowledge someone. To make them feel special. To remember their name. Maybe that was one of the reasons why I was still wearing this uniform. After a performance like the previous night, I was sure some players would have already been sent home.

Those fans greeted me as a player. I engaged them as the person. It wasn't about the name on front or name on the back. It was about the person inside the jersey. Number 4 was my reputation. Vera Jo was my character. Don't get me wrong, it was still a business. From the team's standpoint, I couldn't have multiple games like the one I just had and still be employed. I understood that. But I also realized when you invest yourself in other people, they invest themselves back into you. Nothing would prove to be more valuable or more lasting.

When I was home for Christmas break, if you would have asked me to list what I missed most in Greece, the order would have been—people, teammates, coaches, fans. Oh, and basketball. I created relationships I couldn't wait to return to, ones that would last a lifetime. Thirty years into the future, I could see myself going back to Greece, reuniting in the relationships I was currently building.

The cold air shook me out of my walking daydream. Cold is not cold. Greece cold is not New Mexico cold, not Colorado cold. Layers, and jackets over layers, didn't deter Greece cold. It penetrated everything. It eventually stopped—when it reached bone. Greece cold was damp, too. I didn't order my cappuccino iced. If I didn't pick up the pace and get home soon, it would be. I longed for the warm weather and my old beach days.

The plan was to stay warm in my apartment. Eleni offered an alternative when she called and invited me for a late lunch. For her, I took the polar plunge back into the cold. I arrived to a warm hug, our first since I had left for break. Hugs were her way of adapting to my American greeting.

"I feel like I never left," I said.

"I feel the same way," she replied. "This is another home you have made for yourself. When you find a home, that place always feels welcoming because that place is filled with people who love you."

Moisture formed in both our eyes.

Eleni was right. I was finding homes—with her and Alex, with my teammates, with my fans—by simply treating people right and by investing time and love into them.

My parents raised me right. And now, everyone in Greece raised me higher. I soared when I was with Eleni and Alex, even with both feet on the ground. And right now, those feet were in hot pursuit.

You see, over the break, Eleni and Alex got a pet chinchilla. I chased that chinchilla pretty much non-stop for the rest of the afternoon and evening. Maybe Alex really bought that chinchilla to help me work on my defensive quickness. His mind was always seeking out ways to give the team an advantage. I secretly wondered about his motive.

Was this one of those big-picture moments I was supposed to be seeing?

⊚

Day 4

⊚

I looked for the familiar as a source of comfort after entering the gym Monday for my first practice since the break.

The rims, backboards, flooring were as I remembered. So, too, were my teammates. Well, most of them. I wished those who had opted not to return well in whatever direction life had taken them. And naturally, I recognized Alex.

Since Alex was now in charge he brought his own philosophies to both ends of the court. The differences were striking.

Under Alex, we ran a dribble drive offense that implemented a lot of drive and kicks. For those who aren't accustomed to basketball terminology, the idea behind this offense was for the person with the ball to do their best to drive to the rim. If they were cut off by a defender, that person would then kick (pass) the ball to an open teammate, who looked to catch and shoot immediately. If not, the teammate who received the pass also drove to the rim, and from there it was a continuous drive-and-kick process. Everything was played off the dribble penetration.

At Adams State (my college team), we ran a motion offense loaded with screens—on-ball screens and off-ball. Now, with no screens involved, I was expected to drive past any defender in front of me. I'm not slow, but I'm not that quick, either. I expected to struggle and knew I would have company. It would be a challenge, adding a completely new offensive scheme in the middle of the season.

The newness of the offense frayed my nerves in Athens. I was feeling the strain in practice. I wasn't surprised by either. The actions of confidence come first while the feelings of confidence come second. I wasn't feeling confident in Athens because I hadn't practiced those actions. I hadn't spent any time on the court applying the actions to my repertoire. For that to change, I needed practice to regain that confidence. That's a step that can't be skipped, a process with zero shortcuts. I had to put in the work.

Through my studies in sports psychology, I learned how the body reacts to stress, nervousness, anxiety, and excitement. Here's a quick quiz: When you get butterflies, when your heart rate and adrenaline spikes, and when you tend to sweat a little more, what feeling do you automatically attribute that to?

If you answered, "nervousness," you are like most people, but that isn't necessarily correct.

It's what follows the nervousness that matters.

Let's suppose you are riding a roller-coaster. For most, it's an exciting moment. Exciting *but* scary. Notice where the emphasis is. When we speak about something positive, most times we tend to follow that with the word *but*, which indicates something negative to follow and eradicates the positive. If we can just change the way we speak to ourselves, that changes the way we perceive things in the physical world as well.

It's true.

If I focus on something that is exciting *and* scary, versus something that is exciting *but* scary, which sounds more appealing? I find "*exciting and*" the more attractive choice because we put our focus on the excitement.

A simple change in our thought process to "exciting and," or "yes, and," can ignite a chain reaction in our mindset, unlocking and releasing endless possibilities to what we can uncover and problems we can solve.

Let's get back on that roller-coaster. You're buckled in and it starts to climb and climb and climb. What's going on inside your body? You know that big drop is coming. Is it butterflies? Increased heart rate? Adrenaline? Sweat, even?

Wait. Aren't those the usual suspects, the ones associated with nerves? Yes, they are. Here's why they're back. Physiologically, the body can't decipher the difference between nervous and excited. The body reacts the exact same way, releases the same hormones. The difference between feeling nervous and feeling excited is the word—or the meaning—you choose to give that feeling.

It all comes down to words and a deeper understanding of the meaning behind them.

I applied this new-found knowledge to my basketball career. The impact was a profound shift in my mindset and perspective. I no longer dreaded a racing heart, an overflow of adrenaline. I learned to see those factors as a good thing.

That day was a breakthrough moment—for myself as an athlete and as a person—I only wish I had learned that small mind hack earlier in my career.

This was the latest action I put into my craft. It left me feeling confident about where I was and where this could take me, which I believed was the next level in my evolution as a player.

I felt butterflies.
It felt familiar.
Then again, it felt better.

Day 5

Growth is measured in a myriad of ways.

It can be found in pencil marks on a door frame or on a PhD affixed to a wall. I felt my basketball game growing daily. Ironically, the breakthrough followed the breaking point that was the worst game of my career.

Growth is cyclical and requires stages. In life, a baby can't hop over childhood, skip through teenage years, and jump into adulthood. Basketball follows the same path. Steps are necessary to reach each stage.

First is learning the concept or skill we want to master. My basketball education started as a child. I learned how to dribble, how to shoot, and how to abide by the rules of the game. Sounds basic, I know. Most foundations are. Without one, nothing built on top lasts.

Second is learning to experiment. On the court, I constantly tried replicating other players' moves. I meticulously studied their footwork and imitated what they did. I tinkered with their moves until I made them my own. I learned we all have a different internal rhythm. Just like I can't dance exactly the same way as someone else, I also can't do a move exactly the same way as someone else. There will be similarities, which foster the learning stage. In the experimental stage, this is where we learn how to make certain skills our own.

Third is the performance stage. I spent my freshman year and the summer leading into my sophomore year of college learning and experimenting with the step-back move. It was during the experimentation stage that my confidence developed enough to get to the performance stage of using the move in games.

Then comes the struggle. It's not an actual step in the process. Instead, it's encompassed in all three of the previous steps. There will be struggle as we learn, as we experiment, and as we perform. In this regard, success is the struggle. Many times, most people fall out of the growth cycle because they make a living in the season of struggle during the experimental stage.

Last is thriving. This is when we are acknowledged for our hard work through accolades, goals reached, and the feelings of fulfillment. It's the most important and the most fleeting. We soak in the success, but never for long, which is a great thing. It means we have a new dream, a new goal that returns us to the learning stage.

Growth is a fact of life. The *summa cum lauds* of the world started as beginners, learning and experimenting in their respective crafts. We sometimes try to cheat the process and skip to the performance stage. Once there, too often we become frustrated and find ourselves mired in the struggle. Stay the course and trust the process.

It works.

I am in the growth cycle of my own mentality training. Learning how to deal with challenges, adversity, and overcoming negative self-talk. Experimenting again and again during the course of my career. The struggle of my performance allowed me to break through to the thriving stage of my own mindset of confidence.

Day 6

Actions over words.

Show over tell. With a renewed feeling of accomplishment and confidence with my own ways of thinking, I had been talking a good game. But could I play one? I was about to find out.

Coach Alex scheduled a scrimmage against the men's team so we could iron out the wrinkles in our new offense and defensive systems and tactics. The scrimmage felt like I was playing a video game where I was in control of everything going on.

My mind and body were in alliance. Everything was effortless. Decisions were made instantaneously, like when I needed to read my defender to make a move and explode past him. Or when I needed to read their offense to distinguish my rotation on defense. Playing against stronger, faster, and overall better players, I was still able to score when I wanted and how I wanted. The cliché most often used is being "in the zone." Call it whatever you want. I prefer actions over words, show over tell.

Afterward, I sat in the locker room in a state of contentment. I pondered what it was that was so different from this scrimmage to the last game I had played. Ten minutes passed. Then, five more. Finally, it hit me, like an unexpected slap to the face that came out of nowhere. After it did, I stood up with a sudden burst of energy. It was something I inherently had known all along and have even talked about before. I simply overlooked the obvious. It was total engagement in the task.

Let me backtrack for a bit. In last week's game, the one I referred to as the worst of my career, I was tangled in my own thoughts. Thinking about how my body hurt. The mistakes I had made leading me to worry about making more mistakes, which I did. My psychological defenses became compromised with the fatigue of my body. I lost the ability to manage my negative thoughts and emotions. I allowed them to overwhelm me—becoming a self-defeating prophecy. My emotional energy dropped. I had a sense of not caring about the outcome anymore. I still competed, but not to the killer-instinct point needed. I was in survival mode, doing the minimum to avoid a mental breakdown in public. I gave in to my self-limiting beliefs, negative thoughts and emotions. I allowed them to engulf my being—mentally, emotionally, and physically.

In the scrimmage, however, when I reached the state of fatigue, I stayed in the moment, concentrated on the task. Whether that was breaking a press, reading my defender, guarding my man, or rotating on defense. My mind stayed attentive. I allowed the negative thoughts that came when I made a mistake or got beat on defense to just be. Instead of getting ensnarled, I allowed them to come and go without latching on to me, or me on them. I experienced mindfulness.

I had a good sense of mental toughness in my younger years as an athlete, especially my junior and senior years of college. It's nothing like it was now. As I continued my search for knowledge about mindset and learning through experiences, I wished this realization had happened earlier in my career.

It's the typical *if* daydream. As in, *if* only I had learned this mindset of confidence sooner, how much more would I have accomplished? Then again, from where I was standing at the moment, my dreams were in fruition. As I learned more, I pledged to do more. I would help other athletes learn the essence of confidence and the importance of mindset to help them achieve their dreams and to prepare them for their own paths of success.

Once our skills are honed to meet the demands and challenges of the situation, we will only enter "the zone" under two conditions:

First, our skill and preparation of our craft are developed enough for the task.

Second, we engage fully in the task and accept negative thoughts.

In other words, ball don't care.

Ball don't care about your day.

Ball don't care about your life.

Ball don't care about your feelings

You must trust yourself, believe in yourself, and rely on yourself, irrespective to what you are going through, what you are feeling, and what you are thinking.

Those words reminded me of what Kelly Kruger, my college coach, used to say about discipline.

"Do what needs to be done, when it needs to be done, and do it that way every single time, especially when it's hard or inconvenient."

Actions over words.

Show over tell.

Remove all *ifs*.

Mentally weak athletes have a tell. They engage in their moments when they feel good, but when they are not in the mood or feeling good, nothing gets accomplished. Mentally tough athletes have a show. They engage in their moments all the time, regardless of how they are feeling. They allow their standards to overcome their feelings, instead of allowing their feelings to overcome their standards.

I showed with my mindset and new-found skills in the scrimmage. It made me excited for the weekend's game. It was a must-win for us.

That evening, I joined Alex, Eleni, the manager of the club, and a few of my teammates at a local tavern for dinner. The atmosphere was cozy with live music, blue-and-white tablecloths that seemed to be a go-to for a lot of the Greek taverns I visited, and photos of the local scenic landscape along the walls. The aroma of pita bread hit me as soon as I walked in and instantly made my mouth water.

Alex ordered for the table. The ensemble was pita bread with olive oil, tomato and cucumber salad, French fries sprinkled with grated feta cheese, pork gyros, chicken skewers called *souvlaki*, and *kokoretsi*, which I believe was beef liver. There were no rules of engagement. We reached over each other until our plates were full—family style, as usual.

A Greek combination plate features three items—great food, great conversation (translator needed), and great people. I left with a full belly.

And an even fuller heart.

Day 7

Vera Jo gets the pass on the right wing.

She eyes her opponent. The home crowd is screaming. Three . . . two . . . She puts up the three-pointer. One . . . It's good. IT'S GOOD!!! Vera Jo beats the buzzer. Again. There isn't a silent voice in the stands as her teammates mob her at center court.

I am undefeated in my backyard. Playing under the outdoor lights that dimly light the small slab of concrete outside my parents' house, my record is 1,000,000 wins, zero losses. I kept track. Children have a tendency to do so. I also swished exactly one million last-second shots.

I was a professional back then. Well, in my imagination I was. I wasn't outdoors. I was inside, under the brightest—and hottest—lights. Each and every time, I brought the crowd to its feet and the opponent to its knees.

As kids, the self-visualization and imagination we have are amazing. The memories left me smiling as I sipped my morning coffee.

I was living that dream, save for all the last-second heroics and the undefeated record. Some days, I absorbed the vastness of where I was and what I was doing. Other days, the trap of routine sapped the unbridled joy from it all. I was fortunate in that the struggles left behind slivers of silver linings, ones I could follow back to the path I wanted to walk and live.

Today, it was the walk down memory lane to my backyard that made me stop, think, and take a step back to see all that was before me. Greece was packed with surprises and challenges I'd never before faced, and I wasn't fully embracing them like I should have. Greece is my backyard. I am getting paid to play the game I love, the game I would play for free. (*Shhh*! Don't tell them.) And, I am living in one of the most picturesque and beautiful landscapes to ever exist.

I disappointed myself for not always feeling the appreciation I should have and for taking far too many things for granted from time to time. I built amazing relationships with extraordinary people. They enriched my life in too many ways to list. Yes, being able to say I had the experience of playing professional basketball in Greece was incredible. Yet, knowing I was loved while playing the game I loved was the true blessing. That is not something anyone should ever take for granted.

I switched my routine before practice that morning. I took the bus to Krini, the area down by the sea with the cafés, bars, and restaurants. It was a bit chilly, but I was determined to re-write the script. I got off at the first stop and walked along the street for several minutes. I wanted an unfamiliar destination to spark my sense of adventure. I walked until I came across a fancy looking café/bar near the water. It was a little hard to see from the road, and I had to walk down some steps to get to the entrance.

"This looks like a good spot," I thought.

I walked in and sat at a table next to the window, so I could continue to revel in my appreciation and in the beauty of Greece. I ordered *frappe metrio meh gala*, which is iced coffee semi-sweet with cream, and stared at the sea. No phone. No book. No conversation. I was content being alone with my thoughts.

I didn't steer my mind in any particular direction. I didn't need to. Normally, my thoughts are four steps ahead of life, busy with nonexistent plans of an unknown future. Far too often I was in full stride in the proverbial nonstop race, sprinting from one thing to the next, all in hopes of one day being able to live financially free and peacefully. What we miss, or what we take for granted, is forever gone.

For me of late, that was going day to day without stopping to value the beauty of the sea that was in front of me. I had never lived remotely close to the sea or ocean before. Within a couple months, I had already begun taking it for granted. And I felt ashamed.

I signaled the waiter and asked him, "Do you have a pen I can borrow?" He looked confused, so I gestured with my hand, pretending to write on my napkin. He gave me a thumbs up, reached into his pocket and handed me a pen.

I began writing down everything I was thankful for and appreciated in my life. The list got so long I had to get up and borrow a couple of napkins from the tables next to me.

Without thinking too much of it, I wrote, "the struggle." Yes, I was thankful for the struggles I had gone through in life. The hard times, along with the good, shaped me. The struggles, challenges, failures, and heartaches held the most significance in the lessons I learned. Failure is a great teacher when we let go of our egos and choose to learn, listen, and apply the lesson.

The chaos and the lows I face are the final touches of the symphony God orchestrates in my life. The lows are just as important as the highs to create the masterpiece. It's all a matter of perspective. Would I choose to stop and read the music? Or choose to stay illiterate? Seeing the notes on the page as nothing more than the scribbles of chaos without meaning?

I left the café with appreciation and perspective. There was so much to be thankful for each and every day. This time, I didn't wait until the clock reached *three . . . two . . . one.*

I made it.

In my backyard by the sea, I learned to read the music of my own symphony a tiny bit better. Through adult eyes, I remain undefeated.

Day 8

*Determined to live my promises,
my café du jour tour continued.*

Once more, I walked through unfamiliar doors for the first time. I found six tables, fit snugly next to one another. Each was covered in a white tablecloth, with a candle placed in the center, most likely to add to the atmosphere. The chairs featured blue cushions. Landscape pictures of the Aegean Sea and beaches decorated the walls.

The solitary confinement I had with my frappe lasted for half an hour. As I was getting ready to exit, a few men I recognized from the club entered.

"Ahhh, Vera Jo Bustos. My favorite!"

The greeting was in full throat. All heads turned in our direction. I assumed it was due to the volume and the language. He spoke in English.

"*Geia sas,*" I replied to the group, hoping my smile spoke volumes.

Before I knew it, we were immersed in a conversation I had to really focus on to understand because of his accent. While one man did the talking, the other two went to order their coffees.

"Are you Greek Orthodox?"

It was a question I'd never been asked. "No. I was raised Catholic, but I believe it is very similar from what I have seen."

He smiled at my response. "Yes, yes, yes. They are almost the same. This is good to know. Now, I have a very serious question for you. Will you marry me?"

I stood unmoving and stared unblinking. His poker face was devoid of tells. What if he's being serious? I gambled. I went all in, calling his bluff with laugher. He folded, laughing as well.

"I am only joking."

His words were my relief. More fun ensued. The other two men rejoined the group, and he spoke to them in Greek. One of the men put his hand to his forehead and shook it back and forth. All of them were laughing. I assumed he told them about the proposal.

"Do not listen to him. He is always Mr. Joker." The voice belonged to the man who had shaken his head.

"All right, I have to get back and start getting ready for practice. I am sure I will see you guys at the gym sometime."

"Yes, of course." It was Mr. Proposal.

"Your new fiancé will be waiting for you." It was the third man, adding his two-cents. He playfully hit my "future husband" on the back while saying something in Greek I couldn't understand.

"Bye, guys!"

I laughed myself back to my apartment.

After practice, I told my teammates about the café proposal. I don't know why, but it was funnier the second time.

"Vera, you should have said yes so you can get your Greek passport and stay forever!" At least one teammate was looking out for my best interests.

"Hmmm. You're right. I really didn't think that through, did I?"

Others were quick to offer their advice.

"Vera is more Greek than American. She doesn't need to marry a Greek man for that!"

From there, everything switched to Greek, and I could only listen with my eyes. It wasn't long before my curiosity got the best of me.

"Okay guys, what are you talking about?"

I threw my hands in the air for full effect.

"We are just confirming that you are Greek, that is all."

A teammate answered in English before another one confirmed it in Greek.

"*Neh. Eisai Ellinida,* Vera."

"Ahh, Okay. I suppose you all are right. *Eimai Ellinida.*"

At least once a week, I was reminded how I was Greek. It was a great compliment to be thought of as one of their own, and I never tired of hearing it.

Eimai Ellinida. I am Greek.

I had two final thoughts:

One proposal is plenty.

And, I need to find a new café.

Day 9

What you see depends on what you are looking for.

Sifting through the remains of a defeat minutes old, I collected as much of the positive as I could. I didn't discard the negative because that was part of the story. Still, if we only focus on the hurt, we will continue to suffer. But if we focus on the lesson, we can continue to grow.

Seeds of growth had been planted in the scrimmage. It was time for the first harvest. I immersed myself by staying in the moment and went with the flow of the game. Nothing was forced, neither by me, nor my teammates. We dictated the tempo for most of the first half. We held the lead for almost every second, though our opponent stayed loyal to our pace.

At the break, we trailed by double digits.

What?

How?

The how was easy to answer. Our defense lapsed, their offense capitalized. They drained uncontested three-pointers when they weren't scoring breakaway layups. From being the totter, we were now teetering.

"Not again."

I ran to the locker room with that single thought in my mind.

Coach entered speaking all Greek and nothing but Greek. Let's just say he wasn't whispering. He was infuriated. He had every reason. I didn't ask for a translation. I didn't need one. His animation, gestures and tone were clear in any language. From the few words I understood, he challenged us to guard the ball and challenged some of my teammates to show a little more hustle.

I wasn't going to go down without a fight. I turned to my teammates as we were leaving the locker room.

"We got this guys! We got it."

I gave them each a high-five as we ran onto the court. All responded, save one. She's one of the youngest on our team. She didn't make eye contact when I gave her a high-five. Her head hung still in defeat when we reached the court.

"Hey, don't worry about those last transitions," I told her. "We were all at fault for that. I don't know if they have time machines in Greece, but from what I know, we can't go back in time to change things, right?"

I was hoping for a smile. I received a nod. It was a start.

"All right, then let's just focus on the next play."

I got another nod. Only this time, we were looking eye to eye. If we wanted to mount a comeback, we needed her. We needed everyone. It was uphill. Then again, aren't all climbs?

Like all ascents, this one took time. In fact, we didn't get within three points until the final minutes. But we had put ourselves in a position to win, which is all you can hope for when you trailed by as much as we did.

Their coach stemmed our momentum with a timeout inside the final minute. They needed a basket to ice the victory, we needed a defensive stop and a buzzer-beater to force overtime. One team would blink. We were that team.

They ran a double-screen off the baseline for their best shooter. We defended the play about as well as we could. Their player was simply better, hitting the three-pointer with a hand in her face. Down six with seconds to go and no timeouts left, we pushed the ball up court. A teammate found me on the wing, I found time to catch and release a three-pointer. The shot beat the buzzer. The shot also went in. No one celebrated. We lost by three.

Our faces defined disappointment. I thought about trying to raise the spirits. I scanned the room. This was neither the time nor the place. We dressed in silence, but not everyone went their separate ways.

A couple teammates and I accompanied Alex and Eleni to a tavern near the ancient walls of Thessaloniki. I recognized the place by sight and by sound. The last time I had been there, people danced to live music. We heard the music and singing before we opened the doors.

We sat at a long table along the back wall of the tavern. There was an older gentleman playing a small guitar-type instrument and a younger woman singing beside him. The patrons served as the choir. Already, my mood lightened.

We strayed from the normal family style ordering, opting instead for our own plates. That was a first for me, ordering my own plate. With Alex and Eleni, it was always family style. I ordered lamb.

I knew Greece was known for its lamb, and rightly so. I couldn't tell you how it was prepared, but I can say it was the best I had ever eaten. And it wasn't just the lamb. The potatoes that came as a side were lightly salted and had some type of seasoning on it that I couldn't place. And, of course, Greek wine.

In between singing bouts of popular songs that everyone seemed to know, Alex spoke to all of us.

"You know, basketball is a good teacher. Sometimes you lose, sometimes you win. Winning is important and fun, but you have to remember what the important things are: to do your best, to have fun, and to keep looking on.

"It does no one any good to be sad about losing. Let me tell you something, nobody cares! Nobody cares that you are losing and nobody cares what you are feeling. So, we can't feel bad for ourselves and have our heads low. Keep looking on. That is all we can do. Look on to the next game and prepare."

I nodded. A teammate raised her glass while Eleni poured wine into the last glass.

"*Geia sas.*"

We toasted as one.

The topic of basketball ended and everyone slipped into the comforts of their native tongues. I didn't mind. It's similar to being given a 100-piece puzzle without the box. You are left to solve the puzzle, or in this case the conversations, on your own. But I could only piece things together for so long without finally asking for a translation.

Sometimes, I placed the pieces of the conversation in the right place, and I knew what had been said. At other times, I wasn't even close. I took pride in how much I actually understood. The daily immersion, which sometimes felt like drowning, tipped the learning in my favor. For me, it was the only way to learn.

This conversation sounded serious. I asked a teammate for clarity.

"We are talking about the Greek church," she said, then continued with her explanation, though some words couldn't be translated from Greek.

"It is like the Vatican for Catholics. It is its own independent country within Greece, which has its own laws, very similar to the Vatican."

"Really?" I asked. "I didn't know you guys had that here."

"Yes, everyone is talking about how the church should help with the crisis," she said. "The Orthodox has money to help, but they are hesitant to help Greece with the crisis. Too many politics for anyone to make a decision."

I admit, politics was never of interest to me, regardless of what country it was. But what my teammates thought and felt was. The conversation lasted until the musician played another popular song. Once the tune began, the tavern erupted in applause and cheers.

Everyone who could sang the night away. And everyone included our table, with one exception. And since no one was depending on me to sing, no one looked my way.

---⊚---

Day 10-11

---⊚---

Three years before I entered this world, the Bangles released the song, Walk Like an Egyptian.

If they were to reunite and they saw me that Sunday, their sequel would be *Walk Like a Penguin*.

"I am not sure which is funnier today. Listening to you speak Greek or watching you walk."

It was Eleni.

She was spot on. I resembled her observation. I waddled, exactly like a penguin.

Penguins do it to save energy. I did it because of blisters on my feet from the previous night's game. The blisters wanted no part of me being vertical. Neither did I. But I had been invited to spend the day with Alex and Eleni, so I waddled over. Eleni made coffee, and we watched soccer. I was the entertainment.

So, which was funnier? I had the answer for Eleni.

"Probably listening to my American accent."

There was no hesitation in Eleni's reply. "I think you're right."

We ordered gyros from a place down the street. Thankfully, they delivered. Mine was equal parts gyros, French fries, and onions wrapped in pita bread. I forgot all about my blisters. We couch surfed most of the afternoon and channel checked between the soccer and basketball games being shown on TV.

A suggestion was made to stroll the square and scoff ice cream. I wasn't ready to take my waddle public, but this was my first time eating ice cream since I had been back from Christmas break. I would crawl to the ice cream if I had to.

I hugged my gratitude into Alex and Eleni, thanking them for their hospitality and company before returning to my apartment from the square. My pace was penguin-quick as I attempted to spend the least amount of time in the day's cold. I spent the evening reading and journaling.

The agony of de-feet didn't prevent me from resuming my fresh routine on Monday. It started in a new café for morning coffee. While I was out, I stopped to grab lunch before heading to my shooting workout. Then it was back to my apartment to rest and refuel before returning to the gym for our evening practice.

An outsider never would have guessed that we were coming off a loss based on our effort, energy, and enthusiasm. I can't recall when we've practiced better. I even managed to stifle the waddle. That definitely wasn't something my teammates needed to see. I entertain them enough already, thank you very much.

Alex invited me to go to the theater to watch a movie with him and Eleni. I answered by hopping in the back seat of their small car. With tickets in one hand, popcorn in the other, we found our assigned seats for *Underworld Awakening* in 3D.

I'm a fan of the *Underworld* series and Kate Beckinsale, one of my favorite actresses. The movie was in English, with Greek subtitles. The distraction of the words took some getting used to. But soon I was engulfed in the plot and the action.

Alex pointed to our glasses.

"You look funny wearing those glasses."

He insisted on a photo-op.

A click later, Eleni snapped a retort. "We may look funny, but I will not try to take your picture, you will break my phone with the way you look."

I high-fived Eleni through our laughter.

Smiling, Alex waved away her comeback. *"Otinane."*

In other words, "Whatever."

There are a million reasons why these two are my favorites.

Now, there are a million-and-one.

Day 17

I come from a two-high school town—
West Las Vegas and Robertson.

Or East, as everyone calls it. I attended West, graduated from West, am all things West.

When it came to athletics, West vs. East was and still remains one of the state's last, great rivalries. The Green and Gold of the West side vs. the Red and White of East side. The Dons vs. the Cardinals.

While I was a kid, two of my uncles at two different times held the title of varsity boy's basketball coach. I learned at an early age the personal matters behind the rivalry. Watching such passion between two rivals as a wide-eyed kid sparked my competitive fire. There's just something about Northern New Mexico Basketball that ignites a flame with everyone involved.

Our respective gyms kept everyone packed tight. You didn't need to read lips to understand what was being yelled. You heard every syllable of every word. Don't quote me on this, but I believe this is where *Spanglish*—a combination of Spanish and English—originated. You can't properly define bi-lingual profanity. It's something you need to experience.

Fans packed the games, regardless of the records. But when both teams were considered to be among the state's best in their classification, lines of fans would begin forming in front of the ticket window sometime after lunch. It was quite the obstacle for students who were trying to walk from one class to the next.

I thought all that was behind me.

It was.

Until I witnessed a West Side Story break out in Thessaloniki, Greece.

On Saturday afternoon, I finally had a chance to spend time with Andreas, my former coach. It was the first time we had gotten together since I had returned. He invited me to the Aris men's basketball game. I was looking forward to catching up with him.

Coach Andreas picked me up from my studio and drove us to the gym. The crowd was five thousand people strong. Their chants and drums remained unchanged as did the on-court action. What differed was halftime.

Andreas and I were standing in line at a concession stand. We heard a commotion nearby. It started with shouting. It moved to shoves. It escalated to profanity of which I am fluent in understanding in any language. Police made sure it went no further. They separated the men and sent them on their way.

The West Side Story resumed five minutes later. As we walked back to our seats, a fight broke out in the stands. The section of the gym where the fans played the drums and were the loudest and most obnoxious ran from their side of the gym to join the fray.

Distracted by the fight, both teams stopped their warm-up and watched. It looked a mismatch, as a multitude of men moved forward against four or five. The police couldn't prevent punches from being thrown, having to fight their way through the stands. Once there, they separated the sides and escorted four men out. All wore matching black shirts with an identical symbol.

"This is sometimes common for fights to break out," Andreas explained to me. "The men who caused the fights are fans of Paok."

Paok is another club in Thessaloniki and is the arch-rival of Aris. Hmmm, sounds familiar.

"The rivalry between Paok and Aris is very big, and fans are very loyal to their teams," Andreas continued. "There is almost always a fight that breaks out during the games, which is why we always have police at the games."

"Remind me to never wear a Paok shirt to an Aris game!" I said.

"No way I would ever allow you to wear a Paok shirt in this gym," Andreas said. "That is just asking for trouble."

"Uh huh! That is for sure," I said, nodding in agreement.

I grew up in a rivalry, just never to this extreme. Well, not to my recollection. The passion of the Greek fans, and their love of team, made the atmospheres of the games unforgettable.

The second half was incident free. Aris won by double digits. The fans chanted to the cadence of the drum for the final minute before exploding in applause after the buzzer.

We made our way to the lobby. Andreas was close friends with one of the Aris players so we waited for him to emerge out of the locker room. I spotted a reporter interviewing Aris players. After he finished, he spotted me off in the corner. He approached us and began talking to Andreas. When both looked in my direction, I knew the topic of conversation.

Andreas confirmed my suspicion.

"The reporter is asking if you will do an interview to talk about your time in Greece and say a few words about your team?" he asked, after turning toward me.

I was caught off guard.

"Sure."

My single-word answer was for Andreas. My thumbs up was for the reporter. It became second nature for me to communicate with gestures.

The reporter did not speak English. He called to a woman, who was still speaking with the Aris players. When she arrived, he began speaking to her. She listened and nodded her head to whatever he said. The woman turned to me.

"*Geia sou*, I will be translating for Bill for the questions he will ask you. I will also be translating what you say in Greek so our listeners can understand you as not everyone is so good with English."

"Okay, I will do my best to speak slowly."

"Good. After you say a couple of sentences, take a pause so I can translate what you are saying, then you can continue speaking."

"Okay, let's see how my first translated interview goes!"

I smiled, clapped my hands. Her first question came quickly.

"How has Apollon been playing?"

"The team has been doing good. We have faced some challenges and haven't always come out on the winning side, but we continue to play hard and . . . "

Before I could continue she pulled the microphone away and started speaking in Greek, translating what I had just said.

Whoops, I forgot to pause.

She put the microphone back in front of my lips for me to continue speaking. My train of thought left the station, a passenger on the microphone. My pause was not for effect. I promise.

"Umm, we still fight and try very hard."

I stopped after the sentence. The microphone stayed. Silence is not what she was waiting for. Still, I stood and stared. Finally, she spoke into the microphone to translate my words.

We weren't even close to being back on track. In fact, I was now aboard the butterfly express, heading for who knows where. I've done my share of interviews, starting in high school and lasting through college. They never flustered me. But now, I had to think about what to say, how much to say, and when to pause. It was overload, and there was no *Take Two*.

"How do you enjoy Thessaloniki?"

"I love life here in the city. I think Thessaloniki is really nice. I am always telling my friends and family back in America how awesome it is. I love it here!"

I paused with a huge smile directed right into the camera. The woman pulled back the microphone and began translating. Relief replaced anxiety.

"Do you think you will come back to Greece after this season?"

"Come back? I don't want to leave. I want to stay in Greece!"

My laughter was contagious. She carried it through her translation.

"That is all we have for you."

"Thank you for my first international interview."

We shook hands. I extended my hand to the reporter who didn't speak English and said, *"Evcharisto poli,"* which means thank you very much.

I looked over to Andreas for the first time since the interview began. He smiled at me as the reporter went over to talk with him again. I waited for them to finish and waved goodbye. Andreas returned with the update.

"He says that the interview will be on his site by tomorrow afternoon. He will add highlights of you playing to add to the interview."

"Awesome!"

"He also said that you are his favorite American woman player that he has interviewed."

"Oh yeah? Well, that's not surprising. It is probably because I act like a Greek."

Andreas laughed

"I think so, too."

There wasn't one West Side Story in Greece.

Turns out, there were two.

Day 18

In Northern New Mexico, which is where I was born and raised, it is faith, family, basketball.

The sport is its own religion, instilling a passion inside both players and fans and creates a following where cars snake almost bumper-to-bumper through the darkness of two-lane roads for unending miles. The calling comes early in life and for most lasts a lifetime.

We were called to the gym en masse for a traditional ceremony to celebrate the New Year. That is how it was explained, though sometimes my mind shortchanges the details. Everyone from the club, from young kids to professionals on both the men's and women's side, were present. A priest stood at half-court in front of a makeshift altar. A book and papers rested on top. His robe was black with a gold garment draped over the top. Embroidered symbols adorned the garment. I was unsure of their meaning.

The priest's first words hushed the gym. His voice boomed through the speaker system. He held a microphone in his right hand and a book in his left as he welcomed everyone. He continued by reading from the book.

Drawing from my Catholic background, I gathered he was reading a passage from the Bible or the relative version of the Orthodox religion. He continued for several minutes. His voice was the only sound. Once he finished reading, he looked up and into the faces. He knew this part by memory. So, too, did his followers. The gym replied in one voice to his prayer. I didn't recognize his words, but I received the message. Faith is quirky that way.

Next, the president of the club took the microphone. She spoke quickly, passionately. So much so that her speech had the gym applauding at its conclusion. A translation wasn't requested. I believe if there was something in her message I needed to know, Alex or Eleni would tell me.

A woman who worked for the club began handing out pieces of cake. Now this I hadn't anticipated and needed explained. I turned and asked my trusty translator, Vassiliki.

"There is a coin placed into the cake when it is baked. Whoever gets the coin in their slice is supposed to have luck for the remainder of the year," she said. "Be careful when you bite into it."

"Oh wow, that's kind of cool," I said, secretly hoping that I would find the coin.

I used my fork to autopsy the cake. No coin. Disappointment was sure to be showing in my body language.

The coin found its owner a couple minutes later. Luck shone on one of the young boys from the club. He stood and held the coin aloft. The ovation was the loudest of the day. Beaming, he walked to Ms. Rena, the president, who had a gift bag ready for him. He received high-fives from all those around him upon his return.

I was grateful to be part of this tradition, this celebration. It felt like a continuation of the passion already imprinted on my soul.

I carried this joyous spirit to lunch. I joined Alex, Eleni, and a friend of theirs at a seafood tavern that specialized in octopus, squid, and fish. Seafood had always been a favorite. But the seafood in Greece was on an entirely different level from what I was used to back in New Mexico and Colorado—two states surrounded by land, not sea.

Freshness matters. Preparation, spices, and cooking do, too. The tavern's fried octopus, or calamari, jumped to the top of my favorites list after exactly one bite. One thing did make it better. Ice cream. We each grabbed a cone to go and took what was left of them back to Alex and Eleni's.

We couch-potatoed until eight that night, which was our departure time. We were meeting some of my teammates at a coffee shop to watch a soccer match between two of the top teams in Thessaloniki. The match was in town but was also being televised nationally.

I'm not a soccer aficionado. Still, I enjoy watching those who kneel at the boots of Messi, Ronaldo, Neymar . . . Sorry, those are the only three names I know. Our table drew their allegiances, each side taking turns yelling at the players inside the TV.

Watching them proved to be a religious experience. And by watching them, I was talking about the people in the coffee shop and the people in the stands at the match. The cameras constantly switched from match to people. I admit, the fans captivated me more than the game. It was the cheers, the chants, the boos, the fire. The fire? Yes, there were fires in the stands. Or what looked like fire. I learned later that some fans take flares to matches.

All of me wishes I had been there. I promised myself one day I would. To be at FC Barcelona vs. Real Madrid in Spain, or Juventus vs. Inter Milan in Italy, or any of the other big-named soccer clubs in Europe was now on my bucket list.

I am not sure I would ever convert to soccer as my second religion.

Then again, who knows?

After all, the Lord loves a great mystery, working in those mysterious ways of His.

—⊙—

Day 25

—⊙—

*I was all of three years old when
Michael and the Miracles, better known as the Dream
Team, dominated the 1992 Olympics like no other
basketball team had before or since.*

Others have donned the moniker, Dream Team, only to realize it fits exactly one team. The Dream Team, however, is not in the Guinness World Records.

Athinaikos is.

Welcome, not to my dream, but to my nightmare.

Our third trip to Athens was long enough all on its own. The thought of playing Athinaikos made it feel like an eternity. Haven't heard of Athinakos? Well, for starters, it won the EuroCup during the 2009-2010 season, the first team from Greece to accomplish that feat. The EuroCup is the Olympics for European women's basketball. It's that big of a deal.

It's not Guinness-worthy. This is. From 2008-2012, Athinaikos dominated the Greek League. And by dominate, I mean the team won 105 straight games. That's right, 105-0. That put them in two record books—Greece and Guinness.

I prepared myself mentally. Athinaikos' accomplishments are impressive. And intimidating—if allowed to simmer in your thoughts. I'd been victimized by perception before. Too many times I accepted the hype as gospel, and I suffered for it. I know I can't alter reality. I also know I can control perception.

Athinaikos didn't live up to the hype.

It surpassed it.

The last time the game was close was when we were warming up. I started in survival mode. Instead of competing to win, I was playing not to get embarrassed. Didn't work. Within a couple minutes, I got my shot blocked, got the ball stolen away from me, and had a silly turnover. I wasn't alone in the misery. It was total-team.

There was no rising to the occasion, no historic second-half comeback. This was Athinaikos. But the intimidation dissipated. I saw players, not idols. They were extremely skilled and gifted, but they were human. Just like me. I regained my confidence, enough to not hang my head at game's end.

We lost by almost thirty. And yes, it was that lopsided. But it wasn't titanic. Athinaikos is an excellent team, one of the best in Europe. I'll never accept losing, that's not in my DNA. But I wasn't about to water dead flowers.

On the bus ride back to Thessaloniki, I had another head-to-heart talk. I couldn't always control the feelings that rose within me, but I could control the way I chose to think and respond to those feelings. I entered the game intimidated and fearful. Initially, those feelings controlled me. But they weren't permanent. I allowed my mind to work for me instead of against me. I talked to myself instead of listening to myself and allowing those feelings to dictate my actions.

I didn't run from the challenge. I sprinted toward it. I was proactive instead of reactive. I needed to live the actions of uncomfortableness and fearfulness, of being amidst intimidating situations to practice the actions of courage and confidence.

Mental preparation is a great asset. But the edge it provides can take you only so far. The real test is living in the action.

I craved more of that reality.

———— ⊙ ————

Day 26

———— ⊙ ————

"We need people in our lives with whom
we can be as open as possible.

To have real conversations with people may seem like such a simple, obvious suggestion, but it involves courage and risk."

Thomas Moore is the author of that quote. I'm reminded of his words as I wait for a different Thomas, my agent. As you know, he is more than just an agent. He is a friend and is someone who cares for me as a person, not just as a player. There is no pretense in our conversations. He possesses the courage to tell me what I need to hear, not what I want to hear.

We selected one of our usual hangouts near the sea for mid-morning coffee. The small talk centered on the game and the tale of two halves.

"You looked like you were sleeping the first two quarters," Thomas said with a hint of disappointment.

"Yeah, I was lost in my own thoughts for a while," I humbly replied. "To be honest, I let the Dream Team hype get to me. My body followed the way my mind was thinking."

"I understand that, Vera, but listen, if you want to continue to play in the top league, get a better contract and get paid more, you need to take advantage of the opportunity."

I nodded in total agreement.

"If you would have played the entire game the way you played in the second half, that would have gotten you a lot of attention," Thomas said, his tone more forceful. "You can continue to rise in the ranks of the Euro-League, but you can't have any more bad games."

That last sentence was in reference to a few weeks ago, to the game I call the worst of my career.

"I understand what you are saying," I said, looking directly into his eyes. "I am training myself mentally to rise to such challenges. I am doing better, I promise."

"I trust you are," he said. "I have no doubts we will sign you with a great contract next season, but you have to take care of business this season so I can take care of business for you next season."

"Deal!" I said, extending my hand forward.

I smiled. He laughed.

"Okay, this is a deal."

We finished our coffee talking about my well-being, my trip home for Christmas, and his time with his friends and family over the holiday. I valued Thomas for holding me accountable to the reason I was there— playing professional basketball. And for making sure I was doing well in my personal life.

Relationships that come from a place of care while also challenging you to be the best person you can be are rare and special. If you have someone who fits that mold, don't let them go. The people who hold you accountable are the ones who have your best interests at heart.

After we finished our coffee and conversation, we drove to Aristotle University of Thessaloniki. Thomas had scheduled some muscular strength tests with the Human Performance labs to test for muscular imbalances within my body.

Walking into the university, I thought it looked similar to the ones in America. Long, bland hallways with white tile floors. Offices lined the empty hallway we walked through en route to the labs. We were greeted by an older gentleman. He looked to be in his late sixties with medium length silver hair and glasses that rested on his long and pointed nose.

Thomas greeted the man, and they began speaking in Greek. I didn't focus on their conversation. I was looking behind them into the lab when Thomas introduced me. I snapped back to reality and extended my hand.

"*Geia sou*," I said, extending my hand. The man shook my hand and gestured for us to follow him into the lab.

The lab was large and resembled a weight room full of machines. That's where the similarities ended. These resistance machines were connected to computers. I could tell the computers were set up to monitor and analyze body movements on the machine. A bookshelf served as the back wall. Every spot on every shelf was filled.

My aptitude of reading and love for books drew me to the shelf. The books were all in Greek, of course. I tried to sound out the titles of the books, testing my ability to read.

Sensing my curiosity, one of the students working in the lab approached me. He was young, about early twenties, with short brown hair and an athletic build. He spoke first.

"All of these books are about human performance and studies on how we can improve performance in sports."

"Yes, all of these books look very interesting, even though I don't understand what the titles say."

"I suppose they can be interesting, but I find most of them to be incredibly boring,"

I laughed at his response. "I can relate to that feeling when having to read books for school."

He walked away toward the machines and gestured for me to follow him. "Okay, let's get you set up."

I sat down on the machine, which looked like a leg extension resistance training device used to improve quad strength. I was strapped down to the chair in every way you could think of. There must have been eight or ten straps over me. The student instructed me to cross my arms over my chest to make sure the power generated was only coming from my legs without any assistance from my upper body. One leg at a time, I pushed up against the resistance of the machine and then pulled down just as forcefully against equal resistance.

Once finished, the professor explained the data to Thomas. They spoke in Greek, so I had to wait until their conversation concluded to hear the translation. The professor had a look of surprise on his face while he spoke to Thomas. I sat silent, and patient, and curious.

The results concluded that my hamstrings were much stronger in ratio to my quadriceps muscles. The professor said he was amazed I hadn't suffered a serious injury due to the imbalance. I was given a six-week resistance training plan to strengthen my quads and eradicate the disparity. I was dumbfounded such a disproportion existed to that extent.

Thomas and I pretty much covered everything that needed to be said, so the drive to my apartment was weather-related. The sun had been playing hide-and-seek for a couple weeks. In its place was the fog of low-hanging clouds. On top of that, most of the past week included snow.

Snow? In Greece? Greece is palm trees and beaches. Just look at the postcards. It's not snowmen and snow angels. But it was. It was more shock, less awe.

Thessaloniki sees snow about as often as it sees an American basketball player from Las Vegas, New Mexico. And yet, the Greeks have a phrase for the flakes.

"When a white day comes."

It's basically our "once in a blue moon."

That year, Europe broke records with the cold weather. Thomas blamed me. He said I brought the cold weather with me from New Mexico and Colorado.

He was joking.

I didn't mind.

I like having Thomas in my life.

We have an open-door policy.

Day 32

People say I'm an old soul.

Perhaps they are right. Perhaps not. I'm familiar with some of the characteristics, but not all. Of the ones I do know, most sound like me.

I have a preference for solitude. I am sensitive and empathic, and I can be deeply introspective. I possess both a thirst for truth and wisdom and an inclination toward spirituality.

My current head-first dive into solitude wasn't entirely my choice. The frigid temperature outside had its say in that I only froze when it was unavoidable. So, too, did my on-again, off-again relationship with the internet. The lack of fingertip access to the world was a major source of frustration, particularly when I wanted to reach my family back home.

Holding on to that frustration did more damage than letting go. Eventually, it floated away silently, like a snowflake in the wind, and I was there, alone with my thoughts and only my thoughts.

In the quiet, I read and reflected. When I contemplated over the words others had written or thoughts that crossed my mind, my connection to God amplified. I began to feel more in-tune with my emotions, my feelings, and myself. I had a sense of peace and tranquility, as if my life's problems vanished instantaneously, even if only for a moment. Love pervaded and permeated my inner-most being. Lightness and stillness overcame me. Stillness was not nothingness. Stillness created a clearing for my thoughts. It opened the emotional clutter and allowed that untidy mess to dissipate, without feeling angst or judgement. The result was space to feel, to think, to question, and to dream.

Someone once told me that I speak from the heart, but I never show anyone what's in my heart. He had a point. I only show the world what I want it to see. Yes, it's the real me. But no, it's not all of me. That changes—here and now.

I'm learning that vulnerability is the key to transformation. We all have flaws and imperfections. I certainly do. It takes great courage to embrace those imperfections and live those vulnerabilities and pull back the curtain to reveal our true selves. Too often, we seek only validation and acceptance, and not often enough do we simply say, "This is me."

What is the greater risk, letting go of what people think? Or, letting go of how I feel, what I believe, and who I am?

What we don't realize is our time is limited and we waste too much of it trying to live our lives to the satisfaction of society, friends, even family. We fall into the trap of living with the results of other people's thinking. When that happens, we fail to capture the essence of who God made us to be. We allow ourselves to drift into the wind of nothingness, following the numb flow, away from who we are and what we can become.

The finger I am pointing is directed at me and no one else. I've let the noise of others' opinions silence the voice inside me more times than I care to admit. When I lived for the approval, praise, and validation of others, I became their prisoner. I didn't always possess the courage to follow my heart, my intuition. But slowly, I am getting there.

Notions are like opinions. We all have them. We all speak them. Most are preconceived. You see the connection? Too many spend a lifetime thinking about how they would really like to live and not enough to see with their own eyes and feel with their own hearts.

I am . . .

You choose the words that follow.

Believe them.

Trust them.

Live them.

I am.

Day 34

I crawled into the cocoon I constructed
without knowing the real reason why.

Was it to protect me from the gloomy weather, the cold winter air? Or was it the next logical step from solitude to solitary confinement?

I was lonely. I just didn't know why.

Everyone tucked themselves tightly inside the warmth of their homes. Or so it seemed. My neighborhood became a ghost town. I was alone on my morning coffee adventures that sought a different café each day. It was one of the few times I strayed from my apartment that wasn't basketball-related.

I, too, craved warmth, the kind only a family can provide. I was homesick. I grabbed the calendar. This is where I was. This is where I longed to be. I counted the separation day by day. It didn't ease the situation. It might have made it worse.

It's not like I had been abandoned on a deserted island. The internet provided a link between me and my family. But it wasn't a lifeline. I needed proximity. I needed to look into their eyes, not into a screen. I needed to be present, to love in-person, not over Skype. And, I needed to be loved back, in full-hearted hugs and kisses on the cheeks that meant more than hello.

Then again, when I was present back at home, how often was I concurrently absent? Wasn't I was always going from one thing to another, day after day, allowing the busyness of life to rule me? I never once stopped and was able to *just be,* did I? The saying, "You don't know what you have until it's gone," rang in my ears. Not that I had lost my family by any means. I knew where they were, where they would always be. They didn't leave. I did.

I expected to miss my family, miss my way of life back in America. After all, they are my world. What I didn't anticipate was the shadow it would cast and the paralyzing effect it would have. I got so caught up in what I was missing that I forgot to enjoy what was around me.

You can't make new memories if you are re-living old ones. I wasn't present. I was missing the adventures and lessons I was meant to endure. Part of the reason I was here was to learn how to live on my own, to be okay by myself, with myself and to raise my relationship with God to a higher level.

Traveling to a foreign country and having more time to be alone than ever before in my life, I realized what resounded within me. I understood with complete conviction what my priorities were, what I needed to keep, what I could discard, what I spent my time on, and who I spent my time with.

I also learned that what I left behind was what mattered most, and it would be there when I returned. That knowledge was the first light to enter my cocoon. It was another sign of growth.

Time to emerge.

Day 37

I freed myself from the physical cocoon, but remained wrapped inside the mental and emotional ones.

I lived moment to moment, as I had promised, and washed words of inspiration over myself to make the most of each. It didn't matter. Homesickness continued to sting repeatedly and deeply.

I sought solace in sweat. I devoted extra hours to on-court workouts, weights and study sessions. I broke down games, I broke down opponents. It helped. I escaped the struggles, if only for a couple hours each day. The gym became my sanctuary. Then again, maybe it always has been.

Eventually, other teams would arrive and I would have to depart. Time wasn't playing fair. When I had the ball in my hands or when I was working on getting stronger, the moments flew. When I was at my apartment, they crawled.

The thoughts of eternal solitude weren't healthy. If I couldn't help myself, I would help others. I sat in my studio apartment with my computer on my lap. For the next twenty minutes, a blank word document and I had a staring contest.

We both lost.

Life and its messages sometimes come to us as darkness. So what message was I sending, sitting wordlessly here in the light? I couldn't write what I was feeling, which was doubt and fear. I couldn't write what I was thinking, either, about not being good enough, or worthy enough, or accomplished enough. No one wanted to hear what I had to say or follow my example.

I shut the computer with disgust, with feelings of unworthiness, with . . . I heard my phone. It was Eleni. She invited me for coffee. At that moment, her timing was a godsend. Sometimes friends are messengers to save us from our own misery. Eleni and Alex were such friends.

They were at my apartment within minutes.

"*Geia sou, paidi mou.*"

"Hello, my child."

The warmth of Eleni's greeting melted me into a giant puddle of smiles.

"Is there any place in particular you would like to go?"

"Can we go downtown? I haven't been there in a long time. I think it would be nice to get a change of scenery from the neighborhood."

"You got it, Miss Bustos."

Alex joined the conversation and the smiles.

I don't remember a single word said the rest of the night. I just remember feeling happy—lost in the moment.

Day 38

I awoke, expecting to pick up the pieces.

Turns out, I didn't need to. They had fallen into place. In twenty-four hours, a breakdown became a breakthrough. All I could do was chuckle.

"Training the youth."

I would build on those three words. Exactly what, I wasn't sure. Not yet, anyway. The finished product was down the road. I just toed the starting line. Instinctively, though, I knew this was the right path.

I evicted myself from my apartment, even though it was freezing outside. I walked into a café on the square, ordered coffee, sat down, opened my laptop. Once more, I stared into a blank screen.

This time, there were no doubts, no disappointments, no hesitations. My thoughts rushed from my mind through my fingers to the document on the screen, which was no longer blank. My free-thinking stream of consciousness produced written thoughts on basketball training and mentoring, on academic tutoring, on developing mental toughness and character. My fingers couldn't keep up.

I wanted to make an impact and leave an imprint on future generations. I wanted to train athletes from all around the nation and help them achieve their dreams, using basketball as the foundation.

With these pieces in place, I stopped and looked at the picture. I saw what it was and what it could become. I hadn't anticipated any of this. They say unexpected gifts are the best. This one certainly was.

The gift given to me is something I could give to others.

———◉———

Day 39

———◉———

Here is one thing I never thought I would see playing basketball indoors—my breath.

That's how cold the Paok gym was.

I could make jokes about how penguins were standing outside, waiting in line to buy tickets to that afternoon's league game so they could come in and chill. Or, how there was an igloo-building contest at intermission. But the cold we played in was no laughing matter.

I borrowed a teammate's long sleeve undershirt to wear inside my uniform for added warmth, since parkas weren't allowed. I pre-gamed in layers, a first for me. My body never reached room temperature. My hands stung anytime I caught the ball, that is, when I could actually feel them. I shot knuckleballs that clanged the rims. After attempting one three-pointer, I attempted no more. I moved mid-range but my accuracy never improved. It's called a shooter's feel for a reason.

I was a *slofie*—a slow-motion selfie. I filed my performance under the letter M—mediocre. The game fell under the letter L—loss. It was a close loss, but a loss, nonetheless. There wasn't much room left in that particular folder to add more.

Losing became the norm. It was new to me. It infuriated me. It exasperated my teammates. I noticed the toll it was taking on them, on me. I was accustomed to winning, and the competitive edge inside me was crying out. As I sat in silence, a stream of tears streaked my face. I didn't stop them. It was a solid, ten-minute cry. I hoped for a turnaround. I carried it out of the locker room with me, along with my composure.

Alex and Eleni, my Greek parents, were waiting in the lobby. We were going to a postgame meal at Fridays. Any American meal was always a treat, but I was looking forward to the company even more.

Alex always made me smile, and Eleni always made me feel at home. Both filled me with love at every opportunity.

The last thing I needed was to be left alone with my thoughts, so at the meal's conclusion, I offered a suggestion.

As I looked at Eleni, I asked, "Do you think we can go for a walk?"

"I was thinking the same thing; the weather is not so bad."

We wandered along the sea near downtown. The scenery was fresh, and the water was healing. I inhaled the cool air and aroma from the sea and held it longer than normal while gazing into the mountains in the distance. I wanted to feel the beauty of Greece inside me for as long as possible.

No walk is official without coffee. I promise, as soon as I'm back in the States I'll find a 12-step program for my addiction. We sat and talked in the café overlooking the sea. About what, I can't recall. My thoughts were preoccupied.

It was amazing how close I had become with Eleni and Alex. I was part of their family, their adopted daughter. Nowhere in the contract I signed to play professional basketball in Greece did it say that I would be loved and supported the way I was. If it had, I would have signed for ten years, not just one.

My feelings of homesickness disappeared whenever I was with them. And it made perfect sense. Because of them, Thessaloniki felt like a second home. After all, home is not a place. It's a feeling.

I grew here out of love. I was living abroad for the first time, trading the known for the uncertain. It could have ended disastrously. I could have been another statistic, another American who failed in Greece. Instead, I was succeeding. On paper, the losses would have suggested otherwise. We don't succeed in life on paper though. I was succeeding with life itself. Alex and Eleni were two huge reasons why.

I can only imagine what my life and my experience would have been like if I hadn't had them beside me, easing my fears and erasing my homesickness. Actually, I can't. I can't imagine any life that doesn't include Alex and Eleni. I can't, and I won't. Not now. Not ever.

We left the café and continued our trek. It led us to a massive sculpture carved in stone.

I asked Eleni, "Is that Jesus in the center?"

"Yes, that is Jesus in the middle. To the right is Saint John, on the left is Mary, the Mother of Jesus, and on the bottom is Saint Michael."

I found it intriguing that Jesus, the saints, and Mary were as much a part of the Greek culture as they were in the Hispanic culture. I studied the carving closely as I did each time I explored the sculptures, churches, and pictures of my surroundings.

We left the ancient for the active, joining Alex's sister, brother-in-law, their children, and his parents at a tavern. I rode shotgun to either Alex or Eleni, so they could translate. It became second nature for them to tell me what was being said without me asking. It helped that my vocabulary was ever-improving.

Throughout dinner, I joined the conversation when I could, replying in Greek. Whenever that happened, the table burst out laughing. I wasn't paranoid, just confused.

"Is my accent really that bad?" I asked Eleni, a little embarrassed.

"No! We laugh because we don't expect you to speak Greek so well. Your accent is fine!"

Her words filled me with pride. She patted me on the back and said, "I'm proud of you, my child."

I didn't stay in the present. I couldn't. Here, surrounded by love and family, took me back home, to my mom and dad, to my sisters, to our sitting around the table at dinner. This time, there was no sadness. How could there be? I was loved there as I am at home.

Before the night ended, my heart wasn't the only thing full. My hands were as well. I became the newest object of fascination for Elias, Alex's four-year-old nephew.

Elias asked Alex if I was from another planet because my English sounded alien. He approached me with trepidation. I could relate. That was how I had broached the German airport worker. My attempts at Greek broke the ice, and eventually the relationship melted into a friendship.

Next time we played at Paok, I'd bring Elias. I needed all the warmth I could get.

Day 40

"Just be sure you have your camera."

Alex provided one clue for my Sunday adventure with him and Eleni.

I didn't seek additional details. I didn't need to. I knew today would be one of those days you couldn't fit inside a picture frame. Even with a camera by my side, our excursions were never about 3x5s, 5x7s, 8x10s. They were about moments and memories, about Alex and Eleni, about firsts and forevers.

Our first stop was in Pella, where the ruins of the palace of Alexander the Great remain. Alexander the Great, the King of Macedonia and conqueror of the Persian Empire, is considered one of the greatest military geniuses of all time. He was born in 356 BC in Pella, the ancient capital of Macedonia. We tried to see the palace, but it was closed to the public. No reason was listed.

We tried to loop around the back of the palace on a dirt road to see if we could get a better look. The Indiana Jones in me looked for hidden accesses that led us to the ruins. The back road was a dead end. Only in the movies, I guess. Our last resort was the museum, which contained a building's worth of artifacts and pictures of what the palace used to look like. To our disappointment, the museum was also closed for construction.

Alex muttered disdain under his breath. At least, that's what it sounded like. I could tell they really wanted me to see it. They were right. I did want to walk through time and history.

"Well, if we can't see those old rocks, let's go to see different old rocks."

I didn't understand what Alex meant. He spoke to Eleni in Greek, which added to my confusion. I was content to follow like a puppy that didn't know any better. Well, for a while.

"Where are we going?" I finally asked.

"To the place that used to be considered the marketplace of the palace," Eleni answered. "There are more ruins just a little ways away."

I was back in Indiana Jones mode. In the distance, I could see large beams that I imagined held some type of structure a long time ago. We approached the ancient marketplace, and I noticed the stone floors were still intact. The texture and patterns of the stone created centuries ago fascinated me. It was as if each small stone was sized perfectly and then meticulously placed onto the ground to create a pattern.

I was amazed to see that they were still in such great shape after all those years of being exposed to the elements. We walked around the ruins, and I couldn't help but think that this was the place where Alexander the Great lived. I was convinced he stood where I was standing. I wondered who else had stood there during the previous centuries. I felt the enormity of it all. Most get their history from books. I was standing in it.

I looked at these ruins through a camera lens and through my eyes. I thought of other cameras, the ones found in Hollywood, and pondered the accuracy of the movies that depicted the way of life in Greece and Macedonia. As I ventured on, I imagined how the people had really dressed and what the market would have looked like in its zenith.

I pictured people in different colored robes with ropes tied around their waists, like the actors wore in the movie *Troy*. I saw them wearing sandals that wrapped around their ankles and crisscrossed all the way up to their mid-calves. I watched the marketplace full of hustle and bustle, the women carrying baskets of goods on their hips as they shopped, the salesmen barking and hawking their wares. My imagination has a mind of its own. At this moment, it was in ancient Greece.

I could have stayed longer, but we had places to go and more beauty to see. It wasn't long before we reached the waterfalls of Edessa. The city and falls were in the mountains. Each could be seen clearly from the valley. Their attraction to tourists was obvious. Souvenir shops lined the way. In addition to the falls, Edessa is famous throughout Greece for its cherries.

The waterfalls were a once-in-a-lifetime moment. The thunderous rush of water running over the edge of the cliff and the water traveling down with such force hitting the standing water at the bottom was nature at its most powerful. And for me, its most relaxing. If not for the chill of the breeze, I could have stood there for hours, watching and listening to the magnificent majesty of the waterfall.

Our map had one more circle on it—Florina. Andriana, one of my teammates, met us there. She didn't have to drive far. It's her hometown. We accompanied her to her parents' house for lunch.

Her parents had a beautiful house up in the mountains. The peaks were covered in snow and even though I couldn't see the water, I heard a small stream running through the foothills. I could only imagine how beautiful it must be up in those mountains during the summer although the snow had a captivating and unique beauty all of its own.

We got a tour of the house, which was traditional, a tad old-fashioned yet filled with love. Andriana said her father preferred to keep the house traditional. The floors and stairs were made of wood, and from the smell, I could tell it was real, not the plastic stuff we had become accustomed to back in the States. The house was three stories high, the wooden staircase changing direction with each floor.

In the first-floor living room, an old-fashioned phone drew my immediate attention. But it worked with the room's furniture that faced the windows with the mountainside view. The phone was made of wood. It featured a rotary dial, the kind where you placed your finger inside the hole that corresponded with the number you wanted, rotated it clockwise, and waited for it to return before you went to the next number. No one born after 1990 will have a clue as to what I just described. My mom had an antique phone similar to it, which was the only reason I recognized it.

The bedrooms, kept immaculate, comprised the second level. Standing inside felt like I was in a different era. The furniture had been built to last. The hardwood floors smelled of authenticity, even more so by the rooms' cold draft. Time had been kind, and forgetful, to these rooms. And I wouldn't have changed a thing.

The top level had been modernized. It was the home of a ping pong table, which sat atop a rug that covered the floor. It defined a different kind of cozy. We played ping pong for a few minutes before lunch.

"I think you need to stick to basketball," Eleni said.

The call to lunch ended the laughter and my embarrassing ping pong skills.

As the table spoke in Greek, I drifted into my own thoughts. It happened a lot. I tried to follow for as long as I could. But soon I was off in my own dream world. Hearing English snapped me back into reality, and I happily joined the conversation.

We couldn't stay past lunch. Alex said we needed to get going back to Thessaloniki. As we walked to the car, I noticed a small stone structure in the back yard. I asked if I could take a look. The family gestured that it was okay.

The stone structure had an altar inside with icons, or images of the saints and Jesus. The Hispanic culture refers to them as *retablos*. A lot of the saints, Mary, mother of Jesus, and Jesus, were all present in the family-made chapel. The images were almost an exact replica of what I was used to seeing back home. Although, the features differed in each.

We expressed our gratitude, said our goodbyes and drove to the downtown area of Florina for coffee. Eleni ordered me Greek coffee. The serving was a lot smaller than a regular coffee because it was so strong in taste. I wasn't familiar with that kind of coffee, which resembled a shot of expresso.

"The coffee is healthier and easier on the stomach than the frappe that you are used to drinking," Eleni said.

The smell was overpowering.

"Even if it is healthier and easier on my stomach, with the way it smells I am not so sure I want to drink this," I said.

Eleni and Alex laughed at my hesitation.

"When have you ever turned anything down to try?" Alex asked.

He was right. I hadn't. I shrugged my shoulders, took a deep breath and took a small sip of the coffee. I felt like I was in England, drinking tea because of how small the cup was. Once I tasted it, I could understand why the cup was so small. I was only able to take small sips at a time due to the strong flavor that overwhelmed my taste buds. When I finished, there was a creamy residue at the bottom of the cup where the coffee grains had settled.

"This type of coffee is supposed to tell your fortune," Eleni said. "The older generations used to do this quite often. Our grandparents were rather skilled at reading a fortune from the coffee cups."

I emptied the remaining contents of the creamy remains and placed my cup upside down for it to dry as Eleni instructed.

"Once the coffee dries in the cup, it is then that you can have your fortune read based on the shapes left on the inside," Eleni explained.

Neither Alex nor Eleni had the ability to read fortunes. Wait. So, that's it? No coffee fortune for me? I don't think so. This is not where this story is going to end. One day I will find someone who can tell my fortune from the Greek coffee cup.

That fortune still exists.

It's pictured, but not framed.

In 3x5.

Day 41

*The morning call was as unexpected
as the message was cryptic.*

"Get ready, we have another excursion planned. Dress warm and get your camera ready!"

After giving the team the day off, Alex gave me the minimum about what was to come. But I did as instructed through piqued curiosity. Alex and Eleni were at my apartment within an hour. The last thing I grabbed on my way out the door was my small digital camera. I jumped into the car.

"*Geia sou*! Where are we going today?"

I wasted no time in starting the playful interrogation that would get me nowhere. Alex, always wanting experiences to be surprises, stayed wrapped tight in his secrets.

"You will see soon enough."

That's all he said, which filled me with one part excitement, two parts exasperation. I was never one for surprises. Tell me now, not later. It was a lesson in patience, and I didn't even realize I had signed up for the class.

Eleni also came with a surprise—made to-go frappes. She handed me a Styrofoam cup with the iced coffee inside. Now this is kind of surprise I don't mind. Unexpected, delicious, and most important, I didn't have to wait to enjoy it.

My inquisitiveness could wait. I sat back, sipped my coffee, and sang along to Greek music. My voice was only audible to me. Or so I thought. My singing caught Eleni's attention. She turned around and looked at me.

"Do you know what you are singing?"

I laughed.

"Not the slightest idea, but hearing the songs over and over helps me to identify some words. Some I know, some I have no idea what I am saying."

Suddenly, I was enrolled in Greek 101. Eleni and Alex translated the lyrics so I could have a better understanding in identifying words. By the end of the ride I was ready for Greek 201.

I recognized more than lyrics.

"This road looks familiar."

We were midway through our drive, heading into the mountains. My observation made Eleni smile.

"Yes, it should. Where we are going we have been before."

I studied the scenery in silence. Clues passed by my eyes for the next fifteen minutes before I proclaimed my findings, formed in a question.

"Are we going to Drama?"

I knew I was right by their laughter and Eleni's confirmation, formed in a question.

"We can't get anything past you, can we?"

I don't know which excited me more, my discovery or our destination. Drama was our first excursion after I arrived in Greece. The memories were as fresh as yesterday. There was the old military fort, the one completely in the dark that required flashlights to traverse. There was the hot tub at the resort where we had soaked in serenity. The scenery through the mountains was as we left it—spectacular.

As we drove the winding roads, I could see the village of Drama in the distance. This time covered in snow. The red roofs through the village stood in stark contrast against the white-covered ground. I wondered how many other places a person could be sandwiched between sea and mountains. And the best part was living in Thessaloniki where we didn't have to travel very far to enjoy one, the other, or both.

We arrived at the Aloni Hotel resort on time—lunch time, to be precise. I ordered fried calamari, my new favorite. After, we sat in the lobby by the fireplace, drinking hot chocolate and engulfed in conversation. One of the resort's owners, who is also a friend of Alex's, joined. She didn't speak English, so the conversation ping ponged from Greek to English and back to Greek.

You want Heaven on Earth? This was it. A snow-covered mountain town. A roaring fire. Hot chocolate. Family. I was Alice in wonderland on an adventure I hoped would never end.

I didn't grow much on the drive back. My inner-child wouldn't let me. There would be plenty of time to return to being serious, to responsibility, and to adulthood.

But not here.

And not now.

This was all about innocence and imagination, about mischief and magic, about all things we either lose or bury deep once we become grown. You know what I find funny? When people say, "Stop acting like a child."

Are they saying stop having fun in life?

Are they saying stop looking at the world with wide-eyed wonder?

Aren't children the best part of humanity?

One of the most beautiful things in the world is listening to a child's unbridled laughter.

It's how all of us used to laugh and how all of us secretly wish to laugh again.

It's how I laugh every time Alex calls and I hear the word "excursion."

Day 42

A new morning, another phone call.

Only this time, it wasn't Alex.

It was Thomas.

My agent, as well as my friend, invited me to coffee. He took me to a café that featured a breathtaking view overlooking the sea. In the distance was Mount Olympus, the highest mountain in Greece. He didn't call to talk about scenery.

It was the basketball teeter-totter I rode. I've never experienced the ups and downs of a season like I have here. Sure, there were factors. You want the list? Okay, here it goes. There was living in a foreign country thousands of miles away from home and bouts of homesickness. There was the communication barrier and the stretches of loneliness. There were the high expectations placed on myself to perform and the different style of play. There was the losing, so much losing.

If that's not enough, I could list more.

"I know my confidence has been a bit of a roller coaster, but I feel like I am finding myself as a person and understanding more of my mindset that relates to performing at my best on the court."

If Thomas had doubts, he didn't express them. He understood that I knew I needed to grow mentally, which seemed to be my greatest struggle. He ended our silence.

"You know, Vera, at times you are very tough." He tapped his head around his temple, signifying mental toughness. "And other times, you are nowhere to be found. I tell you why you have been able to remain in this league for so long, and it is not because of your physical capabilities."

He paused to take a sip of coffee. Our eyes locked as I waited for him to continue.

"You have stayed in this league because of your toughness, Vera." Again, he pointed to his temple. "Your skill is what got you here. Your toughness is what has kept you here."

His words triggered an explosion inside me and what flashed before my eyes were the hours spent working on my mental game. Someone was watching, someone had noticed. Actually, it was more than just one.

"Wow, I guess you're right."

I was bewildered by that revelation. I questioned my physical abilities in comparison to the other athletes who were in the league, but I never compared myself to the mental performance side. Now that someone pointed it out, I believed I was ahead of the curve in that aspect of the game. I understood the importance of mental training, but I never understood that's what set me apart from other players.

I needed to sit down and think about this, except I was already sitting down. I knew Thomas needed to go. I knew I needed to stay.

"I will stay here at the café to think about our conversation a bit. I will catch the bus back home. Thank you for challenging the way I see myself."

That moment was a huge discovery for my performance, my confidence, and my mindset. I didn't know where to begin the dissection of it all. I walked my path, yet far too often I was distracted by the paths of others, wondering if theirs were the ones I should be on. I recognized the uniqueness of my path, but I didn't fully appreciate it.

Some waste lifetimes wishing they could live others' lives. I wanted no part of the some. A friend told me two things that only now began to make sense. The first was, "Be you, everyone else is already taken." The second was, "An original is much more valuable than a copy."

I am original. My path is once-in-a-lifetime. As long as I stayed mindful of that, I would continue to grow without shame or guilt of not being further along according to my own judgements.

That is the path I wanted to walk. That is not the path I was currently on. There were times I felt guilty that my journey was too good for me and that I wasn't worthy. That I didn't belong, that I expected next to nothing from myself.

I was a high school state champion in the high jump. I never set the bar low. Yet some days, my standard was no higher than a sidewalk curb. It's impossible to rise to low expectations. If I didn't believe in myself, how could I ask or expect anyone to believe in me?

Everything begins, everything ends in the same place—the mind. Give something power and that something has power over you when you allow it to. I needed to expect great things from myself before I could achieve them. I needed a new way to think. I needed to be my own voice, not someone else's echo.

The times I lost sight of who I am were the times I became what someone else wanted me to be or what someone else perceived me to be. Whichever it was, I was no longer me.

I held myself back. I climbed into the cage, closed the door behind me, tossed the key out of my reach. I sacrificed the gifts I had been given.

As long as I continued that, I would remain where I was, locked with one foot in confidence, one foot in doubt, unable to move in either direction.

While I sat alone with my thoughts and the reflections they produced, I sensed whispers descending from "My Guy." The calling neither decided my fate, nor determined my destiny. But it clarified one thing.

I am unique.

And I will use it to my advantage.

Day 45

Here I am, on center stage,
under the bright lights, all eyes on me.

And I have one thought. I need to . . .
Sorry, I pushed the fast forward button by mistake. Let me rewind.
Here I am, on center court, under the lights of Aris gym, all eyes on
me after I either scored on offense or rebounded on defense. And I have
one thought. I need to stay in the moment.

I'd been on Aris' turf before to watch its men's team play. I had seen
the court from the stands. Now, during pre-game warm-ups, I was looking
up, not down. The gym seemed larger from floor level. Thankfully, it was
warmer than Paok. Even a week later, the memory of that gym left me
shivering.

Prior to tip-off, I quieted my mind and visualized on all possible
scenarios. My mental approach worked. I played one of my best games
as a professional athlete. Our team also never looked better. My stat line
was decent with eighteen points and ten rebounds. What you won't find
in black and white was that I didn't allow fears of making mistakes, and
actual mistakes, to intimidate me or to disrupt my game.

Even in defeat, we could not have done more as a team. I'm certain
of that. I was drained—mentally and physically. The walk to the parking
lot was painful.

"Emai ptoma ta exo paixei."

Instantly, my teammates and others who surrounded me laughed at
my statement. It was a Greek phrase Eleni taught me. Loosely translated,
it meant: "I am so dead I cannot go on." Okay, so I was being a Drama
Queen. I also didn't mind my teammates' laugher. I think they appreciated
my attempts at learning their language.

I could have rested and recovered until morning. But I had plans with
Alex and Eleni. They invited me and their friends to a tavern in the hills
outside the city. The neighborhood and tavern were new to me. We met
the rest of the group outside. I realized I was the youngest of the group by
seven, maybe ten years.

We found a table right in front of the stage. In hindsight, we should
have found a different table. As the night went on, the tavern became

packed and the music grew louder. The live music made it almost impossible to carry a conversation.

The all-male trio was one singer, two guitarists. The guitars were smaller than those I'd seen in the States, and the base of each was more oval. I never asked, only assumed they were traditional.

If I had extended my arm, I would have touched the musicians. Proximity wasn't my ally. In between songs, the singer pulled me from my chair and had me stand next to him while he serenaded me with his romantic love song. I had no idea what words were being sung to me.

You've already read what happened next. At least, the start. Here is the rest of the moment. On center stage, under the bright lights, I became flushed with embarrassment. I needed to find an exit strategy—and quickly. But I couldn't.

He continued to sing and I just stood there, not knowing what to do or where to look. My discomfort became obvious, and the singer motioned for me to dance.

Huh?

I stood there in terror. I had no idea how to dance to Greek music. The blood rushed to my face, the heat intensified inside me. I could only imagine how red my face was. I looked at Eleni, who waved her arms up in the air in a circular motion rotating her wrists. She was trying to show me what to do. If this had been rock-n-roll, I would have hidden under the rock. Instead, I rolled with the punches as best I could.

I continued to watch Eleni. What she did, I did. The mimicry heightened my feelings of awkwardness, and I blushed more than I danced. Well, that's how it felt. I'm not sure how it looked. Thankfully, there is no video. Once the song ended, the singer gave me a side hug and thanked me.

Because our table was within feet of the stage, I was seated inside a heartbeat. Applause accompanied my return. There were other emotions—and motions—as well. Eleni's face was streaked with tears from uncontrollable laughter. Alex recreated my dancing. I shook my head and laughed.

"You did great for your first Greek dance!"

I believe that was Eleni's first—and only—lie she ever told to me.

"I don't know about that, but I will pass with dancing on stage for a while."

Eleni sensed my shyness. She patted me on the back but continued to laugh. I couldn't blame her. Alex gave me a thumbs up.

Let's see. Lionel Ritchie danced on the ceiling and Billy Idol danced with himself. This night, people danced on tables. And in every available open space. I stayed seated. I really didn't need—or want—all eyes on me.

This memory wasn't going to leave me for a long, long time.
Most likely, never.

---⊙---

Day 46

---⊙---

Typical found me at my favorite café,
holding my frappe of choice.

I followed one simple pleasure with a second—lunch at Eleni's. She cooked her version of stir fry, a combination of rice, peppers, shrimp, and deliciousness. I've been grateful for home-cooked meals and spoiled by them, too.

We decided to watch the club's younger girls play a home game. On our walk to the gym, we stopped for ice cream. It had been quite a while since my last scoop. After first taste, I vowed it would not happen again.

I had the option of returning with Eleni to her and Alex's apartment, but I couldn't pass up this cloudless, windless, warm day. Not with tomorrow's forecast predicting the start of a week of rain and gloom.

I walked to the beach, nested in the sand. The sun and sea were hypnotic. I watched as waves stroked the shore with the gentleness of a mother caressing a child. The sea smelled of fish and forgotten memories of my family's fishing trips to the rivers and lakes near our home.

In that moment, time ceased. Only clarity and quiet existed. I discovered utopia in my backyard. It didn't stop there. I pictured my family sitting beside me in constant awe with the beauty of this place. There are no seas in New Mexico. There are some rivers and lakes, but nothing close to this magnitude and magnificence. One day I would bring them here, so they could make their own memories and live their own moments, instead of me telling them about mine.

What follows are the words I wrote that day, in the sand, under the sun, with a view created by God.

As I let my thoughts go freely I think of where God has taken me, all of the blessings he has given, and is still continuing to give as I take in this breath right now, looking into the sea. I take a step back and look at my life through another's eyes. How a small-town girl made it to Greece to pursue her dream in playing professional basketball.

My memories of a kid flashed before my eyes like a movie scene while I gazed into the distance. The countless hours shooting in my driveway—day or night, hot or cold. The times I would have to bribe my younger sister, Sarah, to rebound for me, even though she would never live up to her part of the deal. The intense games of "21" I would play with my cousin Val, which would sometimes get a little rough only to end up in arguments because of our competitive nature. Flash forward to middle school when the "Fab 5" couldn't be separated and our adventures on and off the court would always be cherished. The first time I watched the movie *Love & Basketball*, which was when my dream of playing as a professional really took off.

As I sat there with the sand running through my fingers, memories flew before me like the time the "Fab 5" thought it was a good idea to put Icy Hot on our feet prior to our game because we were so cold. By halftime, we were fighting each other for access to the sinks to rinse off our feet from the excruciating heat of the ointment. Most importantly, one of my dearest memories is when my parents used to coach all of us during those years. The little brat I used to be with them, and yes, guilty to say I even had an attitude problem at that age. My parents were the ones who taught us the fundamentals of the game and instilled the character and values within me that I hold true to this day. Without their foundation, there is no way I would be where I am right now, and that isn't just their effect on the basketball court!

The glorious high school days. The countless hours spent in the gym after practice getting extra shots up and not leaving the gym until I got my ten free throws in a row. My memories of winning two District Championships, which were both thrillers. I still remember the rush I felt after those games, one of which was attended by my future college assistant coach. The reporters I knew at the time would soon become friends, who I am proud to say still keep in touch to this day. The bus trips with my teammates and how much closer our relationships developed over the years. I thought about how much basketball did for all of us at that time, how much we all loved the game.

Then of course my college days. The initial shock I went through being away from home for the first time, how much of a change college ball was for me compared to high school basketball. The intensity of the program I had gone into, so rich in culture and discipline. The hard work we all exerted to become the best we could be with Coach Kruger pushing and challenging us every step of the way.

The thrill of making it to the National Tournament two years in a row—a first in program history. Continuing to break records in making it to the Regional Championship and Sweet Sixteen my senior year. Thinking back to all the records I broke as well. It's amazing to see where we left the program in comparison to where it was when I first went in as a freshman, and that is something I will always be proud of.

I thought of all the sweat and tears I left at that place and some of the great people I have come to know. It still intrigues me to think how I ended up at Adams State over all the other schools and programs that I could have picked from. Everything I went through, the challenges, the adversity, the camaraderie, the leadership, and all the special moments that shaped me into the person I am now.

It seems like only yesterday I was playing in the Regional Championship as I played my last game as a Grizzly. Yet, here I was still playing the game I love in one of the most beautiful places on earth. Words could not describe how blessed I was to have been given this opportunity, to know how much God loves me. I can only imagine what the future held. I have had my times of doubts throughout my journey. Times I felt like a failure, times I felt like I wasn't good enough, times when I felt like it was time to throw in the towel. Amidst it all, there was always that little spark within me that told me to keep fighting. Keep going because it would pay off in the end. Perseverance under the guidance of God can prove to be a miracle in itself. I just had to keep my faith.

One thing I felt within myself that day sitting on the beach was that I am a success in the eyes of God. That is all that really matters after all.

Day 58

It lacked the longevity of the Trans-Siberian and the intrigue of the Orient Express, but I eagerly anticipated my first train trip in Greece.

We were heading to Athens to play FEA. It was our final road trip of the regular season. Instead of chartering a bus as we had on our previous trips, we boarded the public train.

It took six hours to reach Athens. For the first five, I helped a few teammates with their English lessons. For the final hour, they taught me Greek words and phrases. I liked when we worked together, as teammates, and as friends. Sadly, that togetherness unexpectedly imploded.

To this day I don't know how or why it happened. All I know is the feeling I was left with on the basketball court wasn't a good one.

It wasn't just the loss. It was the bizarre way in which we lost. Even as I replayed the game in my mind, it was hard to accurately describe the events that unfolded. But I'll try.

Our team got into foul trouble. And when I say team, I mean just about every player in uniform. Every player except two—another teammate and I—fouled out.

When the fourth quarter started, it was two against five. Then it was one against five, with me being the one. I fought with all my heart. There was one final whistle, one final foul—on me. When I fouled out, the game was called.

Our locker room was full of confusion and contention. No one stayed silent. I felt lost, but not defeated. I played as I was taught—to the final whistle. It was unlike anything I had ever experienced. Some teammates told me not to worry, what happened, happened. I knew I had done my best. My character remained intact and I could live with that.

Since the game ended with our entire team fouling out, there were no stats listed for either team. The official record book shows the final score, 20-0. That number doesn't acknowledge the actual score of the game. I believe it was a way to represent how the game ended. For what it's worth, I finished with 20-plus points.

With everything that had just happened, I figured we would head straight to the train. I figured incorrectly. Margarita, the general manager of the club, surprised us with a detour downtown to see more of Athens and to get a better view of the Acropolis. Naturally, none of this was new to my teammates. I was told she was doing this especially for me before we headed back to Thessaloniki. This act of kindness will stay with me forever.

Margarita had made arrangements for the team to have lunch downtown with a view of the Acropolis. Since we didn't have our usual charter bus, we depended on public transportation. That meant taking the underground metro downtown. When we resurfaced, I was amazed by the mass—and maze—of humanity on the sidewalks and in the street crossings. Tour busses tricked-out into convertibles passed through the streets, with arms and cameras dangling off the top.

We maneuvered through the crowds to get a glimpse of the Acropolis. Due to time, we wouldn't be able to see it up close. Margarita gestured for the group to follow her.

"Margarita says that she has the perfect spot for you to see the Acropolis from a distance so you can still get a good view," Stella informed me.

I gave Margarita a thumbs-up. We managed to stay together. As we walked toward our destination, there was a gap in the tall buildings that allowed me to get a glimpse of the ancient and historic site.

"Wow!"

I had just voiced the final "w" when Spyridoula bumped into me.

"*Pame*, Vera."

In other words, "Let's go."

We followed Margarita to the city's center. Imagine taking a huge marketplace, mixing in an outlet mall, and intertwining both with vendors selling knick-knacks, souvenirs, fruit, goods, leather, and just about anything else you had on a shopping list. Then add live entertainment, where people gathered to watch the individual and group performances. I was captivated by one of those little shows with dancers to the point where I was getting left behind. And I would have had Vassiliki not turned back and grabbed my arm.

"Vera, you must keep up with the group. Don't get lost."

We walked to an opening at the edge of the center where the crowds thinned. There it was—the Acropolis. Off in the distance but still close enough that I could study the architecture of the building and marvel at the sight before me. It's not one of the seven wonders of the world, but it should be. A teammate noticed my fascination.

"Acropolis can be translated as the highest point of the city or even high city. Our ancestors used to build their important temples high up to where the people of the city could retreat in case of an attack."

I continued to learn with my eyes and she continued to teach with her words.

"The Parthenon is very famous with the archaeology and brings many tourists to Greece every year."

I was not up to speed with my Greek history. I acknowledged my confusion in a question.

"What is the difference between the Acropolis and the Parthenon?"

"The Acropolis is the high city or the high hill where the Parthenon is built. The Acropolis is the hill and the Parthenon is that structure that you can see. The Parthenon is just one of the buildings of the Acropolis, it is a part of it."

Her history lesson breathed life into the past and brought more questions from me.

"So is this where the ancient Greeks used to worship Zeus and all of those guys?"

"Yes, I guess something like that. The Parthenon was built as a temple to Athena, who is the patron of Athens. She was also the goddess of wisdom and war."

Greek gods and goddesses. All of a sudden, I found myself having an immediate curiosity to learn more about the Greek gods.

I stood there trying to memorize each and every detail as thoughts of Greek gods and goddesses consumed my thoughts. From a distance, the long and slender marble pillars looked a couple stories high. They were damaged and the tops were jagged, but in my mind, I saw them in their prime.

I couldn't take my eyes off the Parthenon until it was time for us to go. We had a lunch reservation we needed to keep. I would have skipped lunch and stayed, but it wasn't my decision to make.

One day, I would return. That was a promise I made to myself before I turned and joined the others. And the next time I would get as close as humanly possible.

The train ride back to Thessaloniki felt longer. I knew why, but didn't say. Still, it was written on my face. Konstantinos spoke and laughed at me as we got off the train. A teammate provided the translation.

"You were so excited when you first got on the train and by the time we got to Thessaloniki you had had enough!"

The statement hit the target. But missed the bullseye.

I was still confused about the ride I had been on.

But it had nothing to do with the train.

---◉---

Day 60-61

---◉---

I consider myself a fair-weather girl with a United Nations disposition.

In other words, I welcome sun and strangers into my world every chance I get.

The sun arrived first and stayed for a week. I relocated to the beach and sea during the daylight when I wasn't wandering through unexplored neighborhoods. I walked deeper into the stretch of Krini. I continued toward the marina and through the sandy shore.

I had the beach to myself during the weekdays, with the exception of a few elderly men, who sat and drank their coffee on benches. A few people swam in the sea for exercise. When I wasn't walking, I was reading. Or trying to read. I found the ducks and seagulls more interesting when they swam in front of me.

I studied the birds' every detail and was intrigued by the sounds they made as they moved their bodies through the water. I was a bit sad when their interest in me waned, and they swam away in silence. Then I remembered the book I was holding and opened it again. I could have stayed there until the sun went down on that first day, but it started to get chilly and I decided it was time to head back to my apartment.

The following day, I laid out soaking in the sun. One of the swimmers exited the sea in front of me. We made eye contact and he said hello in Greek. The words that followed were too fast and too complex for my comprehension.

"*Kalispera*," I replied, saying "good afternoon" in my Americanized/ Hispanic accent.

"*Pos seh Leni?*"

He asked my name.

"My name is Vera. I play basketball for Apollon Kalamarias. *Emai Americana.*"

I told him I was American. He told me he spoke and understood English. That was good because while I was UN in disposition, I was not UN in translation. We talked for a while, mostly about basketball. Before long, he was on his way, leaving me with my sun.

I can't trace its origin, but I've always loved conversations with random people, even passing strangers. Just being able to talk to someone and about something out of the ordinary was something I craved, almost more than ice cream. A stranger can reveal a topic that sets your mind racing or gives you an outward mindset of thinking. I've always made eye contact and said good morning or hello to everyone who crosses my path.

Even here.

When the occasional person responded with a question I didn't understand, a question I had no idea how to answer, I did what came naturally.

I smiled with the warmth of a sun.

Day 62

Eleni needed to run errands downtown.

I tagged along until my inner Dora, the Explorer, got the best of me. When Eleni went one way to take care of her business, I took off in another direction in search of who knows what.

The *what* turned out to be a church. Inside, I passed a fountain. On a pillar next to it hung a sign.

"Holy Water."

The man who entered before me grabbed a cup, filled it with water and took a drink. He then placed the cup on top of the cross in the middle of the fountain and walked away.

Had the cup been there before?

Is this the tradition everyone follows?

Or was this man just thirsty?

To drink or not to drink? That was the question I asked myself. My soul provided the answer. I slowly dipped my fingers into the holy water and blessed myself with the sign of the cross.

I studied the gazebo-shaped arch that draped the fountain. Painted on the ceiling of the arch was an incredible picture depicting Mary, the Mother of Jesus, baby Jesus, and saints. I believed one was Saint Michael. I couldn't identify the others. Mary had Jesus sitting in her lap. Both looked to be reposing in a metal tub. Three pipes extended from the tub's front with water flowing from each. The water poured into a pool shaped as a cross. People stood and kneeled outside the pool. Two held potted goblets. One, a woman, stood with a goblet in her hand over a man, who was kneeling, waiting for a blessing from the holy water.

Dora, the Explorer's wait ended as well.

Eleni poked her head into the church and gestured with her hand for me to follow. We walked downtown for a while until we came across a nice café next to the sea. My next breath was not of the sea, but of me and my dad and of all our fishing memories together.

Eleni and I ordered our usual frappes. I immediately reenacted the man drinking the holy water. She answered before I asked. Well, after her laugher.

"I think the man may have been a little crazy. That is not something that we do."

I drank my frappe, knowing my intuition saved me from embarrassment.

We stopped for lunch at *Saltsa Bar*. The menu was written in Greek. I believed I had the ability to read Greek at a second-grade level. I could sound out the letters in order to pronounce the word. But what I read I couldn't translate. Eleni was my savior, translating the menu.

I was no longer in an exploring mood.

I ordered a club sandwich.

Day 64

I don't know what an angel looks like.

I've never met one. Well, never anyone who actually introduced themselves as an angel. Maybe they're just like everyone else when it comes to appearances. Maybe they have eyes that hold decades of wisdom, eyes so memorizing that you must look away from time to time. Maybe they are tanned, with silvery hair, and white scruff that looks maybe three days old. Maybe they are kind with a gentle presence.

Maybe they go by the name Evangelos.

I met Evangelos several days before at the beach. Our conversation was brief. And pleasant. Our paths crossed for the second time today. I was at the beach, taking advantage of the game-free weekend. He was at the beach, swimming in the sea. It's how he exercised.

We remembered each other on sight. This time, neither of us had some place to go. So we sat. We talked. Evangelos was a dentist. His practice was in Serbia. He commuted. He spoke Serbian and Greek fluently. His English was a work in progress. I struggled with some of his words, some of his phrases. But I made all the pieces fit.

He said life was difficult because of the financial crises in Greece. He was thankful for the job he had in Serbia. Without it, making ends meet would be a lot harder. He spoke with wisdom learned from life, not books.

Now, it was my turn.

Evangelos came prepared. He unfolded a paper full of questions. It was done for my benefit. I am certain. We struggled the first time we spoke. I couldn't answer his questions because I had trouble understanding them. It wasn't his fault. His English was superior to my Greek. Still is. I was sure he used Google translate. I admired him for it.

At first, I felt like I was being interviewed. I even joked about it. His laughter showed he got the meaning.

"What is your surname?"

"Bustos."

His face illuminated his eyes.

"Ah, I read about you in the newspaper."

It wasn't press clippings that impressed him. It was our first meeting. He said I had a "pure" soul and heart. He described the ways I had found the joys in life and learned how to live stress-free at such a young age.

He could tell that from my energy. The rest of the adjectives were written down.

"Calm, sensitive, kind, and a good appearance."

He spoke each word slowly, accurately. The words were his first impression of me.

"I was sent by a Guardian Angel."

I believed him. I also needed clarity.

Was he sent by a Guardian Angel, or was he my Guardian Angel? I asked him to go deeper. He wasn't sure what I wanted to hear or how to explain it.

"I'm not crazy. Believe me."

I believed him.

I also helped build the bridge that eventually connected us, adding one of my own pieces for every two of his. The completed puzzle was this: God had sent him to have a conversation with me. He told me again that I had a pure heart and that money can't buy joy or happiness.

The next sequence was all Evangelos. I remember it verbatim.

"Many people who do what you do get destroyed because they can no longer find the joys in life. They are too busy focusing on money or chasing their version of success. I have money, but that is not why I am happy. I am happy because I am stress-free, and I enjoy life. I choose to see myself as a success because of the impact I have on others surrounding me. Because I choose not to be buried in non-impactful work. You have a pure soul. Don't become like others and destroy it. Always remember to enjoy life and remember to always be happy."

I choked up to the point of tears. I thanked him for sharing his words, his time. Before we parted, he told me he really enjoyed my company. He also said I was the kindest person he *ever* met. He emphasized the word *ever*.

What just happened? How was it that I could understand so clearly the message he had for me? I was touched in my soul. Had I been touched by an angel? Even after an hour spent in reflection, I didn't have an answer.

I still don't know what an angel looks like.

If Evangelos wasn't an angel, then exactly who did God just send to have a conversation with me?

And did I really need an answer?

Day 65

Breaking up is hard to do.

Just ask England about July 4. Or you could ask Turkey about March 25. Then again, maybe you shouldn't. After all, both were the jilted parties. To make matters worse, the countries that got away continue to celebrate their independence annually.

On this day I can say I've been around for twenty-two Fourth of July celebrations, the ones that take place in the United States of America. Today will be my first time commemorating March 25. The day is a national holiday in Greece, one of two set aside to mark its independence from Turkey. The other is in October. Two days celebrating one break up? Talk about not wanting anyone to forget. *Yikes!*

The 4th is best-known for fireworks. I spent the day learning the cultural traditions of the 25th. Long before it ended, I found a common thread that stitched the two together—family.

I was all eyes, all smiles at the parade. So much so that Alex noticed my child-like giddiness.

"Do you want a balloon?"

I rolled my eyes at him and moved to Eleni's side. Alex couldn't stop laughing at his own joke. I admit, it was kind of funny. And partly true. I would not have objected to a balloon. His humor did more than just make me laugh. He reminded me of my father. Both have similar senses of humor. It's one of the special reasons why I enjoyed being around him.

The parade was intimate. Mostly, it was students, marching either in bands or in school uniforms. Others took to the streets in traditional Greek clothing, a 120-box of Crayola Crayons come to life. The beauty was in the simplicity of it all. It was the second reminder of home.

In Las Vegas, the one in New Mexico and not in Nevada, the 4th is celebrated with *Fiestas*. The town basically turns into one big party over the holiday. Most people who moved away always returned to this day on that particular weekend.

My Auntie Edye lives by the plaza, where the *Fiesta* is held. She's hosted a party for as long as I can remember. Family and friends gather, catching up on life and with each other. That isn't all. The most favorable part is the traditional New Mexican food of *menudo, chicos, posole, enchiladas . . . y todo*. Before it gets dark, we drive to the golf course, pull out lawn chairs and enjoy the firework show.

There were no fireworks this time. But there was food, and most important, family.

After the parade, we drove to Alex's parents' house. It's tradition to fry fish on the 25th. The talented culinary hands of Alex's mother are keeping that tradition alive and well. And, she didn't mind me calling her *yiayia* (grandma).

We ate on the balcony of the apartment, which provided yet another amazing view of the city and the sea. In the distance, I could see the houses that made up the city. They stretched to the edges of the mountainside. When I turned and faced the sea, cargo ships floated lazily. Beyond the mountains, a veil of fog colored the scenery in a translucent shade.

The meal ended with—you guessed it—ice cream. I found a seat on the steps of the balcony. Alex's niece and nephew joined me. It seems they were no longer afraid of this foreign-speaking alien. Their warmth contrasted with the cool ice cream. Their acceptance confirmed that I was the latest family addition.

Once again, a home had opened its door to me. Once more, arms and hearts embraced me. I was born into one incredible family, I was welcomed into another amazing one.

I was twice blessed.

I also was torn.

My time left in Greece was twenty-eight days. I had less than a month to do the impossible. I needed to find a way to have two hearts.

One to take with me.

One to stay here.

---⊙---

Day 84

---⊙---

*I attended a funeral of a man I'd never met face to face,
a man I'd known all my life.*

He's a man I'd prayed to, and a man I'd prayed for. His wisdom is my inspiration, His sacrifice is my blessing. I follow His path but never in His footprints. He never asked anyone to be Him, just be like Him. I can't miss Him, because He's always with me. And still, it saddens me that He is not walking among us.

I attended the funeral of my savior, Jesus Christ.

I was in Perea. It was Holy Week. Alex, Eleni and I were outside the church, along with approximately two hundred others. We waited to enter. The line inched forward. No one leaned to the side to see what had taken so long. Everyone would wait for hours, if necessary. The mood was somber, silent. Out of respect, and admiration.

We entered a church filled to capacity. There were more people than pews. It was anticipated. Wooden chairs traced the walls throughout. Each seat was occupied. Our line inched down the center aisle toward the front of the church. When I reached the altar, I saw a giant wooden cross. Behind it was one word: "*Epitaphios.*" It translated to "the coffin" of Jesus.

The *Epitaphios* was visually stunning. White and red roses were stitched together with other colorful flowers and fashioned in an arrangement that was fit for a king, which it was. A cloth, with the image of the dead body of Jesus, rested on a platform, which resembled a bier. It was topped with an elaborate flower canopy.

I smelled the scent of roses before I saw the inscription. *INBI*. In Greek, that stands for Ιησούς Ναζοραίος Βασιλεύς Ιουδαίων. In English, it means Jesus the Nazarene, King of the Jews.

Eleni approached first and kissed the cross. I followed her example. As did Alex. We walked to the *Epitaphios*. Scattered rose petals extended the length of it. A bible rested on top. It, too, received kisses.

The kissing of the cross out of respect to the *Epitaphios* rekindled the Catholic in me. At Christmas mass, we kiss the baby Jesus on His birthday. Both are traditions worth continuing.

With no place to sit, we headed outside. I noticed for the first time the back wall. Lit candles illuminated it. A woman added to the glow. With eyes closed, her lips whispered a prayer only God could hear. Once outside, we waited for the procession to come to us.

The church bells tolled. Four men emerged, carrying the *Epitaphios*. Each man shouldered a corner. The church emptied behind them. Hand-held candles lit the darkness. I smelled rain. A gap opened. We filled it. A lightness overtook my body, my soul. I, like everyone else, was in mourning. Then again, this wasn't the end of the story, just a chapter. I heard a whisper. I turned. It was Alex.

"Watch your hair with all the candles, young lady."

A wink followed his words.

We continued toward the city square. I smelled the scent of roses. I looked around. We were nowhere close to the *Epitaphios*. It wasn't the breeze. There was none. It wasn't my imagination, either. Of that, I'm still certain. Could the impossible be possible? Why not? I said a silent prayer of gratitude.

The procession came to an opening. We had reached the square. The priest began chanting. The crowd was his choir. We left a few minutes later.

We walked to a tavern near the sea. I noticed a fire in the distance. I asked Eleni for its meaning. She said it was the burning of Judas. It was a symbolic punishment for betraying Jesus. It was a tradition that accompanies the *Epitaphios* procession.

There was also an unofficial tradition that took place after the *Epitaphios*: people eating fish in a tavern. We took part. So, apparently, did every other Greek in the city. We walked a half-mile before finding a tavern with an open table. Some of Alex and Eleni's friends joined us. One taught English.

I participated in the conversation from beginning to end. The topics flitted like bees going from flower to flower. Eventually, the topic was me staying in Greece for a few more months. They insisted that I was the most Greek-looking and Greek-acting American they'd ever met. They claimed that Greece is where I belonged. I promised I would return often.

It was 1:30 a.m. Our dinner was over, but not the night. We stopped for a drink. The bartender placed our drinks before us.

"We must drink our sorrows away to forget that you are leaving us." Alex spoke for himself and Eleni. The words were from their hearts. There are those who say, "Hearts don't break even." In this case, they did.

"I promise I will be back many times. Pinky promise!"

I held out my pinky.

"What am I supposed to do with this?" Was Alex being serious? I paused, then explained that in America we sometimes make a pinky promise by interlocking our pinky fingers to seal the promise. I confirmed my seriousness. It remained hilarious to them.

Our conversations included the bartender from time to time. His English was near-flawless. He wasn't lacking confidence, either. Out of the blue, he knelt before me. He proposed. He offered me a small ring he pulled from his keychain. He said it was his great-grandmother's.

I knew he was kidding. My body didn't. Embarrassment painted my cheeks a bright red. I felt the heat coming off them. This moment dwarfed what happened when I was pulled on stage and serenaded with a love song.

He proposed while I sat with my Greek parents. They offered no respite. Eleni offered encouragement. Not to me, to the bartender.

"This is great! You can marry him and stay in Greece with us forever."

Perfect. An arranged marriage. Thanks, Eleni.

I shook my head.

I laughed.

I did what comes naturally. I said a prayer.

"Jesus, I could use a little help here."

Day 85

"So we fix our eyes not on what is seen, but on what is unseen, since what is seen is temporary, but what is unseen is eternal."

The passage is from 2 Corinthians 4:18.

My eyes were fixed on *yiayia* and Alex's sister. They were in the kitchen preparing dinner. They had been working nonstop for hours. I offered assistance. It was kindly rejected. They told me to go and enjoy myself. Back home, my grandmothers have told me the same thing many times. I watched them work. What remained invisible and is indelible was the devotion to their families, the faith in their souls.

Eleni explained the passion and the tradition and how the day would unfold.

"Easter is a very special time for us. It is tradition, for all who are able, to attend the midnight service of the Resurrection of Jesus. Even children attend although most end up falling asleep in their parents' arms."

I told her I was once one of those children.

"We have the same tradition for midnight mass for Christmas back home. I already know that I will have to drink a lot of coffee to stay awake for mass."

She agreed. "For sure, we will have many frappes before the night is over."

I noticed a large basket of red-colored eggs sitting on the kitchen table. "Do you guys have Easter egg hunts, too?"

Eleni smiled. "No, I believe that is an American tradition. We play a game called *tsougrisma*. The tradition is done after we get back from the Resurrection service. It is a game that involves two players, each with their own egg. You will choose your egg and try to guess which egg is strongest. Many of the men find their own tricks to test the strength of the egg."

Alex interrupted. "I am the ultimate master of finding the strongest egg."

He flexed, Hulk-style.

"So how is it that you test the strength of the egg?"

Eleni's answer was rich in detail. "You will find out after mass, it is a great time. Cracking the Easter eggs is a symbol of Jesus' resurrection from the grave. Red color represents Christ's blood. The egg itself represents Jesus Christ's sealed tomb from which he rose from the dead after He was crucified."

I tried to connect Greek dots with American ones.

"Ah, okay. So that's probably how we adapted the tradition of an Easter egg hunt. The Greek tradition makes complete sense as it relates to Christ."

Alex takes full credit for all things Greek. "Well, of course. Everyone copies us Greeks!"

Eleni explained how *tsougrisma* works, but Alex playfully cut her off. He said I needed to see it for myself. Whatever the game's secrets are remained unseen.

It was time. Midnight approached. There were churches in every neighborhood of Greece. Or so it seemed. The one we attended in Kalamaria square was a five-minute walk from the homes of Alex and Eleni, *yiayia*, and his sister, who are all practically next-door neighbors.

Before I reached the door, *yiayia* called me back inside. She was holding a gift. It was a beautiful and lavishly decorated candle, called *labatha*. The body was baby blue except for the top and bottom, which were white. The candle had a marine look to it, giving it the touch of Greek life on the sea. Starfish, mesh nets, a seagull, and a ship wheel all decorated the candle.

Yiayia spoke to me. When she finished, I looked to Alex.

"She says these special candles are made specifically for Easter. They are given to children by parents, godparents, and grandparents. She says that you are a child of hers, and ours, and will always be a part of her heart and will always be a part of our family."

I hugged *yiayia* through moist eyes. As Greek grandmothers do, she grabbed my cheeks and gave me two huge kisses, one on each cheek.

Our walk to church was less somber than the previous night. What remained unchanged were the people. Tonight, there were in excess of one thousand people standing outside the church. We made no attempt to enter. Alex said the priests would come out onto the balcony to light the flame for all the people to see. I had no idea what he was talking about. I simply followed, trying not to get lost in the crowd.

We meandered through the gathering, scouting the perfect spot with an unobstructed view of the balcony to watch the Eternal Flame being ignited. Once there, Alex handed me a small, white candle with a plastic cover toward the bottom to prevent hot wax from dripping onto my hands.

"Just hold onto this. You will see what it is for very soon." Alex's words added to the anticipation. Ten minutes felt like forty. Finally, doors opened on the second-floor balcony and priests came into view. One stood out more than the others. The darkness prevented me from deciphering the colors or patterns of his clothing. It was his hat that set him apart. It was at least three feet high. He was carrying a lit candle. The others held banners.

He shouted, "*Christos Anesti!*"

He passed the flame, the Eternal Flame, to the priest closest to him. The flame moved from person to person. A sea of darkness expanded into a moving spectacle of light, warmth, and celebration. The light reached me from the hand of Eleni.

"*Christos Anesti!*" Eleni repeated the priest's words before adding her own. "It means Christ is Risen. The response when someone says this to you is *Alithos Anesti*, which means, Truly, He is Risen."

"*Alithos Anesti!*"

I watched the sea of light continue through the square. I was not sure where it ended. The illumination made each person's face glow softly, serenely. People cried. People shouted. People celebrated. Others were deep in prayer. I felt a tear. It was one from my soul, passing through my eye, dying on my lips.

"Let the celebration begin! To the Easter eggs, *pame*!" Alex was more childlike than I about *tsougrisma*. He bragged every step back to his sister's house, saying he was going to kick my butt.

Alex beat everyone to the basket of eggs as soon as we entered. He inspected each egg carefully, with surgeon-like skill. All that was missing were latex gloves. When he found an egg to his liking, he tapped the top of the edge to his front teeth.

Eleni provided play-by-play. "That is his special way of testing the strength of the egg."

Alex tapped three eggs to his teeth, then a fourth, before deciding. "I am ready for battle."

It was my turn at the basket. I imitated Alex. I felt silly, until I realized there was a method to his madness. Not all eggs tapped alike. I picked what I hoped was the winner. When the selections concluded, Alex demonstrated the game with his nephew.

It was one-on-one. One player held his egg out and the other player tapped it with the top of their egg. The goal was to crack the other's egg. You cracked, you lost. The winner stayed and faced the next challenger. Last uncracked egg was champion.

I faced Alex.

I tapped my egg on his.

Crack!

I was finished.

One and done to be exact. I didn't take defeat well. Of course, Alex remained champion. I didn't ask for his autograph. What I wanted from him was his secret. Maybe he'd tell me if he ever stopped bragging. I didn't hold my breath.

Before the night was over, I looked around at all the faces and saw the love and joy of family and friends. I captured this moment as I did all the rest. Not with eyes that are temporary, but with a soul that's eternal.

Day 86

This day proved shorter than counting to ten.

One . . .

We would be spending Easter Sunday with Alex's family on the island of Halkidiki, which is north of Thessaloniki. It's one of Eleni and Alex's favorite places. I'd seen photos, so I knew why. They wanted my first trip to be special. That's why they waited until today.

Two . . .

One more adventure. Everyone in their places. Alex drove. Eleni sat across from him. I commandeered the backseat. We all held our frappes of choice. I looked for my nose prints on the window, the ones from our previous trips. Sadly, they were gone. I made new ones. It would be my last. I heard Eleni and Alex singing. They didn't hear me.

For every two heartbeats of sadness, there was one beat of excitement. My days in Greece were a handful at best. I looked at the seat, at the floor. No Kleenex.

Three . . .

My thoughts struck quicker than lightning. I thought of Greece, of Thessaloniki, of teammates and coaches of Apollon Kalamarias, I thought of my Greek parents, and of their family, which is now mine. I thought of who I was, who I am, who I want to become. We drove past all our usual coffee shops, restaurants, bars, and ice cream shops. This time, I recognized them by name, not just sight. I noticed the billboards of local celebrities, who I had come to know. I read the street signs in Greek to myself and knew I was not lost. I looked to the front seat, first to Alex, then to Eleni. Tears settled into the starting blocks that were my eyes.

Everything that was once foreign was now familiar. It had become my home. I had family and love to prove it.

Four . . .

We approach the island. Alex detoured off the main road. He wanted me to see a particular view. It's a secret, known only to locals. He pulled into an area to park. There was access to the beach. I forgot how to breathe when I stepped from the car and saw the magnificence of the baby blue waters.

"You have seen the Aegean Sea of Greece before but never in Halkidiki. This is one of the most beautiful beaches you will ever see. Much better than those tourist places in the South."

Alex was referring to the southern islands of Mykonos and Santorini, must-see tourist destinations. I was still trying to find my breath.

Five . . .

Our feet sank in the sand as we walked. My eyes plunged deeper into the hues of blue. The water's palette started dark, ended light, before the whitewash crashed on the shore. I was at peace as never before. We left silent traces in undisturbed sand. I said a prayer of gratitude for what Alex and Eleni had given me. Like the sea, my tears ebbed and flowed down my cheeks. I didn't bother wiping. Until you weep, you do not see.

I looked over my shoulder. My tears were not streaming solo. Eleni was crying as well. We hugged love into each other. I held on. Eleni was not letting go.

"You will always be my child."

Her words were soft, loving.

Alex left the tender moment alone. Well, initially. He ended the chick-flick scene. "Why do you women cry? You act like this is goodbye forever. You will be back to Greece, I already know. No more tears, we still have a celebration!"

He was right. Not that we told him. Our hug ended in laughter.

Six . . .

We reached the beach house, the one belonging to Alex's aunt. We were the last to arrive. No introductions were required and my cheeks were blanketed in kisses. Immediately, I was drawn to the backyard. Not by sight, by smell. I'm not sure what it was, other than amazing. When I turned the corner, a lamb was rotating slowly on a spit over a fire. The occasional drip of grease ignited a sudden flash of flame. My mouth watered simultaneously.

Seven . . .

One of the aunts touched my arm and motioned for me to sit down. I considered myself family. They considered me family. Still, they insisted on treating me like royalty. I confess. I am going to miss this Greek hospitality.

Alex's aunt, who I called *thia* (aunt), brought me a beer. She told me in Greek to sit, enjoy, and they were thrilled that I was spending the day with them. She was thrilled? I needed all twenty-six letters of the alphabet to describe my feelings.

The dining table stood in the front yard because not everyone would fit inside. The food was piled from end to end with a vacancy left in the middle. Conversations commenced once everyone was seated. They continued until Alex's uncle arrived with the lamb. Everyone erupted in applause.

Eight . . .

"I don't eat meat."

I looked directly at *thia*. I was joking, but my face was not. I was reenacting a scene from the movie, *My Big Fat Greek Wedding*. Her face was equal parts horror and shock. She looked like someone does when you tell them you have a terminal disease. She didn't know what to say, but she knew where to look.

Alex was laughing uncontrollably. It only added to *thia's* confusion. I broke from character and told her I was only kidding. I referenced the scene from the movie where the newcomer of the family says he doesn't eat meat. She walked away, muttering in Greek. Alex high-fived me.

"You are the ultimate jokester!"

Coming from the master, I'm honored.

Nine . . .

We reminisced about memories made—and shared—the rest of the afternoon. We were still at the table when it was time to leave. I knew I would be back. Eleni and Alex did, too.

"When Eleni and I get married, you will have to come back and be a part of the wedding."

There was no hesitation in my response. No surprise, either. "With a chance to experience a Greek wedding firsthand, you know I wouldn't miss it! I can only imagine how much fun that will be."

I had a reason to return, *the* best possible one. All that was missing was a date. It would come. Most likely when I least expected it. When it did, I knew one certainty.

I would be praying for the days to last longer than counting to ten.

I gave it a trial run.

One . . .

Day 93

Goodbyes hurt my heart.

This one bruised my soul.

Saying goodbye to Alex and Eleni meant I was saying hello to a life separate from my Greek family. I was not ready for this. Maybe, I never would be. It was too soon. It's always too soon when it comes to goodbyes.

We shared tears. And hugs. And promises. We will stay in touch. We will visit at least once every two years. I knew I would return, again and again. I also knew I would never stay. No matter how much I love them, no matter how much they love me, it was not my destiny.

I was at the airport, at my gate, waiting to board the plane. I closed my eyes. Too late to stop the mass escape of tears. I wouldn't be all-cried-out until I landed in Albuquerque. Even then, the sorrow in my eyes reflected the sadness in my heart.

This goodbye also made me think.

I took my first step in Greece as a 22-year-old adventurous kid. I took my final step having learned more about myself than at any other time in my life. College was the starting line in figuring out who I am. Greece was my masters' thesis. I plan on achieving my PhD wherever life next takes me.

My independence unearthed the vulnerabilities and weaknesses I buried deep inside. It opened my heart, it humbled my ego. Finding myself and continuing to mature and develop spiritually, mentally, and emotionally would be life-long. As would overcoming new challenges, fresh shortcomings and every other obstacle that appeared in my path. I didn't know that when I arrived. I do now.

I also never knew just how hard it is to believe in myself at all times, how difficult it is to maintain confidence. Those trenches need to be dug and dug deep. That work is still in progress. My fears didn't stop me. Instead, my courage kept me going. I faced difficulties head-on, I erased the "dis-" from disadvantage, I developed a comfort zone without borders or boundaries.

I lost every basketball game I played in Greece, except two. Didn't matter. The dream was about being the best I could. The dream was about playing. It's no longer a dream. It's reality. It's also my past. The last part hurts. It should. It's another goodbye.

Alex and Eleni taught me more, showed me more, loved me more, than I could ever have imagined. They are irreplaceable. So, too, are the moments we shared.

Because of them, I will be forever mindful of this journey.

The plane left the runway, left Thessaloniki.

I said a last goodbye.

I closed my eyes.

I felt my heart.

It hurt.

More than it ever had.

EPILOGUE

I kept my pinky promise.

I was back on Greek soil sixteen months later, taking one of my most memorable walks ever as Maid of Honor for the wedding of Alex and Eleni.

We shaped more memories, we shared more laughter, we shed more tears. We swore an oath to see each other every two years. We've stayed true to those words.

Each time I return to my Greek home, it feels as if I never left. The language awakes from its coma, its memory restored and complete. Nothing is forgotten. Most is understood. More is added.

I kept other promises, the ones to myself.

I wanted my family to see Greece with their own eyes, and not through my words, my voice, my experiences. Two of my sisters, Deanna and Jenna, did just that. They loved Greece. Greece loved them right back. You're next, Linds, mom, dad and Sarah, my other sister and the mother to my two nephews and niece, whom I adore.

Alex and Eleni brought more love into this world and into my heart. I have a Greek sister—Theodora. I experienced single-child's syndrome with my Greek parents. I admit, it was hard for me to share them at first. That was until Theodora held onto my finger for the first time. My heart was hooked, lined, anchored—for life.

Alex's niece and nephew are bigger, braver. They come running to me, eager to practice their English. I can't hug them all at once, but I can hold them all inside my heart. And I do. When I'm there and tighter when I'm not.

I still keep in touch with my agent, Thomas. *Flash Agency* has taken off, and he now represents some of the best basketball players out of the US and Europe. He continues to spoil me with his time and advice every time we see each other.

Coach Andreas, Margarita, Vassiliki, Stella, and Spyridoula always find time to join in on the celebration when I am there. Margarita gifted me with my Apollon Kalamarias professional jersey. It hangs proudly in my office.

My first professional season was my final professional season. It sounds sad. It wasn't. Western Colorado University offered me a coaching position I couldn't turn down once I returned. Yes, I am likely the only person who has ever lived to choose Gunnison over Greece. I'd make the same decision again.

After two years in Gunnison, I crossed the border into New Mexico. I was home again. I served on the women's basketball coaching staff at the University of New Mexico for five years. It was there that I received—and answered—my life's calling.

From the sparks of guidance that illuminated my path and ignited the roaring fire of passion and purpose, I started two businesses.

The first is VJ's Elite—basketball and mentality training. The name and idea, forged in Greece, came into fruition four years later in Albuquerque. I wanted to train and mentor young athletes, to share my experiences, insight, and knowledge, to infuse young minds and to inspire young dreams. I knew I was never the fastest, quickest, strongest or tallest during my professional days.

But I knew what it was like to dream and I know how to realize them. VJ's Elite isn't about me, it's about them. The goal is to show them their heroes and role models aren't so different from them and their dreams are within reach of their grasp. My story could be their story.

Two years later, Mentality Solutions was established. The business card reads—Mindset Coach, Speaker (Storyteller), Business-Mind Workshops. "Challenging aspiring minds to achieve their peak performance level."

A business card is 3.5 x 2 inches. I am not. I am a degree in sports psychology, exercise science, and sport administration. I am lessons learned from life. I understood the journey, lessons growing my mentality and ways to improve my mental toughness. I would be able to serve more than just athletes. Mental toughness shouldn't be an esoteric term.

I had a blue-print and now I have a second business. Through Mentality Solutions, I currently travel the country, speaking and teaching hundreds of students, athletes, and business professionals at conferences, conventions, workshops, school assemblies, and mentality trainings.

I'll continue to dream. And I'll continue to chase them forever.

I caught one in Greece. One I'll never let go.

When people hear my story, some still ask if I am Greek.

I proudly reply, *"Emai Ellinida."*

I am Greek.

I pinky promise.

Eleni, Vera Jo, and Alex

Thomas and Vera Jo

ACKNOWLEDGMENTS

To My Guy up above, thank you for igniting a dream and passion in my soul to pursue my aspirations and giving me the strength and courage to overcome the challenges and doubts that weighed so heavy within. With You, all things are possible.

I am eternally grateful for you, Alex and Eleni, for opening up your home and your hearts to adopt me as one of your own. The memories shared together are everlasting. I'm beyond blessed to have another family. My Greek family. You will always have a piece of my heart. To my agent, Thomas, thank you for holding my best interests at heart while continuing to push me.

A deep sense of gratitude and appreciation goes out to my editor, Carmen Baca. Your belief in me is what gave me the confidence to believe my story was worth sharing. Thank you for your patience and mentorship through the process of becoming an author. Without your guidance, A Mindful Journey would not exist. I would also like to thank Michelle Kirk for your constant mentorship and advice with the sports psychology aspect.

To my Mom and Dad—Etta and Don. My sisters—Sarah, Deanna, and Jenna. Grandma Vera and Grandpa Joe. Your continued love and support throughout my life has made me who I am. You are a blessing I am grateful for every single day.

Of course, I have to thank you, Linds, for your patience with me during the challenging and stressful moments. Most importantly, thank you for holding me accountable and reminding me what is most important in life.

To all my former teammates and coaches at West Las Vegas and Adams State University. I am thankful to all of you for holding me to a higher standard. Without you all, a professional career would not have been possible.

*My final thanks goes out to you, the reader. Thank you for reading **A Mindful Journey**. As an author, there is no greater honor.*

———◉———

To inquire about a possible appearance or training —
please visit Mentality Solutions at
www.mentalitysolutions.com.

Connect with Vera Jo
Facebook: @MentalitySolutions
Instagram: @vera.jo.bustos
Twitter: @VeraJoBustos
www.mentalitysolutions.com
www.vjselite.com

———◉———